DISCOVERING OURSELVES IN WHITMAN

DISCOVERING OURSELVES IN WHITMAN

❖   ❖   ❖

The Contemporary American Long Poem

Thomas Gardner

UNIVERSITY OF ILLINOIS PRESS
Urbana and Chicago

Publication of this work was supported in part by a grant
from the Andrew W. Mellon Foundation.

This book is printed on acid-free paper.

Library of Congress Cataloging-in-Publication Data

Gardner, Thomas, 1952–
    Discovering ourselves in Whitman : the contemporary American long
    poem / Thomas Gardner.
            p.   cm.
    Includes index.
    ISBN 0-252-01630-0 (alk. paper)
    1. American poetry—20th century—History and criticism. 2. Self
in literature. 3. Whitman, Walt, 1819–1892—Influence. I. Title.
PS310.S34G37   1989
811′.54′09—dc19   88-38843
                                                         CIP

For Laura, Ann, and Allison

Contents

Acknowledgments

I began to read poetry seriously with Philip Booth, W.D. Snodgrass, and John Wheatcroft; I thank each of them for showing me, in different ways, how to make words on the page move. David Hopes gave me similar lessons early on, and continues to do so. I am grateful to Helen Vendler for encouraging me at a crucial time to trust my ideas about John Ashbery, and to Hilbert Campbell, L. S. Dembo, Paul Mariani, and Ronald Wallace for reading earlier versions of this book and making useful suggestions. I am also pleased to acknowledge a Summer Humanities Stipend from Virginia Polytechnic Institute and State University that helped me complete some of the work in tracing Robert Duncan's sources. My wife and children have been very important to my work here; I mean this book's dedication to them quite seriously.

Portions of this book appeared, in early versions, in *Essays in Literature*, *Poesis*, and *Sagetrieb*. I am grateful to the editors of these journals for permission to use this material. A section of the Ashbery chapter appeared in *The CEA Critic* and is reprinted by permission of College English Association Publications.

I am also grateful for permission to reprint the following material:

Excerpts from *Self-Portrait in a Convex Mirror* by John Ashbery. Copyright 1972, 1973, 1974, and 1975 by John Ashbery. All rights reserved. Reprinted by permission of Viking Penguin Inc. Excerpts from *Three Poems* by John Ashbery. Copyright 1970, 1971, and 1972 by John Ashbery. All rights reserved. Reprinted by permission of Viking Penguin Inc.

Excerpts from *Rivers and Mountains* and *The Double Dream of Spring* by John Ashbery. Copyright 1962, 1963, 1964, 1966, 1967, 1968, 1969, 1970 by John Ashbery. Reprinted by permission of Georges Borchardt, Inc. and the author.

Excerpts from *The Dream Songs* by John Berryman. Copyright 1959, 1962, 1963, 1964, 1965, 1966, 1967, 1968, and 1969 by John Berryman. Reprinted by permission of Farrar, Straus and Giroux, Inc. Excerpts from *The Freedom of the Poet* by John Berryman. Copyright 1940, 1944,

Discovering Ourselves in Whitman

Introduction

In an attèmpt to place himself as a poet, Robert Duncan has called attention to the hold that Ezra Pound's disastrous struggle to master "the vital universe" has always had on his imagination.[1] Working to order history—a goal which, Duncan notes, "to Pound's authoritarian superego . . . meant the order of totalitarian ideologies and neo-Platonic hierarchies"—Pound produced instead, in the crumbling of that ambition, what he called "a record of struggle" (CP, 190). Admiring that inadvertently produced record, not the external world mastered but an "ideogram of Self" (CP, 190) made visible in its struggle to impose order, Duncan turned back to Walt Whitman for guidance in deliberately creating his own version of such a self-portrait.[2] It was Whitman, he realized, who, in the "two co-inherent figures" of his work—"the lonely, isolate melodic singer pouring forth from its utter individuality and the power *en masse* of the ensemble in which he sings" (CP, 189)—it was Whitman who most clearly identified and exploited the distance between an individual voice and the larger world (the ensemble, the vital universe) shaped, entered, and drawn from. Finding in Whitman a way to anticipate and use that distance rather than have it unexpectedly yawn open within his work, Duncan took his place within a "succession from Whitman to us as followers of Pound discovering ourselves in Whitman" (CP, 189). What I examine in this book is the way that a number of important contemporary poets, engaged like Duncan in creating self-portraits, have also discovered in the "two co-inherent figures" of Whitman's work ways of framing and finding generative the tensions implicit in singing oneself. That discovery is sometimes conscious and sometimes not. In fact, as I hope to demonstrate by reading a number of long poems in which the problems brought forward by Whitman everywhere dominate but are never traced back to him, the fact that Whitman's influence has been generalized now as one set of tensions within our cultural heritage is perhaps the strongest evidence we have of his continuing "presence."[3]

Following Duncan's lead, I would locate this still-generative set of tensions in the figure "Song of Myself" calls the "embrace." Section 50 of that poem conveniently sketches Whitman's understanding of the term:

> There is that in me—I do not know what it is—but I know it is in me.
>
> Wrench'd and sweaty—calm and cool then my body becomes,
> I sleep—I sleep long.
>
> I do not know it—it is without name—it is a word unsaid,
> It is not in any dictionary, utterance, symbol.
>
> Something it swings on more than the earth I swing on,
> To it the creation is the friend whose embracing awakes me.
>
> Perhaps I might tell more. Outlines! I plead for my brothers and sisters.[4]

Proposing to name what is unknown ("I do not know what it is"), asleep ("I sleep long"), or "unsaid" in his inner world by "embracing" the world external to him ("the creation"), Whitman also carefully acknowledges the limitations of his project: he will, through such a procedure, offer "Outlines," not that world itself. And yet, although full realization of that unknown and therefore potentially alien world seems difficult, perhaps impossible—"it swings on more than the earth I swing on"—Whitman suggests that contact with the visible world—"the friend whose embracing awakes me"—might at least bring him near "To it."[5] As Duncan notes in another essay, the problem brought forward by the embrace—that the "crux of Self, of one's very unique existence as such, is always there in the tension between speaking oneself and the utter commonality of the language that must be the medium of that self"—that problem, although not unique to Whitman, perhaps more strikingly than ever before, is brought "forward into the central drive" of the poem.[6] Working out the implications of such a now-central tension is finally what Whitman and those poets extending his explorations seem to be most concerned with.[7]

Attention has repeatedly been called to Whitman's influence on later attempts at the long poem. For the most part, however, the "Whitman" set at the head of this tradition is not exactly the Whitman to which poets, particularly contemporary poets, seem to be responding. Rather than a figure wrestling with and empowered by the problems of self-rendering, the "traditional" Whitman seems often to be drawn from those sections of "Song of Myself" where the poet has not yet fully engaged the complexities of his position. Roy Harvey Pearce, for example, in his ground-breaking *The Continuity of American Poetry* (1961), argues convincingly that "All American poetry . . . is, in essence if not in substance, a series of arguments with Whitman"[8] and finds the clearest versions of those arguments in the long poems of Pound, Crane, and Williams. Pearce's Whitman—engaged in "redefining the sensible self by putting it into *direct contract* with the world wherein it could be *free, creative,* and *whole"*—(CAP, 75, emphasis mine)—takes on a task which, although difficult, would never be dismissed in such terms as: "My final merit I refuse you, I refuse putting from me what I really am" (SM, 25). Seeking a form to give order to "the informing spirit of his times and his world" (CAP, 61), Whitman, according to Pearce, created an "American equivalent of the epic" (CAP, 72) in which the poet's wresting of a self—an "ideal type" or "cosmic man" (CAP, 93, 92)—from the world surrounding him became a heroic model for each reader's own acts of self-ordering: "What is relatively stable and fixed, because it has no end and no beginning, is the world of which that sensibility becomes conscious, the world in and through which that sensiblity discovers itself . . . since that world contains the poet's readers as well as the poet, his is an insight which, if his readers are bold enough, will move them to transform themselves as he has transformed himself" (CAP, 73, 75). For Pearce, then, poets following Whitman struggle with an ideal in which "the hero releases the *full* creative force of the self, defines the *realia* of his world and takes from them his name, his office, and his phenomenal, existential qualities" (CAP, 83; first emphasis mine).

James E. Miller, Jr.'s *The American Quest for a Supreme Fiction* (1979) extends Pearce's suggestion that in giving form to an entire culture a poet invariably creates a self-portrait, asserting that "At the heart of Whitman's redefinition and re-creation of the form for American use is the placement of the *self* in the center."[9] However, where Pearce uses the phrase "equivalent of the epic" to signal the heroism involved in reworking the outside world into an adequate or "whole" version of the self, Miller uses the phrase "personal epic"—by which he means something subtly different. For Miller, Whitman's model— one adopted by an impressively elaborated sequence of modern and contemporary poets—has two parts: Whitman's work in creating a self-portrait ("personal"), and his attempt to understand that portrait as somehow representative of his age ("epic"). There is a "central tension [that] is played between the lyric (private) and epic (public) roles the poet has assigned himself" (AQ, 43) in which, for the most part, the poet first establishes an image of himself and then moves on to explore its implications in the world at large. "The poet begins with himself, but ends with the world" (AQ, 123), Miller writes. "All the poets that we have dealt with have attempted much the same thing, beginning with their lives, and connecting . . . with America, politics, the universal" (AQ, 321). What disappears in the movement from Pearce to Miller is the role of the outside world as the *medium* "through which that sensiblity discovers itself." Separating self from world and joining them only after the poet's self-description has been completed, Miller shifts the struggle in Whitman from rendering to application.

When we turn to an even more recent account of Whitman's influence, M. L. Rosenthal's and Sally M. Gall's *The Modern Poetic Sequence* (1983), we discover that the outside world—and consequently any reference to the struggle to render by embracing—has all but disappeared. For Rosenthal and Gall, "Song of Myself" is "the first realized modern poetic sequence," by which they mean a poem that "goes many-sidedly into who and where we are *subjectively*" and through "its interacting tonal centers create[s] a semblance of consciousness." [10] Like the long poems that follow it, "Song of Myself" is a response to and a realization of "an emotional center energizing the poem" (MPS, 11); it is a self-portrait that both displays and balances the "sheer variety of tonalities" (MPS, 25) that make up that center. Those tonalities—or "affects—radiant tonal centers of specific qualities, and intensities, of emotionally and sensuously charged awareness" (MPS, 15)—are understood to be fully present. Thus, when looking to Aaron Copland for help in defining this notion of affect—"What, after all, do I put down when I put down notes? I put down a reflection of emotional states: feelings, perceptions, imaginings, intuitions. An emotional state, as I use the term, is compounded of everything we are: our background, our environment, our convictions"—Rosenthal and Gall add the following significant qualification: "The composer's 'emotional state,' defined thus broadly, is a quality of his music similar to what we mean by a poetic affect—although, putting the matter more rigorously, we would say that a passage *presents* the affect rather than *reflecting* it" (MPS, 16). If, moving from Pearce to Miller, a shift of attention away from the problem of rendering was signalled by the slide from "equivalent to the *epic*" to "lyric-epic" (AQ, 36)—the term *epic* serving as a reference to the outside world, the medium to be engaged and embraced—we see that movement completed in Rosenthal's and Gall's emphasis on the long poem as "overridingly lyrical" (MPS, 16). This is a Whitman not particularly engaged in questioning his own method, a poet aware of no need to "bring" his poem "nearer" to the "fathomless human brain" (SM, 42): "To strike an idiosyncratic balance among competing moods and sensations is the overriding aim of lyrical structure. In the volatile realm of the subjective life no such balance can be reached unless the keen sharpness of each tonal energy the poem 'contains' is actively *present. Song of Myself* is engaged throughout in realizing and 'containing' those energies" (MPS, 29, emphasis mine).

We can see how firmly entrenched this view of Whitman as spokesman for the self's ability to master its world, and thereby speak fully for itself, is when we turn to a critic such as Cary Nelson who, when looking in his powerful *Our Last First Poets* (1981) for a way to understand contemporary poetry's "verbal helplessness before history" and its "'disbelief' in its own clarity and power" (and correctly sensing our poets' continued reliance on Whitman), describes our contemporary approach to the embrace as "an ironic continuation of the Whitmanesque embrace."[11] Whereas Nelson's Whitman is "supremely confident of his transformative resources" (LFP, 48), that sense of mastery is subtly called into question by an "early" contemporary poet such as Roethke—"Like Whitman, Roethke reconstitutes nature in his speaking voice, though Roethke makes the violence of the process more visible" (LFP, 41)—and utterly rejected by a "later" figure such as W. S. Merwin, who, confronted with "an almost unmanageable vision of American history . . . based on a record of self-deception at home sanctioning mutilation abroad," writes a poetry "very nearly paralyzed" that "announces the harmonizing dissolution of language" (LFP, 2, 197, 178). In this "unremittingly bleak inversion of the Whitmanesque aesthetic" (LFP, 172), language's ability to embrace the world and thereby "achieve in poetry a vision of selfhood not yet present in actual life" (LFP, 192) is relentlessly undercut by its failure to differentiate itself from, much less master, the world of which it is a part.[12] Poles apart in how they read contemporary poets' attitudes toward the power of language, then, both Rosenthal and Nelson—one by eliminating the world outside, the other by stressing the uniqueness of its overpoweringly resistant contemporary guise—trace these attitudes back to a Whitman seemingly unconcerned with the problems of embracing and working with that world as medium.

If we turn to remarks by several recent poets, however, a subtler Whitman appears—one acutely aware of the distance between self and the medium used to make it visible. Galway Kinnell, for example, in "Whitman's Indicative Words" (1973), attempts "to describe some of the attraction Walt Whitman holds for me" and calls attention to the complex way in which Whitman's voice takes on a "double character, of intimacy and commonality."[13] Common—in that his voice "is outgoing and attaches itself to the things and creatures of the world"—and yet intimate—"it speaks at the same time of a life far within" (WIW, 216)—Whitman's voice enters his surroundings in order to speak for what is inner and nameless: "A powerful sympathy flows from Whitman toward the thing. He loves the thing; he goes out to it; he becomes its voice and expresses it. But to enter a thing is also to open oneself and let the thing enter oneself. So that when Whitman speaks for a leaf of grass, the grass also speaks for him" (WIW, 219).[14] As Kinnell reads Whitman, this formulation has about it an implicit tension never directly acknowledged but continually gestured toward: "It is impossible not to feel in this man who always proclaims his health, this good gray poet who writes constantly about himself yet about whom we know very little, something unavowed, a trouble, perhaps even a sickness, at least an intense loneliness and a more than ordinary fear both of sex and of death" (WIW, 220). Reluctant to publicly display "struggles of any kind," according to Kinnell's speculations, Whitman silently worked through this fear of contact (sex and death both being powerful entrances to the world of commonality). And yet, Kinnell finds evidence that the struggle was everywhere engaged: "The energy which made me feel his declarations of health to be false overflows; the surplus energy that remains in the poems gives them life; and it is this surplus, this life, that convinces. We see the sickness; in the same moment we see the sickness healed. . . . [T]o achieve his exemplary self-portrait—a self-portrait which would also portray everyone—Whitman had to lift the curse. He had to set against his despondency all his gratefulness. He had to clarify his madness and find in it possibilities of joyful health—and do this, moreover, as a work of supererogation: the surplus would be the poems" (WIW, 222, 226).

The "real" poetry, Kinnell argues ("the poems"), is found not in the overstated declarations of health that "overflow" and drain away, but in the "surplus" that remains and convinces. There, as an act of "supererogation" beyond any explicitly stated program, Whitman struggled to see what blocked the desired embrace—he "clarif[ied] his madness"—and found in that acknowledgment a way back to openness—to "joyful health." That struggle with the embrace, Kinnell insists, produced Whitman's portrait of himself as everyone.

John Berryman, in "*Song of Myself*: Intention and Substance" (1957), notes the same tension within Whitman's "passionate sense of identification" but sees the struggle to embrace conducted much more openly.[15] As does Kinnell, he describes the way Whitman opens himself to the world—"The poet—one would say, a mere channel, but with its own ferocious difficulties—fills with experience, a valve opens; he speaks them"—and identifies that openness as "the method by which the 'I' of the poem is gradually expanded, characterized, and filled with meaning" (FP, 232). Berryman reads Whitman as confronting two sets of complications within this method of self-revelation. First, as his attributing "ferocious difficulties" to the channel suggests, Berryman shares with Kinnell a sense of possible limitations within the poet—for example, a "profound dissatisfaction (no doubt sexual in character) that aims at *loss of identity*, in the poem" (FP, 232). Second, and to my mind more usefully, Berryman calls attention to Whitman's work with the complications of the act of speaking through a medium itself. Whitman, Berryman deduces from section 50 of "Song of Myself," distinguishes between "ultimate human reality" (FP, 239)—what "is in me" but "unsaid": "Happiness"—and "the poet's ignorance and guessings" as he works toward that "knowledge" (FP, 235). These guesses, Whitman's "explorations of experience" (FP, 237), are conducted by his "incorporations and followings" (FP, 238) of elements of the world external to him and add up to "a series of experiments on himself—two series—to see what he is" (FP, 237). Because none of these experiments tells the whole story, "Song of Myself," although it "has the form of a paean or exultation—'I celebrate myself'—unconditional, closed, reflexive" is "in fact . . . [a work] of Welcome, self-*wrestling*, inquiry, and wonder—conditional, open, and astonished (not exulting as over an accomplished victory, but gradually revealing, puzzling, discovering)" (FP, 233). Berryman's Whitman, then, both embraces the world and—when those experiments ultimately fail, the medium threatening to dissolve under the pressure to provide full access to the self—marks its limits, "withdraw[ing] from and criticiz[ing] the . . . violent, outtending experience" (FP, 239) of pushing the device too far. And yet, despite such complications—or rather, because of being driven to work through such complications—Whitman's voice sounds finally, at the close of the poem, "like the speech-back-to-us of a being already elsewhere, *in* Happiness as a place" (FP, 241).

Robert Duncan, in "Changing Perspectives in Reading Whitman" (1970) and "The Adventure of Whitman's Line" (1985), takes this response to the limitation of the embrace one step further. For Duncan, more radically yet, the tension involved in using a medium to speak for an inaccessible self is never resolved; Whitman is never able to work out so full "an identification with the creative forces working within masses and populations" that a final "spiritual testament of a self-realization" is obtained (CP, 166,162). That is, he *never* speaks from "Happiness as a place." As Duncan sees it, for Whitman, "Per-

sonality demanded the largest population of human possibilities for
its fulfillment. . . . We have inherited from Whitman . . . an urge that
seeks to scatter itself abroad, to send rootlets out into a variety of
resources in deriving itself" (CP, 173, 175). And that urge—because
some aspect of "the variety and generative potentiality of mankind"
(CP, 164) remains always beyond Whitman's grasp, the medium never
dissolving and becoming the same as the self, and therefore never
offering up the self whole—that urge produces a poetry that grows
"as a man grows, composed and recomposed, in each phase immediate and complete, but unsatisfied" (CP, 164). As Duncan sees it,
Whitman everywhere acknowledges and exploits that tension, finding unexpectedly generative the fact that in his struggle to make visible "his identity, . . . his 'Self' . . . the revelation of the meaning of
the work lies in the tenet of the Whole that is but present, presently
revealed, but not anywhere 'fully'" (CP, 196). The rich drama of this
limited embrace, according to Duncan, is seen most clearly in Whitman's "adventuring" line which, both absorbing facets of the world
and holding itself ready to be modified by new contradictory information eventually to be welcomed into the poem, declares and makes
a portrait out of the fact "that there is no [final] line to be drawn but
only . . . the line of going out there, declaring one's self, problematic"
(AL, 203).[16]

What these three poets respond to in Whitman, I suggest, is precisely what is often overlooked—the way "declaring one's self" is deliberately acknowledged to be "problematic."[17] A struggle is involved
in singing oneself through embracing a medium. For Kinnell, it is
caused by a fear of contact; for Berryman and Duncan, more complexly, by an understanding that medium remains medium, never becoming transparent and providing full access. That struggle, whether
conducted silently or staged as a drama, is what produces Whitman's
remarkable self-portrait. Simply put, tension, for these contemporary
poets, is the central fact of Whitman's work. Accordingly, before
moving on to a discussion of a number of apparently quite different
contemporary long poems that trace out some of the implications
of Whitman's work, I will sketch a reading of "Song of Myself"
that, prompted by the responses of these poets, might stand as a
benchmark—a common example of one way these tensions might be
framed and worked with. Although I would not claim that all of Whitman's thinking on this issue is contained in one poem, I would assert,
along with Berryman, that "Song of Myself" is "the epitome of his
book, where it [Whitman's work with these problems] stands first"
(FP, 228). And, as I previously stated, although I am not suggesting

that "Song of Myself" is always consciously held to mind by each poet I discuss, I do identify Whitman as the writer who brought these still generative problems to the fore.

Following his initial promise to "celebrate" or "sing" the self—not to produce it but, as Stevens would have it, to make a song of it, "Uttered word by word"—Whitman devotes the first six sections of "Song of Myself" to sketching in both the problem he is faced with in managing such a celebration and his solution—the embrace. He begins: "I loafe and invite my soul, / I lean and loafe at my ease observing a spear of summer grass" (SM, 1). By "soul," we come to understand Whitman to mean a core of being whose existence is intuited but never seen directly. That soul, or "Me myself," is both separate from the visible, material world and potentially "proved" (SM, 3) by it. He writes in section 4:

> The sickness of one of my folks or of myself, or ill-doing or loss or lack of money, or depressions or exaltations,
> Battles, the horrors of fratricidal war, the fever of doubtful news, the fitful events;
> These come to me days and nights and go from me again,
> But they are not the Me myself.
>
> Apart from the pulling and hauling stands what I am,
> Stands amused, complacent, compassionating, idle, unitary,
> Looks down, is erect, or bends an arm on an impalpable certain rest,
> Looking with side-curved head curious what will come next,
> Both in and out of the game and watching and wondering at it.

Unitary, ultimately untouched by both the world's material demands and the poet's material self—the speaking "I" of the poem, often understood as the body—the soul stands apart. Whitman puts it this way in a notebook entry: "I cannot understand the mystery, but I am always conscious of myself as two—as my soul and I: and I reckon it is the same with all men and women."[18] Or, in a slightly different formulation: "*behind* all the faculties of the human being, as the sight, the other senses and even the emotions and the intellect, stands the real power, the mystical identity, the real I or Me or You."[19]

This unseen power, then, addressed in the first lines of the poem, is being "invited" to make itself known: "Loafe with me on the grass, loose the stop from your throat, / Not words, not music or rhyme I want, not custom or lecture, not even the best, / Only the lull I like, the hum of your valvèd voice" (SM, 5). Appropriately, the voice of the soul is also spoken of as unitary; it is imagined as singing itself whole—its lulling "hum" unordered by, and thus not "abased to,"

the requirements of words, or custom, or music. What has suggested
to Whitman that this is not an impossible invitation is the memory
immediately following this address, whether actual event or intuition, which supports his bold request.

> I mind how once we lay such a transparent summer morning,
> How you settled your head athwart my hips and gently turn'd over
>   upon me,
> And parted the shirt from my bosom-bone, and plunged your tongue
>   to my bare-stript heart,
> And reach'd 'till you felt my beard, and reach'd till you held my feet.
>
> (SM, 5)

Speaking to the soul, Whitman—that is, the bodily Whitman, possessed of senses, part of the pulling and hauling—calls to mind a
moment when that separate, unseen power became present: an experience described as a kind of sexual awakening of the body by the
soul in which those two separate aspects ("I am always conscious of
myself as two") were for a moment fully (from beard to feet) and
deeply ("plunged . . . to my . . . heart") joined.

And what was it like to be fully awakened to the presence of the
soul?

> Swiftly arose and spread around me the peace and knowledge that pass all
>   the argument of the earth,
> And I know that the hand of God is the promise of my own,
> And I know that the spirit of God is the brother of my own,
> And that all the men ever born are also my brothers, and the women my
>   sisters and lovers,
> And that a kelson of the creation is love,
> And limitless are leaves stiff or drooping in the fields,
> And brown ants in the little wells beneath them,
> And mossy scabs of the worm fence, heap'd stones, elder, mullein and
>   poke-weed.
>
> (SM, 5)

To be fully taken over by the soul, this seems to say, is to be possessed
by something "limitless" and beyond "all the argument of the earth"—
an inner boundlessness Whitman approximates by saying that he
suddenly understood, at the deepest levels, the numberless connections he shared with men, women, creatures, and objects throughout
all time. As "brother" or "lover" to this expanse, he is complexly
united with, and thus defined by, all. And he sees this in a flash.

Because, as several writers have noted, this central experience is
referred to in the past tense—section 5 shows "his discovery of

the imaginative world into which he will plunge, his seizure by the soul," Howard Waskow writes. "The man who speaks to us in the present time, who says, 'I lean and loafe at my ease observing a spear of summer grass,' has returned from both the discovery and the plunge"[20]—the poem as a whole, firmly in the present tense, must be seen as an attempt to build on that intuition. And how is that to be done? Not by waiting on another full merger of body and soul, but by "observing a spear of summer grass," or, because grass is "a uniform hieroglyphic" present everywhere, by observing the visible world, and thereby working back toward that boundless vision.[21] If the infinitely complex network of relations envisioned in section 5 is one way of describing the limitless "potentialities and possiblities waiting latent in the unconscious to be brought into active play and realization as the Self," then making "contact" (SM, 2) with aspects of that network, as lover or brother, would be a way of gradually bringing that latent, silent soul into awareness and song.[22] According to Whitman: "The soul or spirit transmits itself into matter—into rocks and can live the life of a rock—into the sea and can feel itself the sea."[23] The method of "Song of Myself" follows directly from this insight: that the material world offers a medium which, embraced by the poet, allows the soul bit by bit to be rendered visible.[24] Accordingly, section 5 is followed by what has been called a "poetic exercise" in which Whitman takes up the grass at which he has been gazing and uses it, deliberately "mak[ing] metaphors before our eyes"[25]— playing with it and "translating" it in a kind of erotic, linguistic embrace. "Tenderly will I use you curling grass," he writes, desiring to incorporate all its "many uttering tongues," but declaring as well his inability to translate all its hints (SM, 6). The act of reading and translation modeled in this section is marked by a self-aware flexibility that will be fully achieved only in the later sections of the poem: tentative, easily abandoned for new formulations ("I do not know what it is any more than he. / I guess it must be . . . / Or I guess it is . . ."), the various mergings of poet and object capture unspoken aspects of the poet while yet insisting that those aspects are but fragments of a larger, not-yet-visible whole. As Duncan puts it, this translation shows how one might work out a "sense of locality in 'the infinite variety, the past, the surroundings of to-day, or what may happen in the future,' the grand ensemble Whitman evokes" (CP, 168). Producing segments of a whole—the grass is but a single "handkerchief" of the Lord, one of the "babe[s]" of the "vegetation," a member of the democracy of "broad zones and narrow zones," or part of the death-rebirth cycle—the embrace modeled here is both aware of its limits and engaged in bringing to speech what was "not in any dictionary, utterance, symbol."

The middle sections of "Song of Myself" (7–38), Whitman's long, sweeping catalogs and swift vignettes, attempt to put the embrace into action, but do so in such a manner that a remarkably detailed meditation on the problematic implications of the mechanism is worked out as well. The first "stage" of this meditation—I use this term while being aware that the poem is more fluid than such boundaries suggest—could be said to run from sections 7 to 17.[26] Here, as Berryman notes, we follow "the 'I's' identifications *outward*" (FP, 237). Quite deliberately, Whitman pictures himself as a witness in these sections—perceiving and reading the world around him in order to get at the "law" of himself. But, as a number of readers have pointed out, this early series of connections between observer and the world is presented in a manner that emphasizes Whitman's "cautious position . . . [as] spectator to the action and not participant."[27] We have here "the caresser of life wherever moving" who is not ready to fully commit himself to the method of the embrace. He "reads" the world around him, but, not having engaged the implications of becoming these things and thus not having allowed his "soul" to enter them, his translation is an incomplete, shallow one. Aside from the insistently detached verbs in these sections—*note, view, loiter, follow, behold,* and so on—Whitman offers a number of more direct signals to alert us to the problem he wants to bring into focus. Two of the catalogs, for example, end with these descriptions of the poet's non-engaged position:

> Arrests of criminals, slights, adulterous offers made, acceptances, rejections
> 　　with convex lips,
> I mind them or the show or resonance of them—I come and I depart.
>
> 　　　　　　　　　　　　　　　　　　　　　　　　　　　　(SM, 8)

> The city sleeps and the country sleeps,
> The living sleep for their time, the dead sleep for their time,
> The old husband sleeps by his wife and the young husband sleeps by his
> 　　wife;
> And these *tend* inward to me, and I *tend* outward to them,
> And such as it is to be of these *more or less* I am,
> And of these one and all I weave the song of myself.
>
> 　　　　　　　　　　　　　　　　　　　　　(SM, 15, emphasis mine)

In both cases, the language is not unlike that used to describe Whitman's idle, unitary Me myself—"both in and out of the game"—the suggestion being that the soul has not yet been put in a position where it can fully engage itself with or penetrate these material forms. More striking yet are the self-critical implications of the narrative in section 11, where Whitman's detached stance in these sections is mirrored in the fearful, lonesome woman who "hides handsome and richly drest aft the blinds of the window," projected by her unexpressed desire into the midst of the young men bathing below her: "An unseen hand also pass'd over their bodies, / It descended tremblingly from their temples and ribs." The aching inadequacy of this position—suspended midway between union and detachment ("You splash in the water there, yet stay stock still in your room")—is one aspect of the poem that leads Kinnell and Berryman to suggest that Whitman is calling attention to a limitation, perhaps caused by unexamined fears and timidity, in his own "in and out" stance as well. How far this is from the sexual awakening of the body in section 5!

That Whitman has not, as yet, thought through the implications of his mechanism gets further support when he moves to a speculative, reflective summary (18–24) of what sort of self had been achieved through that embrace.[28] The claims in this section—attempting to answer the questions "What is a man anyhow? what am I? what are you?" (SM, 20)—follow directly from the network of identifications asserted earlier. "I know I am solid and sound," he insists, the Me myself now described as embodied in the surrounding world: "To me the converging objects of the universe perpetually flow, / All are written to me, and I must get what the writing means" (SM, 20). By the tone of these sections, we are apparently meant to assume that the manner of reading sketched in earlier—tending toward, then weaving a song of, the richly detailed external world—has proved adequate:

> This is the press of a bashful hand, this the float and odor of hair,
> This the touch of my lips to yours, this the murmur of yearning,
> This the far-off depth and height reflecting my own face,
> This the thoughtful merge of myself, and the outlet again.
>
> (SM, 19)

His bashful caresses making possible the reflection of previously unseen "depth[s] and height[s]" of his "face," Whitman sees himself as successfully carrying out the program he has proposed—his boundless soul increasingly visible in both "victors" and "slain persons" and in both "goodness" and "wickedness." Claiming the ability to merge himself with all that has been materially unfolded through the ages and anticipating that his own "word of the modern" (SM, 23) will itself be embraced and so transformed, he understands himself to be unbound by both space and time: "I know I am deathless, / I know this orbit of mine cannot be swept by a carpenter's compass, / I know I shall not pass like a child's carlacue cut with a burnt stick at night" (SM, 20). Through these sections, however, there remains the sense that these things are perhaps only theoretically true—claimed before he has fully embraced his surroundings and "got what the writing means." Certainly Whitman's assuredness of tone—particularly in sexual matters, in which we are reminded both that the soul's taking on of substance was imagined as a sexual embrace of matter (5), and that Whitman had suggested doubts about the imaginative adequacy of his own attempts to put such an embrace into action (11)—certainly his tone here seems overassured. We hear the unexamined language of wish rather than of achievement, a tone perhaps seeking distance from thoughts of insufficiency: "Smile O voluptuous cool-breath'd earth! / Earth of the slumbering and liquid trees! / . . . Far-swooping elbow'd earth—rich apple-blossom'd earth! / Smile, for your lover comes" (SM, 21).

That note of boasting makes possible the transition to the next stage of this meditation—the crisis passages of sections 25–29 where, as Berryman notes, Whitman works through "a series of experiments" (FP, 237) that test the poem's mechanism and find it, to this point, too naively employed. Section 24 had closed with an apostrophe to the body's ability to mate with all of nature—"You sweaty brooks and dews it shall be you! / Winds whose soft-tickling genitals rub against me it shall be you! / Broad muscular fields, branches of live oak, loving lounger in my winding paths, it shall be you!"—which had suddenly been responded to in equally sensuous terms:

> Something I cannot see puts upward libidinous prongs,
> Seas of bright juice suffuse heaven.
>
> The earth by the sky staid with, the daily close of their junction,
> The heav'd challenge from the east that moment over my head,
> The mocking taunt. See then whether you shall be master!
>
> (SM, 24)

Section 25 attempts to face that challenge by repeating what had seemed adequate to this point. If his eyes cannot face the sunrise, he argues, surely his voice—by claiming a simple correspondence between the rising sun and awakening soul—has the strength: "We also ascend dazzling and tremendous as the sun, / We found our own O my soul in the calm and cool of the day-break. // My voice goes after what my eyes cannot reach, / With the twirl of my tongue I encompass worlds and volumes of worlds." Then, in a key turning point, speech itself, which Whitman describes as "unequal to measure itself"—that is, not only beyond the reach of traditional measure but also not equal to the task of measuring and assessing itself—speech itself splits off from the poet in order to give exaggerated utterance to what it would actually mean to be able to embrace "volumes of worlds": *"Walt you contain enough, why don't you let it out then?"* Which is to say: if you *are* able to embrace all things, why not then produce that boundless soul that ought, by rights, to have been made accessible? Framed this way, Whitman's boasting stands revealed as overstatement:

> Come now I will not be tantalized, you conceive too much of articulation,
> Do you not know O speech how the buds beneath you are folded?
> Waiting in gloom, protected by frost,
> The dirt receding before my prophetical screams,
> . . .
> My final merit I refuse you, I refuse putting from me what I really am,
> Encompass worlds, but never try to encompass me,
> . . .
> Writing and talk do not prove me
>
> (SM, 25)

I take Whitman's admission that he had claimed too much for articulation to reach back through the entire poem to this point—articulation being the self-revelatory act of embracing a medium.[29] At a distance from speech and writing are the "buds" of the Me myself which, although waiting to unfold into growth and visibility, are not responsive to a series of "screams" that only strip away the soil needed for their nurture. Until the problem of articulation is properly examined, the poet is content with silence and the confounding "hush of [his] lips."

In order to get at why his claims for articulation were overstated, sections 26–29 experiment by taking the embrace to an extreme. Rather than the simple confidence to which Whitman at one point in these experiments momentarily reverts—"I have instant conductors all over me whether I pass or stop, / They seize every object and lead it harmlessly through me" (SM, 27)—an embrace deep enough to fully expose the Me myself would affect the poet in this way:

> I hear the train'd soprano (what work with hers is this?)
> The orchestra whirls me wider than Uranus flies,
> It wrenches such ardors from me I did not know I possess'd them,
> It sails me, I dab with bare feet, they are lick'd by the indolent waves,
> I am cut by bitter and angry hail, I lose my breath,

Steep'd amid honey'd morphine, my windpipe throttled in fakes of death,
At length let up again to feel the puzzle of puzzles,
And that we call Being.

(SM, 26)

What work is this? Although the opera "wrenches . . . ardors" from his inner being never confronted before, it does so in such a way that he is left speechless (his "windpipe throttled") and numb ("steep'd amid honey'd morphine"). As at the end of section 25, he must admit that contact of this profundity is finally beyond "writing and talk"; and so, when he breaks free of the numb embrace and enters speech again, he is content to describe the core of "Being" as a "puzzle of puzzles" beyond the reach of writing. We see this pattern repeated in Whitman's second experiment, in section 28, with the sense of touch. Again, what he touches "quiver[s]" him to a new realization of his "identity," but in such a way that he is simply overwhelmed, "flames and ether" making a volatile rush through his "veins." Unable to halt a process that he, in his own naivete, has begun ("Treacherous tip of me reaching and crowding to help them") and ultimately assaulted by that "licentious" world to which he has opened himself, the poet is drained of the "withheld drip" of his heart and "Depriv[ed] . . . of my best." That is, as with section 26, what is silent and withheld is wrenched from him—an experience that leaves him "helpless," witless, and silent ("my breath is tight in its throat"). Again he writes, this sort of embrace is "too much for me"; it leaves him not in possession of his soul but exposed on a "headland" and "desert[ed]" by all of his sense-making faculties. As Berryman would have it, Whitman in these experiments first dramatizes then "withdraws from and criticizes" a view of the embrace which goes too far.

Interestingly, what happens as a result of this testing is not the abandonment of the embrace—if totally carried out, he has shown, it leads not to a painless self-articulation but to silence—but, as we see in sections 30–38, its reformulation as a limited and more thoughtful device. In fact, in anticipation of that change, the intolerable sexual tension we have just seen is shown to us in section 29 as "diffused in tender subsidence throughout the landscape"; Whitman moves, Albert Gelpi notes, "through the tormenting ecstasy of orgasm back to a more dispersed and generalized eroticism beyond the stresses and counterstresses of genital sexuality"[30]

Blind loving wrestling touch, sheath'd hooded sharp-tooth'd touch!
Did it make you ache so, leaving me?

Parting track'd by arriving, perpetual payment of perpetual loan,
Rich showering rain, and recompense richer afterward.

Sprouts take and accumulate, stand by the curb prolific and vital,
Landscapes projected masculine, full-sized and golden.

(SM, 29)

Instead of the inexpressible stimulation occasioned by "blind loving wrestling touch," Whitman witnesses its departure—its "parting
track'd by [the] arriving" not only of semen but of rain, sprouts, and
whole, full-sized landscapes. This broad exfoliation—the "payment"
outward of a temporarily "loaned" connection and insight—is clearly
a more distant, indirect representation and not the heart's hidden,
central, and "withheld drip." The question we are left with, in sections 30–38, is *how*, avoiding naive bragging and its overwhelming
complement, to achieve an embrace both limited and "prolific," a representation indirect and yet "full-sized."

Section 32, where Whitman looks "long and long" at the animals,
models the sort of embrace needed to produce that full projection.
Animals "show their relations to me and I accept them," Whitman
writes. "They bring me tokens of myself, they evince them plainly in
their possession." And *how* does he accept that aspect of himself
made plain in them? By involving himself with them closely and intensely, but with the control of an artist working with a medium.
Acting out such an involvement, Whitman describes himself "picking
out" a particular stallion he loves, embracing it with his heels, and
riding it. He concludes, pointing to limits placed now on such an
embrace: "I but use you a minute, then I resign you, stallion, / Why
do I need your paces when I myself out-gallop them?" Using the stallion, as with the grass of section 6 ("Tenderly will I use you curling
grass") involves both a full engagement with—that is, more than the
cautious peering and loitering of the early catalogs—and an honest
awareness of the limits of this love game. Less than the speechless
self-exposure explored in the crisis sections, this embrace, as the next
sections make clear, quite consciously teases meaning out of its object
(gives it, in a sense, "pleasure") without ever losing the sense that
this brief connection must itself soon be "resigned" and redirected.
The long catalog of section 33 is, of course, the fullest example the
poem provides of such an embrace—the implication being that its
breadth and intensity of engagement were made possible by the
struggle just traced. Deliberately countering the catalog of section 15,
where objects "tend[ed] inward," this section, as numerous readers
have pointed out, calls attention to the poet's full use of the world:

"All this I swallow, it tastes good, I like it well, it becomes mine, / I am the man, I suffer'd, I was there." Interestingly, just as section 15 was concerned with pointing out the inadequacies of its method—it was as much a meditation as a succession of embraces—so section 33 comments on itself as well. Describing the catalog's successive embraces as "flights of a fluid and swallowing soul"—those things he imaginatively swallows giving temporary, workable bounds to a soul essentially fluid and formless—Whitman offers a narrative version of that device which calls attention to *how* those flights might be carried out:

I ascend to the foretruck,
I take my place late at night in the crow's-nest,
We sail the arctic sea, it is plenty light enough,
Through the clear atmosphere I *stretch around on* the wonderful beauty,
The enormous masses of ice pass me and I pass them, the scenery is plain in all directions,
The white-topt mountains show in the distance, I *fling out my fancies toward them*,
We are approaching some great battle-field in which we are soon to be engaged,
We pass the colossal outposts of the encampment, we pass with still feet and caution,
Or we are entering by the suburbs some vast and ruin'd city,
The blocks and fallen architecture more than all the living cities of the globe.
(SM, 33, emphasis mine)

Ascending to a position where he can "stretch around on" the manifold details of this arctic world, Whitman engages and enters that world by "fling[ing] out my fancies toward them"—working with those shattered blocks of ice and remaking them into "a great battle-field" *or* (indicating by that word that these are only translations, limited renderings of soul and scene) a "vast and ruin'd city." This, then, begins to flesh out the theory of translation sketched in section 6.

Whitman extends his investigation of how one works with a medium in the historical episodes dramatized in sections 34–36. Recounting the slaughter of "four hundred and ten young men" at Goliad, a tale he claims to have known "in Texas in my early youth," and the Revolutionary engagement of the *Bon Homme Richard* and the *Serapis*, a yarn "my grandmother's father the sailor told . . . me," Whitman stresses his transformations of those sources.[31] Most striking is the movement from section 35 to 36. In the first section, Whitman speaks in the voice of his grandmother's father, showing us the given tale in its own right: "Our foe was no skulk in his ship I tell you, (said he,) / His was the surly English pluck, and there is no tougher or truer, and never was, and never will be; / Along the lower'd eve he came horribly raking us." Then, as if his mouthing of the older figure's "we" and "us" had pulled him into participation with the scene he had lived with "long and long," Whitman himself takes over the narrative of the battle's terrible closing scenes—in his own voice. In contrast to the great-grandfather's careful orchestration of gun position, leak management, and troop behavior, this new voice— its fancies stretched out to and embracing the material—clearly has different concerns:

The husky voices of the two or three officers yet fit for duty,
Formless stacks of bodies and bodies by themselves, dabs of flesh upon the
    masts and spars,
Cut of cordage, dangle of rigging, slight shock of the soothe of waves,
Black and impassive guns, litter of powder-parcels, strong scent,
A few large stars overhead, silent and mournful shining,
Delicate sniffs of sea-breeze, smells of sedgy grass and fields by the shore,
    death-messages given in charge to survivors,
The hiss of the surgeon's knife, the gnawing teeth of his saw,
Wheeze, cluck, swash of falling blood, short wild scream, and long, dull,
    tapering groan,
These so, these irretrievable.

(SM, 36)

Taking over the tale and allowing his spirit to revitalize its scents and sounds—working out the dreadfully stark contrasts of "formless," "irretrievable" bodies and the impassively erect guns; the delicate sniffs of "sea-breeze" and the "strong" shock of powder; the slight "soothe" of the waves and the "gnawing" terror of the saw— Whitman allows us a glimpse of *how* it is that the self's deepest unseen "bud," "waiting in gloom, protected by frost," unfolds itself through the facts offered up by the world outside of it.

Surprisingly, at first, as if to remind us that such an ability to read is mastered only tenuously—that it is an art in constant need of readjustment—Whitman immediately follows this powerful achievement with two sections that again call the technique into question. It is as if in the space between the fleshing out of the soul of section 36 and the renewed crisis of section 37 the poet pauses and, by allowing the full, noncontrolled implications of a naively employed embrace again to erupt uncontrollably, reminds himself of the difficult tension to be maintained between self and world. Overwhelmed and "possess'd" by what he would embrace, Whitman slips again into a "stunn'd" silence. And why? We see the same pattern as in the movement between the naivete of sections 7–14 and the crises of 25–28—neglecting to consider the risk involved in merging with something other (in this case, acting as if it were possible to totally distance one-self from its claims) leads to a spilling forth of just what was ignored:

I discover myself on the verge of a usual mistake.

That I could forget the mockers and insults!
That I could forget the trickling tears and the blows of the bludgeons
    and hammers!
That I could look with a separate look at my own crucifixion and
    bloody crowning.

                                                        (SM, 38)

Once that "mistake" has been acknowledged, he is free to "remember" and once again work out his relationship to the tales, people, and objects that surround him, a relationship that although maintaining the soul-world division or "fraction" also permits the freely expansive, indirect reading of oneself as part of a grand procession:[32]

I remember now,
I resume the overstaid fraction,
The grave of rock multiplies what has been confided to it, or to any graves,
Corpses rise, gashes heal, fastenings roll from me.

I troop forth replenish'd with supreme power, one of an average unending
    procession,
Inland and sea-coast we go, and pass all boundary lines

                                                        (SM, 38)

The poem closes, as Berryman notes, with a series of "instructions, recapitulations" (FP, 24). The active work of the poem, both that of contact and the meditation making it possible, having been completed, Whitman concludes with what he calls "charges before a journey" (SM, 43). Even as he claims success in "magnifying and applying" (SM, 41) what the world offers him toward his soul's definition, however—"Now on this spot I stand with my robust soul" (SM, 44)—he also acknowledges his awareness of the limitations of all such work: "Man or woman, I might tell how I like you, but cannot, / And might tell what it is in me and what it is in you, but cannot, / And might tell that pining I have, that pulse of my nights and days" (SM, 40). What I take to be his most judicious claim for the achievement of the poem is this formulation:

Not words of routine this song of mine,
But abruptly to question, to leap beyond yet nearer bring;
This printed and bound book—but the printer and the printing-office boy?

The well-taken photographs—but your wife or friend close and solid in
    your arms?
The black ship mail'd with iron, her mighty guns in her turrets—but the
    pluck of the captain and engineers?

                (SM, 42)

Here is what Whitman's self-questioning has been intended to accomplish: "leap[ing] beyond" the external forms of songs, books, photographs, or ships by pointing to the living things (singer, boy, wife,
captain) at the core of those forms brings not the abolishment of the
external by the internal, but the edging of the external ("nearer
bring") toward that fathomless living element. So leaping beyond a
medium by means of an acknowledgment of its limits might bring it
nearer to what can't be touched. "Song of Myself" both declares the
Me myself untranslatable—"I too am not a bit tamed, I too am untranslatable, / I sound my barbaric yawp over the roofs of the world"
(SM, 52)—*and*, by the series of self-struggles initiated by that realization, nudges its rendering toward a fuller imitation of that richness:

I depart as air, I shake my white locks at the runaway sun,
I effuse my flesh in eddies, and drift it in lacy jags.

I bequeath myself to the dirt to grow from under the grass I love,
If you want me again look for me under your boot-soles.

    What I suggest in the chapters that follow is that Whitman's cre-
ation of a self-portrait out of his indirect embrace of a medium can be
used as a model for reading a number of important contemporary
long poems.[33] The first two writers I discuss, John Berryman and
Galway Kinnell, locate the limitation of the embrace in the perceiver,
the poet. For them—writers who see Whitman as a channel with "ferocious difficulties" or as working heroically through a "fear of sex
and death"—the embrace is frustrated by personal problems, and
that tension is best explored by studying what in themselves blocks
contact. Accordingly, Berryman's *Dreams Songs* are structured as an
attempt to tease out and confront the personal difficulties that stand
as blinds between him and the world, while Kinnell's *Book of Nightmares* can be seen to be progressively working through his fear of
death—a fear that at first holds him away from the world but eventually, when understood, draws him toward it. The second set of
writers—Theodore Roethke and Robert Duncan—more usefully understand the limited nature of the embrace as issuing not from a re-
solvable personal problem, but from the act of using a medium itself.
Thus, Roethke's attempt in "North American Sequence" to make his

spirit visible by embracing the currents where a river enters the sea, when acknowledged as impossible to accomplish directly, becomes a study in indirection—Roethke using the nontransparency of the seascape as a spur to work with and follow out, by memory and metaphor, the problems it presents. Likewise, Robert Duncan, in his self-portrait "Passages," reads himself through the boundless sea of humanity's made things. He is well aware that because no single configuration gives him all of himself (and thus cannot be fully embraced as the same as himself), a portrait can only be made out of working with what is problematic in the medium: its incompleteness. For both poets, seeing these different seas as not fully embraceable renames them as mediums and thus makes them workable.

My third set of writers—John Ashbery and James Merrill—are also engaged, in "Self-Portrait in a Convex Mirror" and *The Changing Light at Sandover*, in singing the self through working with something external. For Ashbery, as with Roethke and Duncan, the cold neutral surface of a Renaissance self-portrait both invites and ultimately refuses a full embrace, a limitation that forces him to accentuate its difference from him and frees him to pursue the lines of inquiry that it puts in relief. For Merrill as well, the elaborately clothed otherwordly voices his poem works with are both different from the unseen internal force for which they speak (and thus cannot be embraced fully as adequate or sufficient) and, because of that difference, are useful in touching and holding it together. Most importantly—and here, although farthest from Whitman in terms of direct influence, these two writers seem to me to most forcefully discover Whitman for the present—Ashbery and Merrill make Whitman's embrace primarily a language issue: language being an external medium that both invites and ultimately discourages a full embrace; language being a medium that, when read as not providing full contact, can be wonderfully and imaginatively worked with. These last writers suggest that the centrality of the issues raised in "Song of Myself" might be seen not just in the long, Whitmanesque self-portraits I examine here, but throughout recent poetry. Here I have most immediately in mind such language-centered poets as Jorie Graham, Louise Glück, Robert Hass, Michael Palmer, and, preeminently, Elizabeth Bishop. Bishop, for example, makes poems out of failed and constantly revised embraces—of a fish, an armadillo, a toy circus dancer, a painting; of Brazil, Florida, the Nova Scotia sea. When she is seen as a poet lamenting and yet finding generative the tension between our silent worlds and the frail fishnets we use, however inadequately, to embrace them, Bishop is, according to this way of thinking, as much an inheritor of Whitman's concerns as are the more obviously bardic Berryman or Kinnell. The next step beyond the investigation I am about to carry out, then, would be to focus on language-centered poetry in general, pushing beyond the continuities to be traced here within one evolving, although finally quite specific, form.

NOTES

1. Robert Duncan, "Changing Perspectives in Reading Whitman," in *Fictive Certainties* (New York: New Directions, 1985), p. 191. Cited in the text as CP.

2. The fullest account of this turn in Pound's work is Michael Bernstein's excellent *The Tale of the Tribe: Ezra Pound and the Modern Verse Epic* (Princeton: Princeton University Press, 1980).

3. For a crucial collection of such responses, see *Walt Whitman: The Measure of His Song*, ed. Jim Pearlman, Ed Folsom, and Dan Campion (Minneapolis: Holy Cow! Press, 1981).

4. Walt Whitman, *Complete Poetry and Collected Prose*, ed. Justin Kaplan (New York: Library of America, 1982), p. 246. "Song of Myself" cited in the text by section numbers as SM.

5. This, I take it, is what Whitman refers to, in his 1855 Preface, as the use of indirection: "The expression of the American poet is to be transcendent and new. It is to be indirect and not direct or descriptive or epic." Joseph Kronick, in *American Poetics of History* (Baton Rouge: Louisiana State University Press, 1984), pp. 90–102, makes a useful distinction between what Whitman criticizes as "bald literalism" and his use of such already established forms as language, writing, and history to name indirectly the world and the self. Kronick writes: "To go directly to the creation, he must proceed indirectly along the byways of language, for it is in the byways that the 'new' is discovered" (p. 94).

6. Robert Duncan, "The Adventure of Whitman's Line," in *Fictive Certainties*, p. 200. Cited in the text as AL.

7. I have been assisted in identifying some of the specific ways contemporary poets have explored and responded to the limitations one accepts in rendering what is perceived to be beyond language by the following works on contemporary poetry: Robert Pinsky's analysis of our contemporary reliance on inherited responses to this "dissatisfaction with the abstract, discursive, and conventional nature of words as a medium for the particulars of experience" in *The Situation of Poetry* (Princeton: Princeton University Press, 1976), p. 12; James E. B. Breslin's opposing study, *From Modern to Contemporary: American Poetry, 1945–1965* (Chicago: University of Chicago Press, 1983), of new approaches to "ordering poetry that would not stifle the very movements of consciousness and independence of objects with which they were trying to revitalize poetry" (p. 60) pioneered by the "breakthrough" poets of the late fifties and early sixties; David Kalstone's investigation of different

thematic implications of this problem in *Five Temperaments* (New York: Oxford University Press, 1977); Charles Altieri's analysis of various ways of exploring or covering over "the interplay between a desire to be personal and a desire to acknowledge the multiple rhetorics through which a person may be glimpsed" in his *Sense and Sensibility in Contemporary American Poetry* (Cambridge: Cambridge University Press, 1984), p. 17; and Robert Hass's quite remarkable meditation on poetry's deeply troubled responses to "the discovery of . . . inwardness and the problem of what it can mean, what form it can take in the world" in his *Twentieth Century Pleasures: Prose on Poetry* (New York: Ecco, 1984), p. 41. From a different field, but also useful in identifying specific ways a poet might wrestle with and find generative such questions as, "How does the self represent itself in writing? What enables representation? Are there ways in which the representation of self is compromised or disabled? And, if so, what are the consequences of this disablement?" is Barbara Leah Harman's *Costly Monuments: Representations of Self in George Herbert's Poetry* (Cambridge: Harvard University Press, 1982), p. 35.

8. Roy Harvey Pearce, *The Continuity of American Poetry* (Princeton: Princeton University Press, 1961), p. 57. Cited in the text as CAP.

9. James E. Miller, Jr., *The American Quest for a Supreme Fiction: Whitman's Legacy in the Personal Epic* (Chicago: University of Chicago Press, 1979), p. 37. Cited in the text as AQ.

10. M. L. Rosenthal and Sally M. Gall, *The Modern Poetic Sequence: The Genius of Modern Poetry* (New York: Oxford University Press, 1983), pp. 8, 3, 161. Cited in the text as MPS.

11. Cary Nelson, *Our Last First Poets: Vision and History in Contemporary American Poetry* (Urbana: University of Illinois Press, 1981), pp. 180, 145, 172. Cited in the text as LFP.

12. One can find a similar emphasis on Whitman's transformative mastery in two other significant mappings of his heritage: Ed Folsom's "Talking Back to Walt Whitman: An Introduction" (1981) in *Walt Whitman: The Measure of His Song* and Hyatt Waggoner's *American Visionary Poetry* (Baton Rouge: Louisiana State University Press, 1982). Tracing "the continuing presence of Whitman" (p. xxi), Folsom calls attention to a "degraded present" (p. xxxix) now perhaps able to overpower Whitman's transforming vision. "Could Whitman's vision transform the new sensual emptiness into a spiritual ideal again," Folsom's Hart Crane asks, "or would Whitman's vision, too, collapse and surrender if forced to confront the twentieth century . . . ?" (p. xxxvi). Beginning with a Whitman capable of "*freely absorbing* the vast variety of an expanding America," Folsom logically finds one ironic culmination of his influence in a figure such as Allen Ginsberg, whose "absorptive lines, imitating Whitman's, seem to accumulate empty or absurd images rather than the rugged, ennobling catalogues Whitman *could so easily collect* as he wandered the roads of America. The country has changed, and Ginsberg charts the change by simply opening up Whitman's flowing line to sterile contemporary reality" (p. xxxv, emphasis mine). Even Waggoner, establishing Whitman as the pri-

mary master of a kind of poetry concerned with "uniting 'mind' and 'matter' or 'nature' and thus narrowing the Descartean gulf between the two" (p. 43), although he stresses the interpreter's working with the visible in order to discover "patterns of meaning and value not easily perceived by most of us most of the time" (p. 5), also seems to drift toward a poetics of "imaginative power . . . [in which] the 'seen,' the perceived world, . . . seemed *to lead directly* into the 'unseen,' to visions of the completion of what was potential in the seen" (p. 60). (The context for this last remark is an account of the diminishment of such power in the close of Whitman's career.) Waggoner as well, since "the times seem as unpropitious for the poetic recovery of many aspects of Whitman's vision today as they proved to be for Crane," speculates that we may be living through a waning of faith in such apparently uncompromised mastery.

13. Galway Kinnell, "Whitman's Indicative Words," in *Walt Whitman: The Measure of His Song*, p. 216. Cited in the text as WIW.

14. See also Kinnell's discussion of medium in *Walking Down the Stairs: Selections from Interviews* (Ann Arbor: University of Michigan Press, 1978), p. 64.

15. John Berryman, "*Song of Myself*: Intention and Substance," in *The Freedom of the Poet* (New York: Farrar, Straus, and Giroux, 1976). Cited in the text as FP.

16. A useful technical account of the way in which Whitman's opening of the "combinational possibilities" (p. 285) of the sentence might be seen as an influence on Duncan's understanding that "the sentence is a mobile unit, its movement . . . reflected in the interplays of completeness and incompleteness" (291) can be found in Enikö Bollobás, *Tradition and Innovation in American Free Verse: Whitman to Duncan* (Budapest: Akadémiai Kiadó, 1986). Ed Folsom, as well, closes his essay "Talking Back to Walt Whitman: An Introduction" with an account of the connection between Duncan's and Whitman's lines, seeing, as I do, the "sustaining power" of the lines themselves.

17. This is less the case in Whitman criticism not directly concerned with the notion of his influence on recent work. Paul Zweig, to mention just one example, very usefully writes about "Song of Myself" in this manner: "How much like Whitman, to have written a provokingly unliterary poem (a frank outpouring, pure 'nature') which yet plays humorously, even erotically, with the theme of its own creation. . . . The poem is a body . . . but also a flirtatious commentary on itself as a poem . . . a meditation on the capabilities of language." See *Walt Whitman: The Making of the Poet* (New York: Basic Books, 1984), pp. 251, 254.

18. Gay Wilson Allen, *The Solitary Singer: A Critical Biography of Walt Whitman*, rev. ed. (New York: New York University Press, 1967), p. 138.

19. *Notes and Fragments*, ed. R. M. Bucke (1899, repr. Folcroft, Pa.: Folcroft Library Editions, 1972), p. 60.

20. Howard J. Waskow, *Whitman: Explorations in Form* (Chicago: University of Chicago Press, 1966), p. 159. See also Agnieszka Salska, *Walt Whitman and*

Emily Dickinson: Poetry of the Central Consciousness (Philadelphia: University of Pennsylvania Press, 1985), pp. 42–44.

21. Duncan, very suggestively, reads the grass as "language," "the green blades of words" (CP, 192).

22. Albert Gelpi, *The Tenth Muse: The Psyche of the American Poet* (Cambridge: Harvard University Press, 1975), p. 179. Although primarily concerned with the psychological implications of this process rather than the techniques of self-rendering that I am investigating, Gelpi's chapter on "Song of Myself"—where he shows that "Whitman's language is serving an exploratory function, releasing the nameless and striving to name it" (p. 165)— has been central to my reading of the poem. See also Bernard Duffey's discussion of one of the implications of this process, that the self identifying itself in this manner might be a "vacuum," in *Poetry in America: Expressionism and Its Values in the Times of Bryant, Whitman, and Pound* (Durham, N.C.: Duke University Press, 1978), pp. 108–17.

23. Quoted in Gay Wilson Allen, "Walt Whitman's Inner Space," *Papers on Language and Literature* 5 (Summer 1969): 10.

24. Daniel O'Hara's use of the work of Paul Ricoeur in understanding "the textual production of the self" in autobiography has been helpful for me in thinking about how one embraces texts, one of the primary ways, I will argue, Whitman's mechanism is extended by contemporary poets. O'Hara, in *Tragic Knowledge: Yeats's Autobiography and Hermeneutics* (New York: Columbia University Press, 1981), fruitfully links "Ricoeur's concern . . . with the 'living' metaphors of the poet and what the philosophic hermeneut can make of them, how he can repeat in a speculative, conceptual form the 'surplus of meaning' created by his 'living' metaphor" (p. 42) with what an autobiographer does in reading, embracing, and speculatively repeating figures encountered in his life.

25. Waskow, *Whitman: Explorations in Form*, p. 165.

26. Among the various proposals for marking the divisions of these middle sections, I have found Gelpi's (8–17; 18–24, 25–30; 31–38), Berryman's (6–19; 20–32; 33–38), and E. Fred Carlisle's (6–17; 18–32; 33–38) in *The Uncertain Self: Whitman's Drama of Identity* (East Lansing: Michigan State University Press, 1973) to be of the most use in understanding the progression of Whitman's meditation.

27. Waskow, *Whitman: Explorations in Form*, pp. 168–69. See also Carlisle, *The Uncertain Self*, p. 184.

28. See also Gelpi, *The Tenth Muse*, p. 187.

29. For more on Whitman's struggle with the limits of articulation see Zweig, *Walt Whitman: The Making of the Poet*, pp. 259–60.

30. Gelpi, *The Tenth Muse*, pp. 196, 197. See his entire discussion of sublimation, pp. 196–201.

31. For an important discussion of Whitman's "constructive" and "destructive" transformations of the past, see Paul Bové, *Destructive Poetics: Heidegger and Modern American Poetry* (New York: Columbia University Press, 1980), pp. 133–53.

32. Gelpi reads the "mistake" here as "excessive negative capability"—a slightly different term for what I've labeled a naively employed embrace.

33. Helen Vendler's remarks on Stevens's use of Keats's parent "To Autumn" have been useful to me in thinking about ways of responding to a model: "In commenting on a received aesthetic form, an artist can take various paths. He may make certain implicit 'meanings' explicit; he may extrapolate certain possibilities to greater lengths; he may choose a detail, center on it, and turn it into an entire composition; he may alter the perspective from which the form is viewed; or he may view the phenomenon at a different moment in time." See *Part of Nature, Part of Us* (Cambridge: Harvard University Press, 1980), p. 21. Vendler's work, particularly her demonstration of how one can talk about a poet's "reflective and constructive acts" (p. 13) in *The Odes of John Keats* (Cambridge: Harvard University Press, 1983), has been a useful guide for the kind of readings I develop in this book.

CHAPTER 1

❖ ❖ ❖

IN ILL-HEALTH

John Berryman's *Dream Songs*

Of the poets in this study, John Berryman is the most explicit in pointing to "Song of Myself" as a model for his *Dream Songs*.[1] In an interview with Joseph Haas, for example, he notes: "The idea was, sort of, the way Whitman put his idea about *Leaves of Grass*. The idea is to record a personality, to make him visible, put him through tests, see what the hell he's up to, and through him, the country—and to commit him to his country."[2] Likewise, in an interview with Peter Stitt, he remarks: "The model in *The Dream Songs* was the other greatest American long poem—I am very ambitious—'Song of Myself'—a very long poem, about sixty pages."[3] That Berryman was committing himself not simply to the recording of a personality but to a specific method for making the self "visible"—Whitman's "passionate sense of identification" (FP, 232)—is insisted on throughout the work, perhaps nowhere more directly than in Song 242, which begins:

> About that 'me.' After a lecture once
> came up a lady asking to see me. 'Of course.
> When would you like to?'
> Well, *now,* she said. 'Yes, but I have a lunch-
> eon—' Then I saw her and shifted with remorse
> and said 'Well; come on over.'

That "me," Berryman goes on, explicating his quotation marks, is that aspect of himself made visible through embracing another. Asked by the woman to close his office door, he again shifts uneasily but finally focuses clearly:

> So I rose from the desk & closed it and turning back
> found her in tears—apologizing—'No,
> go right ahead,' I assur-
> ed her, 'here's a handkerchief. Cry.' She did, I did. When she got
>   control, I said 'What's the matter—if you want to talk?'
> 'Nothing. Nothing's the matter.' So.
> I am her.

Or, as the clearly intended Whitman echo would have it: "I am the man, I suffer'd, I was there."

What this song cares about, however, is not just Berryman's eventual identification with the woman, but the self-obsessed misreading of the situation that initially prevented him from seeing her clearly. By calling attention to his struggle to shed that misreading, Berryman here—as he does throughout *The Dream Songs*—lines himself up with what he saw as Whitman's struggle in "Song of Myself" with those "ferocious difficulties" that would inhibit the world's "pouring and filling me full" (SM, 26). Accordingly, when the "death" of his poem's hero and the accompanying reduction of his body give Berryman a chance to think about poetic ancestry, he arrives at the following formulation, his hero, Henry, becoming:

> smaller & smaller, till in question stood
> his eyeteeth and one block of memories
> These were enough for him
> implying commands from upstairs & from down,
> Walt's 'orbic flex,' triads of Hegel would
> incorporate, if you please,
>
> into the know-how of the American bard
> embarrassed Henry heard himself a-being,
> and the younger Stephen Crane
> of a powerful memory, of pain,
> these stood the ancestors, relaxed & hard,
> whilst Henry's parts were fleeing.
>
> (S 78)

The "relaxed" Whitman who incorporated Hegel into American "know-how" and the "hard" Stephen Crane, possessed of a painful, "powerful memory"—these two figures offer Berryman a way of visualizing, in order to put "in question," the manner in which difficult "commands . . . from down" impose inescapable limitations on the expansive "orbic flex" that, following Whitman, he would be a channel for in this poem. Although such a scheme necessarily casts "Walt" as a figure able to open himself fully to the world, it is important to stress that Berryman's putting the possibility of such openness "in question" is, of course, modeled on Whitman's own self-critical practice; if Whitman, in this way of speaking, seems firmly rooted "in Happiness," *The Dream Songs*'s investigation of "Crane's" difficulties are a sufficient reminder that the Whitman overshadowing the poem as a whole only slowly and painfully made his way there.

The Crane reference in Song 78 offers a fairly precise insight into the "ferocious difficulties" Berryman saw limiting his free channeling of the surrounding world. The two tags given here to Crane—"of a powerful memory, of pain"—are Crane's own words, both men-

tioned in Berryman's *Stephen Crane*, a critical biography published in
1950. Crane, who claimed his *Red Badge of Courage* as "an effort born
of pain, of despair almost," was for Berryman a striking example of
the way in which an individual creative will is both shaped by and
knows itself in opposition to the "limitations" under which it finds
itself placed.[4] In Crane, Berryman claims, we see boldly displayed
"the war . . . brilliant and dark, of Liberty against Necessity":

> It may be that in lives where the will is huge, it forces itself outward in
> many directions and thus comes more constantly and wrathfully into
> contact with Necessity than do the wills of most men. . . . Crane's ap-
> pears to be such a life. His work, as the chief outcome of his life, has
> the same character, and he recognized this character in the activity that
> produced it. He was replying to a younger writer towards the end,
> when years of thought condensed: "An artist, I think, is nothing but a
> *powerful memory* that can move itself at will through certain experiences
> sideways and every artist must be in some things powerless as a dead
> snake." The sentence would repay a long analysis, but it will have to
> suffice that the liberty of "move itself at will" is gravely conditioned.
>
> (SC, 6, emphasis mine)

Berryman claims Crane as an "ancestor" not simply for his unblink-
ing examination of the ways in which the free movement of a "powerful memory" is conditioned by inherited "pain," but also—one
realizes after careful study of the final chapter of *Stephen Crane*—
because of the strikingly parallel "ferocious difficulties" each struggled with. Attempting to locate, in Crane, the source of his art's repeated "overwhelming form of anxiety, where control has failed and
a regression occurs, driving the emotion back behind the point at
which particular danger is occurring" (SC, 305), Berryman searches
for what he calls "an earlier general terror . . . a trauma," an "early
conflict." He points, finally, to Crane's "Oedipal guilt-sense toward
the father, whose place he wishes to take with the mother" (SC,
310)—a sense of guilt complicated, for Berryman, by the early death
of Crane's father: "a treatise elaborate indeed would be required to
distinguish from the Oedipal elements in this aggression against
the father, first, the sense of desertion and impoverishment (with
the consequent resentments) arising from his death when Crane
was a boy, and second, the intellectual rebellion consciously waged
by Crane against him" (SC, 314). Berryman—who shared Crane's
"dominant mother . . . [and was] early 'deserted' by his father"
(SC, 303)—also labels here, however tentatively, some of his own inherited difficulties.

By imposing Crane's particular set of "limitations" on Whitman's final "orbic flex" in order to arrive at an adequate understanding of his own situation, Berryman also demonstrates a way of extending Whitman's self-critical meditation on the limitations of the embrace. Using his own wrathful struggles with "Necessity" to tease out the influence of personal difficulties not always visible in Whitman, Berryman rewrites "Song of Myself" as a war between illness and identification, a standoff between freedom and necessity. Berryman's version of himself in *The Dream Songs*, Henry, is "a human personality, free and determined," "troubled and bothered by his many problems."[5] Consequently, where Whitman declares in "Song of Myself," I, now thirty-seven years old in perfect health begin, / Hoping to cease not till death," Berryman counters: "I, Henry Pussy-cat, being in ill-health / & 900 years old, begin & cease, / to doubt" (S, 365). That "ill-health" constantly wars against Henry's desire to embrace the world and make visible "that 'me.'" As Berryman puts it, in a moment of reflection near the end of his work:

> Henry saw with Tolstoyan clarity
> his muffled purpose. He described the folds—
> not a symbol in the place.
> Naked the man came forth in his mask, to be.
> Illnesses from encephalitis to colds
> shook his depths & his surface.
>
> When he dressed up & up, his costumes varied
> with the southeast wind, but he remained aware.
> Awareness was most of what he had.
>
> (S 370)

Although, in *The Dream Songs*, Whitman's dream of self-creation—the inner man coming "forth to be"—is "muffled," and although his passionate identification with others—putting on "costumes"—is now made difficult by illness, what Berryman would argue is that "awareness" of these limitations is, as it was for Whitman, adequate compensation.[6] In fact, as the following reading will suggest, the structure of the poem is designed specifically to explore the manner in which such awareness might be seen as a logical outgrowth of Berryman's inherited model.

The Dream Songs are composed of 385 eighteen-line poems collected in two volumes. Two critics who have examined Berryman's manuscripts—Jack Barbera in "Shape and Flow in *The Dream Songs*" and John Haffenden in *John Berryman: A Critical Commentary*—point out that the poems are not organized according to order of composition, nor, with a few exceptions, according to the chronology of events

described.[7] What order, then, do the songs fall into? This question
has perplexed many writers on Berryman, leading to charges of in-
coherence on the one hand, and over-elaborate numeric "solutions"
on the other. But if we keep in mind the tension between illness and
identification, a remarkably simple structure emerges. If Whitman's
meditation in "Song of Myself" exposed the inadequacies of a naively
employed embrace then reformulated that gesture as a limited, more
thoughtful device, Berryman's poems could be said to take place *between* these two stages—struggling to map in more detail the steps
from exposure back to speech. The first volume of the poem is divided into three books: the first book is an elaborate debate that
Henry holds with himself about whether hiding from the world is a
proper response to what it has done to him: destroyed his first union,
thereby taking away any possiblity of Henry's simply and naively embracing the world. The second book—guided by "Crane"—is an
analysis of Henry's limitations and an exploration of those things that
keep him from identifying with the world. And the third book—in a
sense rejoining the Whitman model after working out the personal
implications of the "space" between the exposure of the embrace in
Whitman and its reformulation—shows Henry in action: performing,
touching, and loving the world, but, like Whitman in sections 30–38,
doing so in a manner qualified and informed by the analysis of illness
in the previous books. The second volume of *The Dream Songs* follows
the same pattern, although at much greater length, sacrificing much
of the poem's intensity. The poem concludes with a seventh, and
summary, book that, like Whitman at the close of "Song of Myself,"
looks over the previous songs, comments on them, and gives instructions to the reader.[8]

The first song, its three stanzas moving from a debate to an analysis
of ills and then to a decision to talk, offers a miniature version of the
structure I have just described:

> Huffy Henry hid   the day,
> unappeasable Henry sulked.
> I see his point,—a trying to put things over.
> It was the thought that they thought
> they could *do* it made Henry wicked & away.
> But he should have come out and talked.
>
> All the world like a woolen lover
> once did seem on Henry's side.
> Then came a departure.
> Thereafter nothing fell out as it might or ought.

> I don't see how Henry, pried
> open for all the world to see, survived.

> What he has now to say is a long
> wonder the world can bear & be.
> Once in a sycamore I was glad
> all at the top, and I sang.
> Hard on the land wears the strong sea
> and empty grows every bed.

(S, 1)

Unlike Whitman, Berryman finds that his poetry begins *after* the chance to embrace the world openly has passed. "Once in a sycamore I was glad," he writes, but that time is gone, the poet left only with the crashing of the "strong sea" and an empty bed. Retreating into an "unappeasable" sulk, Henry—that is to say, that part of himself that Berryman has contrived to distance himself from so that he might study, cajole, even manipulate certain of his tendencies—Henry is in a defensible but unfortunate position. "I see his point," Berryman comments, then counters: "But he should have come out and talked." A similar pattern can be seen in Books 1 and 4, in both cases the debate showing the struggle involved in the decision to come out and talk. But before doing so, the poet, in Books 2 and 5, must understand and repeat back to himself just what has hurt him. Once the world was protective, "a woolen lover / . . . on Henry's side," but "then came a departure"—not identified here but pictured in the poem as his father's suicide, the movement out of the womb, even the loss of Eden.[9] By analyzing both the effects of this "departure" and the sort of survival that yet remains possible, Berryman is then able, in Books 3 and 6, to move beyond his perfect aloneness and, in a version of Whitman's catalogs, offer the "long wonder" of his hesitant, incapacitated embrace of "the world."

Most of the songs in Book 1 are responses to its epigraph, an almost impossible call to embrace the world drawn from Carl Wittke's *Tambo and Bones*: "Go in, Brack Man, De Day's Yo' Own." (As numerous critics have pointed out, the minstrel show and its various figures furnish Berryman with the different voices necessary for peopling the inner debate of these early books.)[10] That embrace seems impossible because, as the interlocutor reminds us in Song 4—or the poet reminds himself—there is "a law against Henry." Staring at a woman in a restaurant, Henry, in a parodic, but ultimately serious version of Whitman's desire to be poured and filled full, "hungered back," imagining himself declaring: "'You are the hottest one for years of night / Henry's dazed eyes / have enjoyed, Brilliance.' I advanced upon / (despairing) my spumoni." Despairing at the fact that he can't touch her, that it has "all go[ne] wrong," Henry is left only with his spumoni. That law, as Song 8 suggests in its thrice-repeated drop from possibility to limitation, has been imposed from the outside; it is a conditioning not of Henry's choosing: "They took away his teeth, / . . . They lifted off / his covers . . . / . . . They weakened all his eyes." As the promise of the weather improves in that song, finally flowering, Henry suffers the progressive weakening of his senses. His exposure by what "they" have done in destroying his eyes, teeth, and ears— that is, just those faculties needed to make contact with the world—is enough to make him retreat from the epigraph's call. His covers lifted off until his limitations "showed," Henry seems ready to refuse Whitman's call to sing the self; he would "see himself less" (S, 8).

Accordingly, much of Book 1 is taken up with songs musing over ways simply to walk away from his apparently legislated-against struggle to love the world. Song 15, recounting an anecdote about a "haughtful & greasy" woman lashing out at a world where "many graces are slipped," offers this summary of ways to reject the call to "Go in":

> Women is better, braver. In a foehn of loss
> entire, which too they hotter understand,
> having had it,
> we struggle. Some hang heavy on the sauce,
> some invest in the past, one hides in the land.
> Henry was not his favourite.

A foehn is a warm, dry wind—the wind of "loss entire" referred to in Song 1. Women are braver because, unlike Henry at this point, they struggle with the problem, living with the loss so long that they "understand" and can make use of it. In contrast are those who escape contact through drinking ("the sauce"), nostalgia ("the past"), or—in the option dominating Henry's concerns because of the suicide of his father—"hid[ing] in the land." With this pattern in mind, we can see many of the apparently unrelated songs in this first book as examinations of the temptation to hide. In Song 7, for example, old movies sound a siren song of regression:

> He wishing he could squirm again where Hoot
> is just ahead of rustlers, where William S
> forgoes some deep advantage, & moves on,
> where Hashknife Hartley having the matter taped
> the rats are flying. For the rats
> have moved in, mostly, and this is for real.

What is "real" in Song 11 is the empty bed of Song 1 ("it seems we don't have no good bed to lie on, / forever"), in response to which Berryman, in a long, counterpointed sentence, proposes a different rest:

> While he drawing his first breath,
> while skinning his knees,
>
> while he was so beastly with love for Charlotte Coquet
> he skated up & down in front of her house
> wishing he could, sir, die,
> while being bullied & he dreamt he could fly—
> during irregular verbs—them world-sought bodies
> safe in the Arctic lay:
>
> Strindberg rocked in his niche, the great Andrée
> by muscled Fraenkel under what's of the tent,
> torn like then limbs, by bears
> over fierce decades, harmless. Up in pairs
> go we not, but we have a good bed.
> I have said what I had to say.

The first sentence recreates childhood as a series of scrapes and losses: leaving the womb ("drawing his first breath"), "skinning his knees," falling "beastly" in love, "being bullied," doing "irregular verbs." Juxtaposed is a sequence of escapes: "wishing he could, sir, die," dreaming "he could fly," or, a final sanctuary, to have been frozen like the Arctic explorers Fraenkel, Strindberg, and Andrée, whose bodies, found after thirty years, had been rendered insensitive to decades of mauling.[11] What seems finally to be under consideration in this song is the final escape of suicide (thus the somber evasion of the last line), for if pairs *are* broken up ("Up in pairs / go we not"), death remains an alternative "good bed."

Despite the law against Henry and the sweet lure of escape, there are moments in this first book when the poet suggests that, although heartbroken, damaged, and betrayed, he might somehow embrace the world. However rare, those moments serve to indicate that Henry's debate with himself has not yet been settled. Song 2 is a simple, and early, example. In a section of town with so little human commerce that he speculates the rapture might have occurred ("is he come?"), leaving him behind once again, Henry is able, nevertheless, to dance an abandoned minstrel shuffle:

> Le's do a hoedown, gal,
> one blue, one shuffle,
> if them is all you seem to réquire. Strip

> ol banger, skip us we, sugar; so hang on
> one chaste evenin.

That ability to hang on despite his enforced chastity is examined more extensively in Song 5, where each stanza ponders a different response. Martyred ("St Stephen / getting even"), Henry hides in the first stanza; far from those who have stoned him, he "sats in de bar & was odd, / . . . at odds wif de world & its god." Stanza two reverses the pattern; no longer odd, Henry's open gaiety is so infectious that the entire outside world joins in:

> Henry sats in de plane & was gay.
> Careful Henry nothing said aloud
> but where a Virgin out of cloud
> to her Mountain dropt in light,
> his thought made pockets & the plane buckt.
> 'Parm me, lady.' 'Orright.'

On a plane, passing over a statue of the virgin atop a mountain, Henry is so excited when the clouds clear and she seems to drop down a ray of light that he claims the plane's turbulence as his own inner rocking and bucking. This feeling of union seems so powerful that when Henry apologizes to a lady he bumped in the turbulence he seems also to be talking to the virgin—who answers back! The third stanza, backpedaling, establishes a middle ground between the two—essentially the middle ground that Henry will seek to inhabit throughout *The Dream Songs:*

> Henry lay in de netting, wild,
> while the brainfever bird did scales;
> Mr. Heartbreak, the New Man,
> come to farm a crazy land;
> an image of the dead on the fingernail
> of a newborn child.

Each pair of lines in this stanza shows Henry as both "free and determined": he is in "de netting" but sings; he is like Crèvecoeur—in French "Heartbreak," author of *Letters from an American Farmer*[12]—limited by his heart and the crazy land but farming nonetheless; or he is a newborn, carrying an image of the dead with him even as he is told "De Day's Yo' Own." In each case, both action and limitation are inexorably linked.

In Book 1, then, as the sequence of three final songs continues to insist, the debate between hiding and touching is simply set into motion, never resolved. Song 24 presents the clearest moment of passionate identification in the book. The song is an account of Henry's trip to India, a visit in which, although "vexations held a field-monsoon," he was able, one morning, to embrace that exotic world, joining passion to medium:

> The mad sun rose though on the ghats
> & the saddhu in maha mudra, the great River,
>
> and Henry was happy & beside him with excitement.
> Beside himself, his possiblities;
> salaaming hours of a half-blind morning
> while the rainy lepers salaamed back,
> smiles & a passion of their & his eyes flew
> in feelings not ever accorded solely to oneself.

But that moment does not last. In Song 25, Henry begins a self-admiring listing of his various triumphs—"Henry, edged, decidedly, made up stories / lighting the past of Henry, of his glorious / present, and his hoaries"—only to have the interlocutor whisper "Euphoria, /Mr Bones, euphoria. Fate clobber all," at which point Henry collapses:

> —Hand me back my crawl,
>
> condign Heaven. Tighten into a ball
> elongate & valved Henry. Tuck him peace.
> Render him sightless,
> or ruin at high rate his crampon focus,
> wipe out his need. Reduce him to the rest of us.

Henry's flight—he would be a child again ("hand me back my crawl"), a self-enclosed ball, or tucked back under his original woolen covers—is described here as a refusal of expressly Whitmanesque characteristics, "elongate & valved Henry" being a deliberate echo of Whitman's courting of his soul: "Only the lull I like, the hum of your valvèd voice." And what is it that triggers this astonishing collapse? The euphoria Whitman warned himself against was "conceiv[ing] too much of articulation"; Henry's problem seems to be that he has forgotten "fate"—that is, in a narrowing of Whitman's struggle, the particular set of early events that continually return to "clobber him" and limit *his* articulation:

> I am going away.
> There was something in my dream about a Cat,
> which fought and sang.
> Something about a lyre, an island. Unstrung.
> Linked to the land at low tide. Cables fray.
> Thank you for everything.

Something about an island—Clearwater Island, off the coast of Florida, site of Berryman's father's suicide—returns, and the cat ("Henry Pussy-cat") who indeed had come out and fought, sung, and danced, finds himself overwhelmed. His lyre unstrung, his connection to the mainland vanished, and his cables frayed, Henry closes the song, reluctantly, in isolation.

Song 26 simply sets in motion one last time all the possibilities we have examined. Its first line ("The glories of the world struck me, made me aria, once"), which refers to the vanished world of the full embrace in Song 1 ("Once in a sycamore I was glad / all at the top, and I sang"), is juxtaposed to the interlocutor's thrice-repeated question: "What happen then, Mr. Bones?" The song leaves two starkly different responses to being shocked out of the world of simple song, either a new interest ("women's bodies") that led in time to "a sense of others" or, delightedly abandoning that effort, "I had a most marvelous piece of luck. I died." Book 1 chooses neither answer; it is an elaborate, self-critical debate. Going in, as Berryman had suggested about Whitman and has now seen for himself, is not as simple as one reading the epigraph might suppose.

The epigraph to Book 2 is drawn from Jeremiah's complaint that his enemies gather round to jeer at his suffering—"I am their musick"—and the poems that follow, accordingly, attempt to discover the cause of that suffering (that sickness, mu-sick) and stare the problem down:[13] "He stared at ruin. Ruin stared straight back." The book opens by recalling the powerful act of identification of Song 24:

> The greens of the Ganges delta foliate.
> Of heartless youth made late aware he pled:
> Brownies, please come.
> To Henry in his sparest times sometimes
> the little people spread, & did friendly things;
> then he was glad.
>
> (S, 27)

The exfoliating delta is an image of both the friendly "little people" who "spread" themselves before Henry, and of Henry himself, lately made aware of his limited, "heartless youth," who has now opened himself, pleading to have his spareness filled. In a sense, the delta is a Whitman-like state of mind in which Berryman prays his readers will remain (reserving his place) while he conducts the actual business of Book 2—exploring death:

> My friends,—he has been known to mourn,—I'll die;
> live you, in the most wild, kindly, green

> partly forgiving wood,
> sort of forever and all those human sings
> close not your better ears to, while good Spring
> returns with a dance and a sigh.
>
> (S, 27)

His father's suicide is the primary limitation Henry must explore, the source of his illness and of the diminishment of his senses. Accordingly, the book centers on an address to the father in Song 42; the songs before 42 prepare for that encounter by staring down the facts of death, suicide, and revenge, while the songs afterward move away, in time, to various consolations.[14]

In the book's early songs, Henry's loss is never named directly. Song 28, for example, recounts a dream in which Henry, lost in the snow, tired and without food, waits for a rescuing St. Bernard ("the barker"). As in Song 1, Henry has suffered a "departure," but as long as his loss remains unnamed, "the strange one" whose presence would return Henry's voice and prayers seems held from him at an almost infinite distance. Song 29 comes closer to naming Henry's bad "position":

> There sat down, once, a thing on Henry's heart
> só heavy, if he had a hundred years
> & more, & weeping, sleepless, in all them time
> Henry could not make good.
> Starts again always in Henry's ears
> the little cough somewhere, an odour, a chime.

The thing that has broken his heart seems simply a heaviness to which no action ("weeping") or amount of time can adequately respond. So dominant that any sound or smell recalls it, that heaviness remains a tangling of rage and responsibility for which Henry has no adequate object:

> But never did Henry, as he thought he did,
> end anyone and hacks her body up
> and hide the pieces, where they may be found.
> He knows: he went over everyone, & nobody's missing.
> Often he reckons, in the dawn, them up.
> Nobody is ever missing.
>
> (S, 29)

Book 2, then, attempts to provide the involved reckoning with the missing dead this nightmare demands; it is, as Song 30 puts it, a "collating" (and ultimately a proper labelling, as "father") of the bones by which "some of my dying people [have been] indexed: 'Warm.'"[15]

The middle songs of the book reckon with the death indirectly, through literary sources. Song 33 tells the story of the "boy-god" Alexander who, in Plutarch's *Life of Alexander*, "wroth & of wine," throws an apple at a guest, eventually killing him with a "spear-ax" in the ensuing melee. Significantly, Henry identifies not with Alexander's rage but with the feelings of responsibility that follow:

> For the sin:
>
> little it is gross Henry has to say.
> The king heaved. Pluckt out, the ax-end would
> he jab in his sole throat.
> As if an end. A baby, the guard may
> squire him to his apartments. Weeping & blood
> wound round his one friend.

Drawn to the stricken king's regression rather that the "sin," Henry has much "to say" about the survivor's self-reduction: left alone ("sole"), the king would kill himself, ruin his voice, or become a baby, his weeping useless to restore his "one friend."[16] Song 34—addressed to Robert Fitzgerald, with whom Berryman was sharing a taxi when they heard of Hemingway's suicide[17]—thinks through the insistent indirection of these "death" poems. "My mother has your shotgun," the poet begins, linking himself to the ill Hemingway ("he didn't feel the best") and reaching, at least imaginatively, for the same solution—a shotgun "pried / to his trigger-digit, pal." Henry's illness, we overhear him telling himself in the second stanza, was initiated by his father's death at forty:

> Now—tell me, my love, *if* you recall
> the dove light after dawn at the island and all—
> here is the story, Jack:
> he verbed for forty years, very enough,
> & shot & buckt—and, baby, there was of
> schist but small there (some).

That insistent turning away from his own youthful reaction to an equivalent—the shattered stones on the beach—becomes the subject of the third stanza:

> Why should I tell a truth? when in the crack
> of the dooming & emptying news I did hold back—
> in the taxi too, sick—
> silent—it's so I broke down here, in his mind
> whose sire as mine one same way—I refuse,
> hoping the guy go home.

Refusing to approach the "truth" directly, Henry holds back at "the crack" (the gun, the shock, his own splintering) of his father's death and at the news of Hemingway "in the taxi." Allowing himself, instead, to break "down here," to be shattered only in his recreation of *Hemingway's* state ("in *his* mind") is a defense, a way of "hoping" his father's dreadful ghost would "go home." It is only after a series of such refusals—most notably a set of poems on the death of Frost—that Henry finally decides to get off the fence and face his illnesses directly. "But this is where I livin," he finally admits," where I rake / my leaves and cop my promise, 'this where we / cry oursel's awake" (S, 40).

What Henry cries himself awake to, of course, is the impact on him of his father's death. Song 42, sparked by a broken leg in December 1962, addresses the father directly: [18]

> O journeyer, deaf in the mould, insane
> with violent travel & death: consider me
> in my cast, your first son.
> Would you were I by now another one,
> witted, legged? I see you before me plain
> (I am skilled: I hear, I see)—

One-legged, single-witted in his focus on his father's "violent travel & death," Henry brings all of his senses to bear on seeing "plain" the implications of that act: "Would you were I by now another one?" That is, would you have me become another suicide? The question out, Henry is able to confront the full force of that loss: "I hear. I think I hear. Now full craze down / across our continent / all storms since you gave in, on my pup-tent. / I have of blast & counter to remercy you / for hurling me downtown." Although "winged" by a cab and "your stance on the sand," Henry is able to stand up and offer his own counterblast, to remake what was shattered by his father. "Think[ing] it across," no longer retreating from his situation, Henry withstands the "blistered wish" to "flop, there, to his blind song / who pick up the tab." Henry, that is, resolves to survive, devoting himself to studying and taking responsibility for the "tab" left for him. Book 2 turns outward at this point, as if in confirmation of Henry's decision to face his limitations. Although, as in Song 49, he is often overcome by "Tremor, heaves, . . . sweaterings," he just as consistently realizes that "From daylight he got maintrackt, from friends' breath, / wishes, his hopings" and turns himself back to the world. Having faced down the source of his illness, if not yet having become capable of embracing the world around him, Berryman ends the book uneasily, longingly speaking to himself, through the voice of the interlocutor, of the Whitmanic greenness left behind: "Somehow, when I make your scene, / I cave to feel as if // de roses of dawn & pearls of dusk, made up / by some ol' writer-man, got right forgot / & the greennesses of ours" (S, 50).

In Book 3 Henry finally comes out and talks. The book is dominated by songs about working and performing—accomplishments carried out, however, under some sort of limitation. The first song in the book is representative; returned from the hospital, "abandoned" in his workroom, Henry is bothered by the viselike sun: "That was all right. / He can't work well with it here, or think. / A bilocation, yellow like catastrophe. / The name of this was freedom" (S, 52). The name of Henry's freedom is limitation—the limitation of a catastrophe clearly seen and oppressive, but one under which Henry can still work, for if he cannot work "well," he can yet work ill. Song 67 describes Henry's task—and that of all self-portraitists—as an operation in which "the patient is brought back to life" under the most difficult circumstances: "I am obliged to perform in complete darkness / operations of great delicacy / on my self." In another song he fancies himself performing on the stage with Bessie Smith ("I heard, could be, a Hey there from the wing, / and I went on"); he imagines himself blowing a horn: "so, as I say, the house is givin hell / to *Yellow Dog*, I blowin like it too." [19] Here, too, there are limitations. Henry imagines Smith collapsing on stage ("I see she totterin") and realizes that she could never be admitted to a white hospital: "sick-house's white birds'" and blacks must go "to the birds instead" (S, 68). Henry's metaphor for jazz (and, by implication, for his own performances in this third book) combines both its brilliant colors and the squalor of its conditions; it is like "hangin Christmas on some tree / after trees thrown out." Song 70 considers Henry's performance on the crew team; he was a "hero" but "bloody" because "his seat got wedged / under his knifing knees." As in each of these displays, "It was not done with ease," yet Henry continued to row:

> he rowed rowed rowed. They did not win.
> Forever in the winning & losing since
> of his own crew, or rather
> in the weird regattas of this afterworld,
> cheer for the foe. He set himself to time
> the blue father.

As Henry interprets the metaphor, his life is like rowing in the regatta of the *after*world—after, that is, the death of his blue father, the limitation whose "shell" Henry accurately times for us and against which he also competes. Perhaps the ideal version of individual artistic freedom struggling against loss is the austere garden that Henry visits at Ryoan-Ji Temple, a large "sea rectangular of sand" in which "fifteen changeless stones" rest, having established "the thought of the ancient maker priest." Berryman writes: "Elsewhere occurs—I remembers—loss. / Through awes & weathers neither it increased / nor did one blow of all his stone & sand thought die" (S, 73). The "one blow" of the priest's thought resembles Henry's "blast & counter" of Song 42. Although Henry's triumphs are more tenuous and flexible, they too are blows establishing the self in the face of loss.[20]

What, in all its limitation, is actually performed in Book 3, the poet bringing himself back to life, is the act of embracing others. Although, as Song 53 declares, such an embrace is potentially dangerous, quoting Saul Bellow's complaint about reading newspapers, "I have to identify myself with everyone in it, / including the corpses, pal," for the first time in *The Dream Songs* Henry worries about others. He frets over the slow process of desegregation ("After eight years, be less dan eight percent, / distinguish' friend, of coloured wif de whites / in de School, in de Souf"); he identifies with the Korean War dead: "Away from us, from Henry's feel or fail, / campaigners lie with mouldered toes, disarmed, / out of order, / with whom we will one" (S, 61). More lightly, he gives a song to staring at a rabbit (S, 62) and another to lusting after a woman: "the thought he puts / into that young woman / would launch a national product" (S, 69). Clearly, then, he has for the time being moved out of the cave where he was a bat, moist and crisisless, and, in the name of his own blindness "inside," joined the human race:

> Instead of the cave! ah lovely-chilly, dark,
> ur-moist his cousins hang in hundreds or swerve
> with personal radar,
> crisisless, kid. Instead of the cave? I serve,
> inside, my blind term. Filthy four-foot lights
> reflect on the whites of our eyes.
>
> (S, 63)

The closing poems of the book offer a summary of Henry's new condition. Song 74, in fact, seems to mock some of the poet's early positions: "Pulling together Henry, somber Henry / woofed at things." In particular, by slyly describing his poetic method, he mocks the notion of overpowering pain ("What the world to Henry / did will not bear thought") that has been his major theme: "Feeling no pain, / Henry stabbed his arm and wrote a letter / explaining how bad it had been / in this world." Now though, in contrast to that letter's account of "the horror of unlove," Henry has become his own master, a taster, like Whitman, of the world around him: "Spry disappointments of men / and vicing adorable children / miserable women, Henry mastered, Henry / tasting all the secret bits of life." Song 75 celebrates the result of Henry's work. His poem is a sapling that has been pissed on by dogs, by critics, but has grown to an "unshedding bulky bole-proud blue-green moist // thing made by savage & thoughtful / surviving Henry"—such a grand accomplishment that "the flashing & bursting / tree" strikes "passers from despair." And Song 76 is a quiet resolution of Henry's despair about his father. If life comes to loss ("a handkerchief sandwich"), still Henry wants to taste it all. "You is from hunger, Mr. Bones," the interlocutor tells him. Now, he is able to manage that taste:

> in a modesty of death I join my father
> who dared so long agone leave me.
> A bullet on a concrete stoop
> close by the smothering southern sea
> spreadeagled on an island, by my knee.

By "modesty" Henry means a smaller version of the death, a manageable joining with the father through art. (The play with ago-along-gone-one-agony in the word "agone" also seems to indicate distance.) Now, Henry is able to sing about the death: "arm in arm, by the beautiful sea, / hum a little." If Henry's father left him alone, then through these poems Henry will join him: "—I saw nobody coming, so I went instead." The book ends with Henry "shaved & . . . duded . . . up," "his head full / & his heart full," having to some degree dealt with his pain, opened his heart, and taken in the world. Like Whitman at the end of "Song of Myself," "he is making ready to move on," although as the next book indicates, the success is only a temporary one.

The next four books, published as *His Toy, His Dream, His Rest*, repeat that structural pattern—a debate, an account of Henry's ills, a catalog of identifications, and an added summary—although in a greatly expanded version. The 77 songs of the first volume have become, multiplied by four, the 308 poems of the second volume. Although the same struggle to embrace is being broken down and studied, this second volume, in repeating those earlier moves, tends to blunt the force of Berryman's analysis; consequently, the discussion can move more quickly here. Book 4 is another investigation of retreat, a series of poems delivered from the grave where Henry has been, as the epigraph puts it, "scared to death." The "successful" Henry at the end of *77 Dream Songs* is replaced by a Henry whose eye is "darkened" and whose smile is diminished (S, 78), a Henry who has "flared out of history" and into "the world of generosity." The device of having the poems delivered from the grave is a witty and effective way to dramatize Henry's debate about hiding. His reasons for fleeing are by now familiar. He would like to be able to avoid "ill-wishes," including those of his father: "Herewith ill-wishes. From a cozy grave / rainbow I scornful laughings. Do not do, / Father, me down. / Let's shuck an obligation" (S, 82). And as Song 86 suggests, death does indeed relieve him of responsibility. In response to such lashings of guilt as those examined in Song 29 ("never did Henry, as he thought he did / end anyone & hacks her body up"), his lawyer can now plead "Not Guilty by reason of death," arguing that any crime since Henry's passage must have been committed by another.

But this is a hard freedom, for to be free of turbulence is to be without a body ("It's buried at a distance") and without any way of taking in the world ("bits of outer God") or expressing it. Song 83 dramatizes that condition. Henry remembers, from his life, a boil that caused him problems with sitting and making deadlines, an entirely "undignified" turbulence of which he is now relieved: "Isn't it slim to be slumped off from that." But his rehearsal of the advantages of the grave—he is "content on one's back"; there are "no typewriters"—reminds him of what he can no longer do. Although "I have much to open, I know immense / troubles & wonders to their secret curse," expression here is silenced; in life, his mouth "shut" and fingers "stilled" by his "fiery salt mines," he simply "stood up" to type, now there is no way to "howl my knowings." These songs, then, are another extended debate about the problematic implications of hiding in the ground as a response to loss:

> 'O get up & go in'
> somewhere once I heard. Nowadays I doze.
> It's cold here
>
> The cold is ultimating. The cold is cold.
> I am—I should be held together by—
> but I am breaking up
> and Henry has come to a full stop—
> vanisht his vision, if there was, & fold
> him over himself quietly.
>
> (S, 85)

"Get up & go in" is a version of the epigraph to Book 1 ("Go In, Brack Man, De Day's Yo' Own") and reminds us of Henry's difficulty in acting on that call in the earlier book. Clearly, as his wistful tone suggests, it was a mistake to give up the body that held him together, a mistake to let go his senses and his exfoliating self.

It is no wonder, then, that Henry proposes "returning to our life / adult & difficult" (S, 87) in order to climb "the lower slopes" of Parnassus and gaze at people: "heading not for the highest we have done / but enigmatic faces, unsurveyed, / calm as a forest glade." He begins to play with the notion of who will wake his senses, what woman will glide past his "sleepy eyes" and lisp "we do" in a "Marriage of the Dead." Who will "fill" his coffin?:

> O she must startle like a fallen gown,
> content with speech like an old sacrament
> in deaf ears lying down,
> blazing through the darkness till he feels the cold
> & blindness of his hopeless tenement
> while his black arms unfold.
>
>   (S, 89)

She must, that is, revive his senses, let him see, feel, and hear again so the world may enter. Finally, in the last song, Henry is dug up, "disencumbered" for the moment and with "no bills"—although, as in Book 1, the debate about coming out and talking being still alive, he is pictured in the last stanza as Lazarus trying "to get his own back," trying to dig himself back into the grave.

Song 110 of Book 5 contains a situation characteristic of that book as a whole. Henry is recounting a disturbing story about a police interrogation of a couple over the drowning of a child, and he sings:

> It was the blue & plain ones. I forget all that.
> My own clouds darkening hung.
> Besides, it wasn't serious.
> They took them in different rooms & fed them lies.
> 'She admitted you wanted to get rid of it.'
> 'He told us he told you to.'

Admitting that his own "clouds" hung in the way of full sight, blocking him from a clear identification with the people involved, Henry provides the reason for Book 5's investigation of his various illnesses—the need to understand what the limitations of his vision are, what pain obscures his sight. Book 5 takes and generalizes Book 2's focus on the darkening clouds of his father's death. Whitman, in his 1855 Preface, boasts that a poet will tell the world for precisely what it is: "The great poet has less a mark'd style, and is more the channel of thoughts and things without increase or diminution, and is the free channel of himself. He swears to his art, I will not be meddlesome, I will not have in my writing any elegance, or effect, or originality, to hang between me and the rest like curtains. I will have nothing hang in the way, not the richest curtains. What I tell I tell for precisely what it is."[21] Berryman, realizing that he is not "the free channel of himself," describes the poet as "a mere channel, but with its own ferocious difficulties," and one way for him to work with these difficulties is to imagine them as clouds or curtains, certain illnesses, which change or distort his vision. So, in Book 5, we examine the various blinds that hang between Henry and the world: "Here matters hard to manage at de best, / Mr. Bones. Tween what we see, what be, / is blinds. Them blinds on fire."

The book begins, appropriately enough, in the hospital, with the title of Song 92—"Room 231: the *forth* week"—offering an indication that Henry is once again ready to come out of hiding. As if to remind us of the previous posthumous songs, the poem opens with Henry yearning again back toward the ease of death, but, although teased by the desire to be an unthinking tulip and sirened to by whiskey and suffocation, he withstands the attraction and focuses on charting his rattling black nerves. He marches "forth" in Book 5, eyes bleary or fevered, but marches:

> Soon it will fall dark. Soon you'll see stars
> you fevered after, child, man, & did nothing,—
> compass live to the pencil-torch!
> As still as his cadaver, Henry mars
> this surface of an earth or other, feet south
> eyes bleared west, *waking* to march.
>   (S, 92, emphasis mine)

Henry realizes that for an artist, at least in this book, illness has use; it is something to be studied and probed: "He railed a stale abuse / upon his broad shortcomings, then lay still. / That middle-sized wildman was ill. / A hospital is where it all has a use, / so is a makar" (S, 94).

What are those blinds between the soul and things? Why has Henry's black heart been broken? Although the "illnesses" of marriage, of being forced to live his mother's life, of the collapse of his work, are all mentioned, once again, the dominant reason Henry's blinds are on fire is the suicide: "It all centered in the end on the suicide / in which I am an expert, deep & wide" (S, 136). Book 5 almost completely exhausts this downward pull. Early in the book, while still in the hospital, Henry responds to a "surly cop" by thinking of him as "a meathead, and of course he was armed, to creep / across my nervous system some time ago wrecked" (S, 95). The label *meathead* and memory of Whitman's condemnation in "Song of Myself" of those "Here and there with dimes on the eyes walking / To feed the greed of the belly the brains liberally spooning" combine to trigger a violent fantasy. Henry, in the realm where "foes are attached with axes," is actually raging at his father:[22]

> with trembling hands hoist I my true
> & legal ax, to get at the brains. I never liked brains—
> its the texture & the thought—
> but I will like them now, spooning at you,
> my guardian, slowly, until at length the rains
> lose heart and the sun flames out.

Henry imagines spooning the guard's "meathead" at his father. To shift the fantasy, we might also say that Henry throughout *The Dream Songs* has been spooning his own brains ("the texture & the thought") at his father, in hopes that the rains (or reins) diminish and the sun reappear. Even odder is the ludicrous pun on "spooning"—as if in Henry's rage he is also making eyes at his father.

The father appears again near the middle of the book in a song about Jarrell's suicide: "his friend's death made the man sit still / and freeze inside" (S, 127). The fact that Jarrell's death "had been adjudged suicide, / . . . dangles a trail longer than Henry's chill," a trail ending finally in the still unresolved death of his father: "My air is flung with souls which will not stop / and among them hangs a soul that has not died / and refuses to come home." The ghost does come home in the last three songs of Book 5. In Song 143, the interlocutor sings Henry a song "the like of which may bring your heart to break: / he's gone! and we don't know where." Henry picks up the song from the interlocutor, narrating in his voice the tale of his father, who "decided on lead."[23] Finally, as if the act of saying it releases him, Henry leaves his father buried in Oklahoma and declares his love: "That mad drive wiped out my childhood. I put him down / while all the same on forty years I love him / stashed in Oklahoma." The tab, however, is not completely clear; although the love is declared, Henry is still kept ill by the problem: "I repeat: I love him / until *I* fall into coma." Song 144 is a reminder of what the knowledge "we all are dying" does to us; when young, "death grew tall / up Henry as a child" with the result that, like a hospital orderly who wants "to be a Trappist but not to pray," Henry has lost faith in organized versions of truth: "the truths that are revealed he is not buying." The knowledge of death is like a sickness held inside, "death tugging within him, wild / to slide loose & to fall"; it is like a swelling pear splitting his skull, a dark man in the forest, an oxygen tent. And yet, Henry has been through this panic before and realizes, with a touch of easiness in his thinking, that "sorrow follows" such knowledge, but "for the time being only." Finally, in the last song, Henry uses his senses to touch his father and take him in—"I touch now his despair"—although in typical Berryman fashion, the touching is significantly qualified:

> I cannot read that wretched mind, so strong
> & so undone. I've always tried. I—I'm
> trying to forgive
> whose frantic passage, when he could not live
> an instant longer, in the summer dawn
> left Henry to live on.
>
>   (S, 145)

Book 6 is 133 songs in length, or almost as long as the first five books combined. It is most reminiscent of the catalogs of "Song of Myself," for it is here that Henry attempts to direct his "passioning attention" outward to take in the "New World." The focus is no longer on the "death of love" but on Henry's attempts to "grope forward, toward where no one else has been." As with Book 3, Berryman's Whitmanesque aim to "speak a mystery, only to you" (S, 175) by embracing his surroundings is significantly qualified by the illnesses just examined. Song 168, echoing Whitman's confrontation with the limitations of his method in section 28 ("You villain touch! what are you doing? my breath is tight in its throat, / Unclench your floodgates, you are too much for me"), reminds us of the ever-present personal limitation to Berryman's drive to make contact and speak:

> I have a story to tell you which is the worst
> story to tell that ever once I heard.
> What thickens my tongue?
> and has me by the throat? I gasp accursed
> even for the thought of uttering that word.
> I pass to the next Song:

For the most part, however, Henry's illnesses, having been examined previously, lead to union with the world rather than silence:

> I have strained everything except my ears,
> he marvelled to himself: and they're too dull—

owing to one childhood illness—
outward, for strain; inward, too smooth & fierce
for painful strain as back at the onset, yes
when Henry keen & viable

began to poke his head from Venus' foam
toward the grand shore, when all them ears would be
if any.
Thus his art started. Thus he ran from home
toward home, forsaking too withal his mother
in the almost unbearable smother.

(S, 166)

Running through his various infirmities—strained eyes, brain, nervous system; cracked ankle and arm—Henry exempts his ears from failure. Why? Because, "owing to one childhood illness" which we are well aware of by now, they were rendered "outward[ly] too dull" and "inward[ly]" "too smooth and fierce" to be hobbled by any of the "painful strain" involved in the struggles of Henry's "art." In fact, it seems that that initial illness made those ears capable of recreating—in, admittedly, a more limited fashion—the "home" and self that Henry, smothered, was forced to leave. Splicing those broken connections together again (recall the frayed cable of Song 25, the "remercied" father of Song 42), his ears now seem capable of marvelous acts. And what is true about one sense here seems true about the other four senses in different parts of Book 6. As Song 183 puts it, distancing Henry's loss ("the worst thing of all") by claiming "he only remembers it as having been had, / not as itself," and echoing Song 5 ("Mr Heartbreak, the New Man, / come to farm a crazy land"), Henry is now able to move on: "Passing out of pity into the New World / I amounted up. I sum it at five scents." It is comic, of course, to say that Henry's new work is worth only 5 cents, but we are also to notice by the pun that Henry has retained some use of all of his five senses and will, like Whitman, be able to pull the world into himself: "All this I swallow, it tastes good."

Book 6 offers several models for how Henry is to take in the world and sing forth his "long / wonder the world can bear & be" (S, 1). In Song 243, on an "undead morning," Henry runs through various possibilities to describe himself—"I . . . shuffle my poss's"—and settles on Odysseus lashed to the mast as his men row past the sirens:

Lashed here, with ears, in the narrows, memoried,
like a remaining man,
he call to him for discomfort blue-black losses,

> gins & green girls, drag of the slaying weed.
> Just when it began again
>
> I will remember, soon.

Odysseus without earwax, sirened to by his father, who offers escape from his "blue-black losses" (by way of gin, girls, or suicide), Henry is "memoried," the "remaining man" left alone after Song 1's departure. Although he anticipates the full force of his memory returning, "Just when it began," he is able to survive and listen. He is bound (by netting, by limitation), but his ears are open and eventually he will sing back what he has heard:

> Dance in the gunwales to what they cannot hear
> my lorn men. I bear every piece of it.
> Often, in the ways to come,
> when the sun rises and fulfils their fear,
> unlashed, I'll whistle bits.
> Through the mad Pillars we are bound for home.

A second model is found in the work of great artists, anguished, but singing:

> who had for all their pains above all pain
> & who brought to their work a broken heart
> but not as bad as Schubert's:
>
> that went beyond the possible: that was like a man
> dragged by his balls, singing aloud 'Oh yes'
> while to his anguisht glance
> the architecture differs.
>
> (S, 258)

Broken-hearted but singing "Oh yes"—that seems to be Henry's version of himself in this book. Or, perhaps more comically, this:

> They laid their hands on Henry, kindly like,
> and swooped him thro' the major & minor orders
> and said to him: 'You're in business.'
> 'OW' he responded. It was raining at the time,
> or cascading, or the seas were climbing up out of their borders,
> when he took up Is-ness.
>
> (S, 229)

In the catalog of Book 6, then, for all his complaints, Henry begins to be filled. Songs 216 and 217, for example, putting into play Berryman's Whitmanesque desire to "commit [Henry] to his country," attempt to work out the implications of the fact that "in my country only / cast is our lot" and conclude, as Song 218 has it, that contact with others serves, again in Whitman's language, "for letting out love." Song 237 goes even further by using one of Whitman's refrains ("I was there" from section 33 of "Song of Myself") as Henry recounts the murder of the Reverend Edward Wheeler and his lover Eleanor Mills:

> When in the flashlights' flare the adultering pair
> sat up with horror under the crab-apple tree
> (soon to be hacked away for souvenirs)
> and with breasts & brains waited, & with ears
> while masked & sheeted figures silently—
> 'Kneel, I–love,' he stammered, 'and pray,' Henry was there.

In the second stanza, again echoing Whitman, both of them shot, the woman with her throat slit, "her tongue & voice-box out, his calling card / tipped up by his left heel, Henry was toward." Yet, as if to remind us that Henry's limitations are even fiercer than Whitman's, when the two are imagined as united together—"larynx & tongue restored"—"Henry was not there."[24]

Book 7 records Henry's voyage to Ireland, a journey which he had taken once before, thirty years previously. He writes at one point of the natural tendency to look back:

> I seem to be Henry then at twenty-one
> steaming the sea again in another British boat
> again, half mad with hope:
> with my beloved Basque friend I stroll the topmost deck
> high in the windy night, in love with life
> which has produced this wreck.
>
> (S, 283)

This is a useful strategy with which to end a book, for just as the increasing distance away from America allows a clear look at the country—"Where things look more inter'sting, where things / American are seen / without America's perpetual self-laud" (S, 280)—and just as the reminders of his early hopes allow Henry to assess what he has accomplished in his life, so too the poet continually measures his accomplishments in this book ("this wreck") against his early, half-mad hopes. As with the final section of "Song of Myself," the act of ending the poem—assessing his results, summarizing his themes, pleading for the work's structure—becomes the book's dominant concern.[25] Song 308 is labelled "An Instruction to Critics," and many of the poems seem to be just that, as if Henry at the end was thinking over his book and wanted, perhaps, to point his readers in certain

directions. On the debate between hiding and loving, or being pene-
trated or not by the things of this world, for example, he writes:

> Surely I've said enough,
> my mind has been laid open
> for thirty years, as when I spoke of love
> & either could not get it or had too much of it,
> impenetrable Henry, goatish, reserved,
> whose heart is broken.
>
>   (S, 297)

And on his major themes and their ultimate antagonist: "Working
& children & pals are the point of the thing, / for the grand sea awaits
us, which will then us toss / & endlessly us undo" (S, 303). Or finally,
on his age-long struggle with his father's ghost: "an angry ghost
appeared & leaned for years / on his front stoop; elderly Henry
spread his wings / one by one by one // until the traffic could not see
it more" (S, 357). Most of these comments are straightforward versions of what we have been tracing throughout *The Dream Songs*, testifying by the directness of their language to Henry's success in thinking through his various ills, but also suggesting—in their almost
journalistic bluntness—that the strength of this poem lies in those
earlier sections where Berryman *struggles* with embrace.

The last two songs, although also summary poems, are more interesting, perhaps because they refuse to claim the poem as a complete
success. Song 384, visiting the father's grave again and making the
familiar charge that the father broke the connection, that *he* is the
"one / who cannot visit me, who tore his page / out," demonstrates
that "indifference" still has not come. Henry imagines himself dig-
ging up his father's casket, tearing apart the grave clothes, "& then
Henry / will heft the ax once more, his final card, / and fell it on
the start." What are we to make of this? The father has been notably absent from the last book, and his presence here is surprising.
In one sense, the attack can be read as a ritual completion of Henry's
demolishing of his father's hold over him: just such a murder has
been suggested throughout *The Dream Songs*. But the rage seems
to be equally directed at the poem itself, as if, in a dark version of
Whitman's confession of being finally "untranslatable," Henry would
erase his work by axing "the start." Perhaps, as Song 385 suggests,
Henry's task was impossible in the first place. The tone of this last
song is resigned—"grievy, brisk"—as Henry's mind moves first from
the thought that his daughter is "heavier" to the heavy turkeys killed
for Thanksgiving—"Everywhere in enormous numbers turkeys will

be dying / and other birds, all their wings"—and then to a sense of brooding over his own work:

> They never greatly flew. Did they wish to?
> I should know. Off away somewhere once I knew
> such things.

Turkeys aside, Henry certainly did wish his work to have wings and greatly fly. Song 359, for example, uses wings to describe Henry's release from childhood grief to moments of love: "Take down the thing then to which he was nailed. / I am a boat was moored on the wrong shelf. / Love has wings & flies." If once Henry knew "such things," now, concluding, he realizes that his knowledge may have been limited and inadequate.

Why? The final stanza makes reference again to Crane and Whitman:

> My house is made of wood and it's made well,
> unlike us. My house is older than Henry;
> that's fairly old.
> If there were a middle   ground between things and the soul
> or the sky resembled more the sea,
> I wouldn't have to scold
>
> > > my heavy daughter.
> > > (S,385)

Henry's mind moves from his literal, wooden, well-made house to an implied comparison with his own work—the house of *The Dream Songs* whose roof has been "lefted off"—and once again the implication seems to be that his own work is not made as well as he had once dreamed. To put it in Whitman's terms, Henry has not established an emotional ground between things (people, animals, objects) and the poem's central soul. Henry's complaint about the sky and the sea is a good summary of his limitations, referring as it does to the famous opening sentence of "The Open Boat": "None of them knew the color of the sky." Berryman has written extensively about this story, commenting on Crane's opening sentence in particular:

> The men are watching the sea, with anxiety about the waves, . . . and watching the horizon, with an equal anxiety to see it . . . [The sentence] has the effect, shall we say, of bringing the reader's gaze—as if taking him by the neck—*down* from the skyey expectations of the title and subtitle to what is *level* . . . and a matter of human efficiency. Crane's opening sentence is *anti*-heroic, that is to say, standing as it does like a blunt sentry, in the forefront of what looked to be an epic of the sea.

Anti-heroic, and ironic, in view of the 'big' opening (high-keyed, ex-
alted) that the reader presumably expected.

(FP, 178)

So, too, Berryman in *The Dream Songs* attempts to take his readers by
the neck; expecting a poem modeled after "Song of Myself" to be epic
and heroic, our gaze has been forced "down" from those "skyey"
expectations to the "level," "hard sea" (S, 1) of loss, limitation, and
pain. In failing to discover either the firm ground between the soul
and things prophesied by Whitman, or a convincing resemblance between Crane's gray, tightening sea and Whitman's apparently expansive freedom, Berryman has "level[ed]" our initial expectations about
his model. In doing so, wonderfully enough, he has displayed the
rich flowering of its built-in limitations.

NOTES

1. *The Dream Songs* (New York: Farrar, Straus, and Giroux, 1969). Cited in
the text by song numbers as S.

2. Quoted in James E. Miller, Jr., *The American Quest for a Supreme Fiction:
Whitman's Legacy in the Personal Epic* (Chicago: University of Chicago Press,
1979), p. 234.

3. Peter Stitt, "The Art of Poetry XVI," *Paris Review*, no. 53 (1972): 191.

4. John Berryman, *Stephen Crane* (1950, repr. New York: Farrar, Straus and
Giroux, 1975), p. 22. Cited in the text as SC.

5. Berryman, "Acceptance Speech for the National Book Award" (New
York: The National Book Committee, 1969), as quoted in John Haffenden,
John Berryman: A Critical Commentary (New York: New York University Press,
1980) and Richard Kostelanetz, "Conversation with Berryman," *Massachusetts
Review* 2 (1970): 346. For a summary of Berryman's views on the use of the
persona Henry, see Peter Stitt's "John Berryman's Criticism and His Poetry,"
John Berryman Studies, no. 10 (1977). William J. Martz in "John Berryman"
appearing in *Seven American Poets*, ed. Denis Donoghue (Minneapolis: University of Minnesota Press, 1975), p. 202, describes Henry as "an alter ego, a
device whereby the poet may look at himself, talk about himself, talk to himself, and be a multifarious personality." Martin Dodsworth in "John Berryman: An Introduction" appearing in *The Survival of Poetry*, ed. Dodsworth
(London: Faber and Faber, 1970), p. 123, describes Henry as Berryman's "better self. Henry represents a vulnerable, innocent, and childish self which
must be saved from the attacks of an impertinent and hostile world outside."
M. L. Rosenthal and Sally Gall write, in similar terms, "'Henry' is perforce
Berryman's self-mirroring protagonist, seen in a glass that splits and distorts
the reflection," *The Modern Poetic Sequence: The Genius of Modern Poetry* (New
York: Oxford University Press, 1983), p. 417. Cited in the text as MPS.

6. See also Dodsworth's comments in "John Berryman: An Introduction," pp. 127–30 on the reference to Whitman in Song 78, especially his notion that "as the hold on his own personality becomes less secure, the poet is increasingly able to identify with the perilous lives of others. . . . *The Dream Songs* are an expression of love for people, for the variety of the world, that does not overlook what is rotten in the world." For general comments on Song 78 see Miller, *The American Quest*, pp. 235–36, and for comments on Berryman's use of Whitman throughout *The Dream Songs*, pp. 235–75. I do not find Miller's thesis that the songs are "in the broadest sense about Berryman's personal transfiguration from one kind of poet [Eliotic, impersonal] to another [personal]" particularly convincing. Ronald Wallace, in *God Be with the Clown: Humor in American Poetry* (Columbia: University of Missouri Press, 1984), in terms quite close to mine, describes (p. 172) *The Dream Songs* as "a kind of parody of 'Song of Myself,' embuing Whitman's barbaric yawp with more sadness, doubt, worry, and fear than Whitman would have acknowledged." My thinking in this chapter can be seen as a response to one of the best essays on the poem, Denis Donoghue's "Berryman's Long Dream," *Art International* 13 (20 March 1969): 61–64. Donoghue argues that Berryman began with a Whitman-like notion of the poet as a medium and the self "as an ever increasing body of experiences. As the experience accrues, the self expands." But Berryman tired of the rigors of this position and fell back on "one voice, doctrinaire, edgy, magisterial." My position is that Berryman never gave up this notion of the poet as medium, although the influence of his "ill-health" significantly qualifies the success of the self's expansion.

7. Jack Barbera, "Shape and Flow in *The Dream Songs*," *Twentieth Century Literature* 22 (1976): 146–62, and John Haffenden, *John Berryman: A Critical Commentary*. Haffenden provides a "Chronology of *The Dream Songs*" that conclusively demonstrates that the poem's order is not simply chronological. Barbera comments (p. 150) that "Berryman's method in these first three Books seems to have been not so much writing Songs to fit a preconceived theme as writing Songs and then selecting among them and figuring out some plan by which to organize them."

8. Barbera refers to an outline dated May 21, 1964, that "indicates that Berryman considered the themes of the first three Books to be loss, death, and terror (and partial recovery)," "Shape and Flow," p. 150. Haffenden refers to "another loose work note (probably dating from late in 1966) which indicates that Book V represents 'hospital,' Book VI the hero 'stunted' in Minneapolis, and the final Book, a grand release summed up in the word 'Out!'" *A Critical Commentary*, p. 61. These general terms are, I think, compatible with the structure I have described.

9. In his annotations to *The Dream Songs*, Haffenden, p. 81, quotes one of Berryman's letters: "I've always supposed Dream Song 1 to be about his father's suicide, exposing him to the insolence of the world" and also discusses Berryman's references to Eden and the womb. For more on Song 1, see Joel Connaroe, *John Berryman: An Introduction to His Poetry* (New York: Columbia University Press, 1977), p. 261.

10. See, for example, Connaroe, *John Berryman*, pp. 95, 120, 198; Haffenden, *A Critical Commentary*, pp. 47–49; Miller, *The American Quest*, pp. 144–46; and Wallace, *God Be with the Clown*, pp. 173–80.

11. For more on this expedition, see Haffenden, pp. 39–40. He wrongly, I think, describes this as a poem about childhood security. See Songs 18 and 21 for examples of how the deaths of "master" poets consistently sing to Henry of the possibility of suicide.

12. Ibid., p. 83.

13. See Gary Arpin, "'I Am Their Musick': Lamentations and *The Dream Songs*," *John Berryman Studies*, no. 1 (1975): 2–6.

14. For a survey of the importance of the father, see Miller, *The American Quest*, pp. 260–65.

15. Connaroe, *John Berryman*, p. 123, writes that the "subject of death . . . dominates this section."

16. See Haffenden, *A Critical Commentary*, pp. 93–94 and Barbera, "Shape and Flow," pp. 147, 155 for more on this song.

17. Haffenden, *A Critical Commentary*, p. 94.

18. John Haffenden, "A Year on the East Coast: John Berryman, 1962–63," *Twentieth Century Literature* 22 (1976): 139–40.

19. See Haffenden, *A Critical Commentary* (pp. 102–3), who mentions that the song played was probably "Empty Bed Blues."

20. See also Song 72 in which Henry swings his daughter from "disastered trees" in a garden overlooked by judges.

21. Whitman, *Complete Poetry and Collected Prose*, p. 14.

22. Connaroe, *John Berryman*, p. 104.

23. This is open to question; there are no marks to indicate a new speaker.

24. An interesting meditative addition to this long catalog in Book 6 is the group of poems on Delmore Schwartz (146–57; 275), which frames Henry's embraces. Henry's passionate, confused response to Schwartz' death demonstrates both his desire to identify ("I have tried to be them, God knows I have tried") and the ultimate limits of that desire.

25. See the epigraph to book seven: "I thought he's lovin me but he was *leavin* all the time."

CHAPTER 2

❖   ❖   ❖

THE WAGES OF DYING IS LOVE

Galway Kinnell's *Book of Nightmares*

It is written in our hearts, the emptiness is all.
That is how we have learned, the embrace is all.[1]

These lines, appearing in 1980—nine years after Galway Kinnell's deliberate grappling with "Song of Myself" in *The Book of Nightmares*—make explicit what, for Kinnell, were the personal grounds for Whitman's work in that poem. That Whitman's use of the embrace was both limited by and formulated in rich reaction to the fact of "emptiness"—what we love vanishes—seems to Kinnell both inescapable and never directly displayed in the poem. If Whitman "clarified [the] madness" that stemmed from seeing that desired embrace blocked and found in that personal clarification the basis for a new sort of openness—"joyful health"—that struggle was, according to Kinnell's reading, conducted only as an act of "supererogation."[2] What Kinnell challenges himself to do in *The Book of Nightmares*, then, following Whitman's lead, is to meet head on the "curse" of human emptiness.[3] Although he and Berryman identify different personal difficulties preventing the poet's full embrace of his surroundings (an inherited illness, the dread of death), they both point to, and attempt to unpack the rich implications of, what Kinnell calls the single "moment" in Whitman in which the limitations of the embrace are exposed and the device is then reformulated.[4]

One way to begin to understand the deliberateness of Kinnell's unfolding of that moment is to look first at his use of the embrace in two significant early poems, "The Bear" and "The Porcupine." In both poems, Kinnell powerfully imagines himself into a union with an animal. In the first, a hunter trails a bear for seven days, living, in the hunt's final stages, on the animal's blood and droppings. The ritual identification is completed when the hunter finally encounters the dying animal, cuts it open, and climbs under the skin. In so doing, he gains not only warmth and sustenance but also a new means of expression; as he sleeps, he dreams of himself as the bear, first

"lumbering flatfooted / over the tundra," then collapsed and await-
ing death, with the wind blowing "across / my sore, lolled tongue a
song / or screech, until I think I must rise up / and dance" (BR, 62).
Likewise, in the second poem, remembering a porcupine shot from a
tree ("On the ground / it sprang to its feet, and / paying out gut
heaved / and spartled through a hundred feet of goldenrod / before /
the abrupt emptiness") Kinnell dreams of himself as that animal,
"pricking the / woman beside me until she cries" (BR, 58). Again, this
connection gives him a way to identify and speak of his own feelings
of confusion and failure: "I have come to myself empty, the rope /
strung out behind me / in the fall sun / suddenly glorified with all my
blood" (BR, 59). In both poems, although the step-by-step process of
merging poet and medium is carefully worked out and the newly ac-
quired language is explored, little attention is given to the conditions
that make the union possible. That is, just as he had observed about
"Song of Myself," Kinnell works out the connections between these
two worlds without focusing on what prompts that contact in the first
place. In these early poems, Kinnell is content simply to suggest that
an inner emptiness in the central figure—he is "starved" in one
poem, "vacant as a / sucked egg" in the other—is the source of his
openness to the dying animals.[5] In *The Book of Nightmares*, in contrast,
that initial emptiness becomes a central rather than an incidental concern—so central that one almost overlooks the fact that the poem is
also a self-portrait formed out of the series of limited embraces Kinnel
initiates in grappling with this problem. In bringing his personal confrontation with the problem of emptiness into the foreground, Kinnell comes close to directing our attention away from the equally important struggle with the mechanics of the embrace also conducted in
his poem.

Appropriately, *The Book of Nightmares* begins with Kinnell walking
through a black landscape marked by the ashes where tramps "must
have squatted down, / gnawing on stream water,/ unhouseling themselves on cursed bread" (BN, 3). As the remains of these failed com-
munions demonstrate, the world of this poem, the context within
which its meditation unfolds, is, from the beginning, cut off and
cursed with aloneness. Kinnell is marked as well, suffering what he
later describes as the "irreversible sorrow" (BN, 74) of having lost a
lover "whose face / I held in my hands / a few hours, whom I gave
back / only to keep holding the space where she was" (BN, 3). Here
in its simplest form, the empty space Kinnell cups in his hands is the
problem implicit in Whitman with which *The Book of Nightmares*
struggles: the embrace is never full because it does not last—in Berry-

man's terms, "empty grows every bed." Like those abandoned men before him, Kinnell builds a fire which, instead of comfort, offers only echoes of that loss. In the snapping and spitting wood, he hears "the snap / and re-snap of the same *embrace* being torn"; in the hissing rain he senses:

> the oath broken
> the oath sworn between earth and water, flesh and spirit,
>   broken
> to be sworn again,
> over and over, in the clouds, and to be broken again,
> over and over, on earth.
>
>   (BN, 4)

And worse, as he sings into the fire, what he hears is his voice changing, cherished memory twisting into bitterness: "the one / held note / remains—a love-note / twisting under my tongue, like the coyote's bark, / curving off, into a / howl" (BN, 4). *The Book of Nightmares*, fundamentally, is a poem meditating on its own song which, springing from a broken embrace and sung over empty hands, threatens to twist into an account of ashes and bitterness. As with *The Dream Songs*, it asks whether it is possible to move beyond that "self-hugged," abandoned howl back to an embrace of this "broken" world—whether, beginning with a limitation toward which Whitman only gestured, his passionate openness is possible.

The remainder of this first poem—first of ten—concerns Kinnell's daughter Maud, but as he tells the story of her birth and early years, we see that her presence is primarily a means of describing his own self-reflexive desires for his song. At birth, he remembers, Maud was exiled from wholeness ("the flipping / and overleaping, the watery / somersaulting alone in the oneness / under the hill" [BN, 5]) and abandoned into the world. And yet, her first response to this broken connection, as "her tie to the darkness" was cut, was not to mourn the loss of wholeness but rather to open her arms and embrace, in all its limitation, this new emptiness:

> they hang her up
> by the feet, she sucks
> air, screams
> her first song—and turns rose,
> the slow
> beating, featherless arms
> already clutching at the emptiness.
>   (BN, 6–7)

Then, imagining Maud grown up and in the same situation in which he now finds himself ("orphaned, / *emptied* / of all wind-singing, of light, / the pieces of *cursed bread* on your tongue" [BN, 8, emphasis mine]), Kinnell prays that in that future time she will remember the songs "of being and perishing" he sang to her as a child: "not the songs / of light said to wave / through the bright hair of angels, / but a blacker / rasping flowering on that tongue" (BN, 7). And, crucially, he prays that those black songs, stored in "the silent zones / of the brain" will return to her richly as songs of comfort and connection: "may there come back to you / a voice, / spectral, calling you / *sister*! / from everything that dies" (BN, 8). He prays, that is, for Maud to regain the open-armed union with the dying world she had as a child—"the light heart / we started with, but made of time and sorrow" (MA, 11), he writes in another poem[6]—for that would be a sign that *his* song of being and perishing, sung then over her cradle and sung now into this fire in the rain, had come to more than a howl of pain. His struggle with the emptiness not yet begun, and his daughter not yet in a position to describe back to him the effect of his song, Kinnell simply stares into his cupped hands, wonders, and "open[s] / this book" (BN, 8).

The five poems following this prologue attempt to nudge that howl of abandonment back into a love song. They do so through a series of partial identifications with dying, with already dead, creatures—a hen, a drunk, a soldier, a seer. As Kinnell studies these subjects, weaving himself in and out of their worlds, constructing different structures to make that union possible, he finds those patterns making visible his own unstated fears about death, extinction, and abandonment. Unlike Berryman, who moves to his songs of identification only *after* working through his various illnesses, Kinnell attempts to do both simultaneously. What he finally discovers thematically—that emptiness empowers the embrace, rather than negates it—is just what these incomplete, although forceful, identifications have demonstrated silently. "Now that the fear / has been rummaged down to its husk," Kinnell writes in another poem, " . . . there is time, still time, / for those who can groan / to sing, / for those who can sing to heal themselves" (MA, 57–58). If the poem begins with the slip from song to groan having already been made, the book as a whole attempts—as Kinnell said about Whitman—to heal itself by finding in that fear a new way of singing.

"The Hen Flower," second poem in sequence, spells out the challenge of this movement.[7] The hen, Kinnell writes, is like an infant, able to "let go" of fear and throw itself "on the mercy of darkness" (BN, 11). Hens, he feels, are drawn to what we dread most—that moment when our conscious attachment to the things of the earth is broken: "head / thrown back / on the chopping block, longing only / to die" (BN, 11). "If only / we could let go / like her," he muses to himself, then begins a series of drifting connections, imagining himself into her position. They are linked physically: he is lying face down on a pillow, "biting down on hen feathers," with "bits of the hen" he had for dinner still stuck in his teeth (BN, 11). They are linked emotionally: he remembers killing a hen and the sensation— part physical, part imaginative—as he dangled it from his hand: "wing / of my wing, / of my bones and veins, / of my flesh / hairs lifting all over me in the first ghostly breeze /after death" (BN, 12). And finally and most explicitly, they are linked conceptually: just as the hen has wings but is "unable / to fly," so he has been "made" to embrace but is "unable to hold another" in his arms. Just as he cups emptiness in his hands, so the opened cadaver of a hen reveals, in "the mass of tiny, / unborn eggs, each getting / tinier and yellower as it reaches back toward / the icy pulp / of what is," what Kinnell calls "the zero" (BN, 13).

This progression drives Kinnell away from an impression of the uniqueness of his position. He is not yet able to let go like the hen—he still dreads death—yet the various connections he has spelled out between himself and that other creature have helped him begin to read his own condition. In fact, he is reminded of an earlier "reading" of the omnipresence of death. All things vanish:

> When the Northern Lights
> were opening across the black sky and vanishing,
> lighting themselves up
> so completely they were vanishing,
> I put to my eye the lucent
> section of the spealbone of a ram—
>
> I thought suddenly
> I could read the cosmos spelling itself,
> the huge broken letters
> shuddering across the black sky and vanishing.
> (BN, 13)

Although the poem ends with Kinnell still in bed and afraid, he has learned that his position is not unique ("even these feathers freed from their wings forever / are afraid" [BN, 15]) and that it should be

possible to learn from others how to understand that fear. Having
identified the problem ("Listen, Kinnell, / dumped alive / and dying
into the old sway bed, / . . . let go"), he has also been led to a new
method—reading the "broken letters" of himself and "the cosmos"
through the "spealbone" of others.

One of the reasons that it is so difficult to let go of that fear, Kinnell
begins to understand in the next poem, "The Shoes of Wandering,"
is that, without an established system of belief, we must each invent
our own way of facing death, step by stumbling step. Unlike the
hen or a child, we no longer have an instinctive acceptance of that
emptiness on which to rely; nor, by the same token, do we have
"the mantle / of the great wanderers, who lighted / their steps by the
lamp / of pure hunger and pure thirst" (BN, 22). Instead, Kinnell's
struggle, as he *"flounders through chaos"* without a lamp, will be one
of continually losing and finding his way—a condition he rightly
dreads.[8] He reads that fear in this poem by literally putting himself in
another's shoes, buying the "dead shoes" of a stranger at a Salvation
Army store and walking out, painfully, "on the steppingstones / of
someone else's wandering" (BN, 19). Returning to his hotel, homeless
again, Kinnell collapses in another bed and the drifting sense of identification intensifies:

> And the old
> footsmells in the shoes, touched
> back to life by my footsweats, as by
> a child's kisses, rise,
> drift up where I lie
> self-hugged on the bedclothes, slide
> down the flues
> of dozed, beating hairs, and I can groan
>
> or wheeze, it will be
> the groan or wheeze of another—the elderfoot
> of these shoes
>
>   (BN, 20)

As the heat of his body brings the old smells back to life, Kinnell
is momentarily forced away from his "self-hugged" closeness; his
breathing is opened to the drunk's and soon takes on the other's
wheeze: "the groan / or wheeze of one / who lays bare his errors by a
harsher light" (BN, 21). The point here is that as Kinnell "shudder[s]
down to [the drunk's] nightmare," he is able to see his own groaning
fears intensified, laid bare under a "harsher light" than he is able
to turn on himself. The nightmare, accordingly, is a fevered, height-

ened account of life as a stumbling journey across "swampland streaked with shined water," through "jungles of burnt flesh, ground of ground / bones," and down the bloody road of time. The journey, he notes, is conducted down the paths of his own "brainwaves." As those waves are intensified, Kinnell sees in surreal colors that what is most to be feared about the nightmare of loss through which he wanders is that there is no alternative to this "temporal road." There is no full union: *"you will feel all your bones / break / over the holy waters you will never drink"* (BN, 23).

The fourth poem picks up at morning in that same desolate hotel. Kinnell hears a bell-tower's chime, then traces out the implications of the suggested pun: "—chyme / of our loves / the peristalsis of the will to love forever / drives down, grain / after grain, into the last, / coldest room, which is memory—" (BN, 27). Although we would love the things and creatures of the world "forever," they are, and we are, soon broken and ground down, reduced to the cold, distant fragments of memory by the forces of time nightmarishly described in the previous poem, and by our own impossible need to handle and hold them forever. This striking label for memory makes possible the introduction of another figure through which Kinnell can read himself: a woman named Virginia, who lives along the Juniata River, a region Kinnell has seen mistakenly described as "now vanished, but extant in memory, / a primal garden lost forever" (BN, 28). Like the drunk and the hen, Virginia can be said, because of the mistake, to speak from the ground-away, vanished land of memory. She is already lost to the poet. As her letters indicate, she is a kind of visionary who, in fact, does sense that she has already left this broken world. She is "an actual person I've had a long correspondence with," Kinnell comments in an interview. "She is a mystic, a seer. . . . She sees past the world and lives in the cosmos" (WDS, 108). What Virginia tells him from her vanished world—she signs her letters "faithless to this life" and "in the darkness"—are, for this poem, the same, increasingly familiar facts, delivered in the impassioned language of mandalas, figure eights, and demon lovers: the body is a *"dear shining casket,"* God's "prey," and does not last.

Perhaps more interesting is the manner in which Kinnell tries to put himself in Virginia's place, a slightly different manner of reading himself than that used in the two previous poems. First, he imagines the destruction of her first world, its "primal garden" being overrun by "root-hunters" who lever-up and pull away the potent mandrake roots:

> On this bank—our bank—
> of the blue, vanished water, you lie,
> crying in your bed, hearing those
> small,
> fearsome thrumps
> of leave-taking trespassing the virginal woods at dusk.
>
> (BN, 29)

Next, he asks himself what a seer would do when confronted with such a loss: perhaps concoct a magic ritual in which the violated roots are ground up (as those we love are broken down by time's "digestion"), then fermented and drunk. What sort of knowledge would such a potion bring? Kinnell invents a speech in which Virginia describes his surprising vision on awakening: not the lost, "virginal" world recovered, but a world composed only of the "scraps / and jettisons of time mortality / could not grind down into his meal of blood and laughter" (BN, 29); not a world made new, but this one where what we love is "drawn / down by the terror and terrible lure / of vacuum." But what she also lets him see is that the continual disappearance of the world brings with it an openness toward the scraps that remain, that although his lost lover will not be returned, a new sort of face will materialize in his empty hands: "a face materializes into your hands, / on the absolute whiteness of pages / a poem writes itself out: its title—the dream / of all poems and the text / of all loves—'Tenderness toward Existence'" (BN, 29). What Virginia has done, then, insofar as the poet has been able to enter her position, is give Kinnell another voice with which to reject the improper dream of transcending this world. From her superior position, already beyond this world, she has allowed him to suggest that the empty hands of a shattered embrace might be filled by a poem, turning itself—like Whitman—tenderly toward existence. Although the poem ends with Kinnell, in his own voice, on his own "dark shore," still holding on to his fear ("I lie without sleeping, remembering / the ripped body / of hen"), an advance has been made (BN, 30).

"In the Hotel of Lost Light" moves that advance a bit farther. It is set in the same hotel, Kinnell stretched out on the bed in which the drunk died and watching a fly:

> I watch, as he
> must have watched, a fly
> tangled in mouth-glue, whining his wings,
> concentrated wholly on

time, time, losing his way worse
down the downward-winding stairs

(BN, 35)

Now, however, the fly that had been whining and struggling against time, a figure for Kinnell's own stumbling journey down his "temporal road," is seen to transform itself by accepting the inevitability of its death:

Now the fly
ceases to struggle, his wings
flutter out the music blooming with failure
of one who gets ready to die, as Roland's horn, winding down
from the Pyrenees, saved its dark, full flourishes
for last.

(BN, 35)

The fly functions as a kind of summary—as it "lets go" (Poem 2) of its struggle to permanently embrace the world, it blossoms. Maud ("the blue / flower opens"), the hen ("hen flower"), and Kinnell's dark crib song ("a blacker / rasping flowering on that tongue") have been described in similar terms, and now we see why: they bloom with "failure," for in ceasing to hold, self-hugged, onto life, an unfolding or opening occurs. As we have seen in both Whitman and Berryman, giving up the impossible struggle to embrace the world naively, and giving up any resultant bitterness, they flower into the dark, full recovery of "Tenderness toward Existence."[9]

But, it is one thing to see this blooming in a fly, quite another to accomplish it oneself. Again, to begin approaching this knowledge, Kinnell draws on someone outside of himself—a medium. He notes first that he rests in the same lefthand sag of the bed in which the drunk died ("my body slumped out / into the shape of his" [BN, 35]), then—like the hunter in the body of the bear, or his warm feet in the old, dead shoes—he finds himself filling out the other's emptied form and gaining a new voice:

Flesh
of his excavated flesh,
fill of his emptiness,
after-amanuensis of his after-life,
I write out
for him in this languished alphabet
of worms, these last words
of himself

(BN, 36)

Taking dictation from the drunk, borrowing his alphabet of concerns, Kinnell begins to describe death in terms that are, if not yet those of "one who gets ready to die," certainly those of one experimenting with a new sense of expectancy. So, in his creation of the drunk's words, death is described as a flowering of sorts ("I blacked out into oblivion by that crack in the curb where the forget-me blooms"), a change of colors ("I painted my footsoles purple for the day when the beautiful color would show"), or simply a shucking-off of flesh ("*To Live* / has a poor cousin, / who calls tonight, who pronounces the family name / *To Leave*, she / changes each visit the flesh-rags on her bones" [BN, 36–37]). In all of these descriptions, we hear the first notes of a healing, a new song, delivered with some hesitancy and, as yet, solely in another's voice, in which the "shards and lumps" of what we love "re-arise / in the pear tree, in spring, to shine down / on two clasping what they dream is another" (BN, 37).

The sixth poem, "The Dead Shall Be Raised Incorruptible," challenges that new song. It argues that rather than the vision of death as a flowering ("Violet bruises come out / all over his flesh, as invisible / fists start beating him a last time; the whine / of omphalos blood starts up again, the puffed / bellybutton explodes" [BN, 37]), we prefer, as a culture, the dream of incorruptibility—death as an extension of life. Rather than those broken fragments "re-arising" in a proper attitude toward what remains, we insist that they "be raised incorruptible"— miraculously untouched by death. And it argues further that the institutions and policies we have created to keep death at bay have the same root as Kinnell's own fears and thus are also, as they will be for Robert Duncan as well, voices he must acknowledge playing within himself. The obvious example, for a poem published in 1971, is Vietnam. Kinnell begins this poem with a three-part structure designed to expose that shared dream. First, he describes a burning "piece of flesh" abandoned on a battlefield, then the remains of other bodies scattered behind a hospital: "carrion, caput mortuum, / orts, / pelf, / fenks, / sordes, / gurry dumped from hospital trashcans" (BN, 41). The tone here—supported by the unfamiliar ·language—is one of deep disgust, a disgust linked to the presence of death of which these shattered body parts forcibly remind us. The next two scenes offer examples of what we have done to suppress that dread. In one, Kinnell imagines a Vietnam-era tailgunner, confined to a mental ward and obsessively reliving a series of indiscriminate killings. They were killings, we realize as we overhear, made attractive by the sensation of his weapon in action: "'It was only / that I loved the *sound* / of them, I guess I just loved / the *feel* of them sparkin' off my hands . . .'"

(BN, 42). In the other scene, Kinnell chants the familiar, equally obsessive litany of television: "Do you have a body that sweats? / Sweat that has odor? / False teeth clanging into your breakfast? / Case of the dread?" (BN, 42). The connection between these three scenes is the last word quoted—dread. Fear of death is translated into fear of the flowering flesh of the body and then into the search for a means of disguising its nature. That product, whether a gun or deodorant, this poem suggests, replaces the "feel" and "sound" of the broken world with the shine of technology. "Technology," Kinnell explains in an interview, "is the latest of the methods we use to overcome the fear of death. The sense of dominion it gives us allows us to suppress the knowledge of our own mortality" (WDS, 98–99).[10] What the opening poems of *The Book of Nightmares* try to do is just the opposite—make visible again what we have suppressed.

The voice Kinnell takes on in this poem to "read" his position is that of our entire dying race delivering a last will and testament; he calls himself "Christian man," remarking in an interview that it is a term he uses to mean "technological man" (WDS, 98). Acknowledging the various acts of domination that have separated him from the earth, and, through the itemizing suggested by the form of a will, forced to see himself as eventually broken and shattered ("My stomach, which has digested / four hundred treaties giving the Indians / eternal right to their land, I give to the Indians"), Kinnell looks at the life he has lived with "eyes that can't close" then "give[s] the emptiness my hand" and "ask[s] a ride into the emptiness" (BN, 43–44). This marks a turning for the poem; after facing and acknowledging the most extreme results of our fear of death, Kinnell is now able to let that fear go, no longer seeking to suppress his knowledge of the emptiness.[11]

The Book of Nightmares turns outward at this point and begins to examine the expansive embrace prompted by no longer denying death. Two brief scenes at the close of the sixth poem anticipate that second, and new, movement. First, a soldier with his body ruined by war runs from battle (*"my neck broken I ran / holding my head up with both hands"*) but, rather than howling or groaning, clings to his life and the world whose beauty is suddenly clarified for him: *"the flames may burn the oboe / but listen buddy boy they can't touch the notes"* (BN, 44). So, too, when Kinnell imagines a final, postwar world populated only by the scraps of humanity's leavings (as in Poem 4), he discovers that even these fragments ("memories left in mirrors on whorehouse ceilings, / angel's wings / flagged down into the snows of yesteryear") stubbornly cling to existence: *"do not let this last hour*

pass, / do not remove this last, poison cup from our lips" (BN, 45). In both
scenes, as Kinnell remarks in an interview, there is a "pray[er] for
earthly experience to continue no matter how painful and empty it
has become" (WDS, 109). What the first movement of *The Book of
Nightmares* has done, then, is rummage the fear of death down to its
husk, arriving at a stubborn celebration of earthly existence. Once
that fear has been made visible through the voices of others, the argument of the poem goes, it can be overcome, and death can be seen
to heighten and empower the embrace. Of that new knowledge, Kinnell comments in an essay, "That we last only for a time, that everyone and everything around us lasts only for a time, that we know
this, radiates a thrilling, tragic light on all our loves, all our relationships." [12] Or, in the soldier's panicky phrase that now reveals unexpected significance: *"This corpse will not stop burning!"*—it flowers into
something new. In fact, one suddenly realizes, it has been no accident
that Kinnell, obsessed with death, has made his way to this argument
by reading himself through other dying creatures; for what has been
acted out by these readings is precisely that fact that such a shared
condition (they are all corpses-to-be) might issue forth in powerful,
although indirect, union.

In the last poems of the sequence, Kinnell concentrates on working
out the tragic radiance of human relationships within his own family
and does so in his own voice. But, although he moves on to embrace
the world, each of these next three poems is also centered on a problem; each struggles with the temptation to forget what was learned
and to give in again to fear. In a sense, there is a constant stumbling,
as Kinnell learns and relearns, finds and loses his way. With each
public misstep, he insists on the struggle involved in seeing and accepting the implications of embracing what dies.

The seventh poem, "Little Sleep's-Head Sprouting Hair in the
Moonlight," is addressed to Maud one night when she wakes screaming from a nightmare. Kinnell lifts her from her crib, embraces her,
then interprets—or rather, misinterprets—the significance of that action. "You cling to me / hard, / as if clinging could save us," he writes.
"I think / you think / I will never die" (BN, 49). That is, he supposes
she clings because of her fear of the night and of death, clings to be
saved. Moved by her apparent need for his power and "permanence," he attempts to act that role, protectively whispering "I would
brush your sprouting hair of the dying light, / I would scrape the rust
off your ivory bones, / I would help death escape through the little
ribs of your body, / . . . [until] lovers no longer whisper to the presence beside them in the dark, *O corpse-to-be* . . ." (BN, 49–50). Giving

up all he has learned—those we love will inevitably become corpses, that is why we love them—Kinnell falls back on the desire to lift Maud free from the rhythms of this dying world. But then, after a moment, the earlier imagery of the book comes rushing back in. She clings not to be saved from loss but because of loss, not because he represents permanence but because he will be lost some day: "Yes, / you cling because / I, like you, only sooner / than you, will go down / the path of vanished alphabets, / the roadlessness / to the other side of the darkness" (BN, 50).

In a sense, Kinnell has tested himself and the earlier sections of the poem here. As if to repeat that lesson out loud, repeating his imaginative gesture at the end of the first poem, he imagines Maud at his age, walking through "the black stones / of the field, in the rain, // and the stones saying / over their one word, *ci-gît, ci-gît, ci-gît*" (BN, 51). What he whispers this time is his hope that, surrounded by stones testifying to her losses—or as the first poem would have it, "orphaned, / emptied"—she will have relearned what she knows now as an infant: *the wages / of dying is love*" (BN, 53). Anticipation of the "still undanced cadence of vanishing" need not lead to madness or bitterness or to the reaching out for illusory tokens of permanence—no, he whispers, it can lead to a passionate attachment to the vanishing things of this world: "Kiss / the mouth / which tells you, *here, / here is the world*. This mouth. This laughter. These temple bones" (BN, 52). He is whispering, we realize, to himself, repeating back the "healing" his song, in embracing the drunk, fly, and so on, has almost inadvertently been demonstrating all along.

The eighth poem tests the embrace out in Kinnell's own marriage. He is in bed with his wife, who is pregnant with their second child. Perhaps in response to her changed body, he describes them as "two mismatched halfnesses lying side by side in the darkness" (BN, 57). In a sense, the phrase encapsulates Kinnell's version of one possible reason Whitman's embrace must remain a limited gesture. According to Aristophanes, he muses, we were originally part of a perfect union from which we were torn away: "each of us / is a torn half / whose lost other we keep seeking across time / until we die, or give up— / or actually find her" (BN, 57–58). That theory explains both the universal sense of loss we all hold deep within and the misfitting embrace with his wife. Would it be possible to regain that original wholeness and thus avoid the need to embrace a stranger? Might we embrace fully? Kinnell is tempted to say yes. Perhaps the lost lover of the book's opening poem was his "true" other and, for a moment, he had "actually found her, / held her face a few hours / in my hands;

and for reasons—cowardice, / loyalties, all which goes by the name 'necessity'—/ left her" (BN, 58). Perhaps, if he had known, it would have been possible to avoid "necessity" and, as Berryman would have it, to have remained in that "sycamore . . . all at the top," entering a world not defined by loss:

> Suppose I had stayed
> with that woman of Waterloo, suppose
> we had met on a hill called Safa, in our own country,
> that we had lain out on the grass
> and looked into each other's blindness, . . .
>
> I think I might have closed my eyes, and moved
> from then on like the born blind,
> their faces
> gone into heaven already.
>
> (BN, 60)

With that union, he would have remained in his "own country," blind to this imperfect world and its straining and clutching after brief comforts.

But, he immediately realizes, it is precisely this world and its pleasures that are the glories of life; and it is "the wound itself," that painful sense of from what we have been torn, that causes us to sing and clutch and desire, accomplishing, "for a moment, the wholeness the drunk Greek / extrapolated from his high / or flagellated out of an *empty* heart, // that purest, / most tragic concumbence, strangers / clasped into one, a moment, of their moment on earth" (BN, 58). To dream of regaining that original wholeness, then, is to deny the transient, tragic lights of the earth and to be blind to desire. Instead of wholeness, Kinnell admits once again, we have the riches of momentary human embraces—the memory, for example, of him and his wife, clasped as one, on Whitman's "beautiful uncut hair of graves":

> the bees glittered in the blossoms
> and the bodies of our hearts
> opened
> under the knowledge
> of tree, on the grass of the knowledge
> of graves, and among the flowers of the flowers.
>
> And the brain kept blossoming
> all through the body, until the bones themselves could think,
> (BN, 59)

Such an unfolding of human potential (recall the other images of flowering) is made possible only by loss—the knowledge that drives us to vision, and consciousness, and desire. That Kinnell stresses the *"knowledge* of graves" as the ground for his embrace points quite consciously toward what he has added to "Song of Myself." Where Whitman, in "joyful health," can declare "to die is different from what any one supposed, and luckier," Kinnell has forced himself to work through his own line of inner debate that might issue forth in such openness. It is, for Kinnell, the knowledge of loss that prompts our songs, the "call back across the darkness / of the valley of not-knowing / the only word tongues shape without intercession, // yes . . . yes . . ." (BN, 61).

This eighth poem concludes with the prediction of "a kind of fate" toward which Kinnell and those he loves stumble, hand in hand: "some field, maybe, of flaked stone / scattered in starlight / where the flesh / swaddles its skeleton a last time / before the bones go their way without us" (BN, 61). This field of arrowheads is an imagined place where our ties with the earth are broken; it is the context for the embrace. In the ninth poem, Kinnell imagines actually walking through this field, and as he walks, he confronts one last time the temptation to flee its brokenness. He tries to release himself from the world's rhythms in two ways. First, he links himself with what seems the stones' drive away from the broken world:

> I walk out from myself,
> among the stones of the field,
> each sending up its ghost-bloom
> into the starlight, to float out
> over the trees, seeking to be one
> with the unearthly fires kindling and dying
>
> in space—
>
> (BN, 66)

But even as he speaks, he realizes that the blossoming stones are continually "falling back, knowing / the sadness of the wish / to alight / back among the glitter of bruised ground" (BN, 66). The bruised earth is all there is.

Second—reversing the direction, but under the same temptation— Kinnell imagines descending from that broken field to an inner chamber of the earth: "the unbreathable goaf / of everything I ever craved and lost." There he encounters an alchemist ("An old man, a stone / lamp at his forehead, squats / by his hell-flames, stirs into / his pot / chopped head / of crow") with the supposed power to transform the lapsed and ground-down fragments of life into something transcendent. Instead, as with the seer of Poem 4, examination reveals: "Noth-

ing. / Always nothing. Ordinary blood / boiling away in the glare of
the brow lamp" (BN, 67). And it is this discovery—gained and lost
throughout the book—that the "ordinary blood" of the earth is all
there is to turn to, that frees Kinnell to make his strongest account of
connection.

> I crawl up: I find myself alive
> in the whorled
> archway of the fingerprint of all things,
> skeleton groaning,
> blood-strings wailing the wail of all things.
>   (BN, 68)

His groans are the world's; the wail of his bones and sinews is the
wail of all dying things.[13] Avoiding the last false option of transcen-
dence, he acts out his version of Whitman, deliberately "sett[ing]
against his despondency all his gratefulness" (WIW, 226) and embracing his surroundings.

The final poem in the sequence serves as a summation: it reaches
back and quite consciously revises a number of the book's opening
images in light of Kinnell's deeper understanding of the embrace.
First, returning to the "black ashes, black stones, where tramps /
must have squatted down," Kinnell thinks again of the fire he built in
response to his loss. Rather than sputtering out into black, dead remains, it (and the poem for which it is a figure) has proved a radiant
center: "it warms / everyone who might wander into its radiance, / a
tree, a lost animal, the stones, // because in the dying world it was set
burning" (BN, 71) Second, the black bear, which had appeared in the
first poem as a model of instinctive acceptance of life's rhythms, appears again in the same pose. But now, the bear "understands" that
Kinnell has worked his way back to its position; the poet and the bear
have merged:

> he understands
> a creature, a death-creature
> watches from the fringe of the trees,
> finally he understands
> I am no longer here, he himself
> from the fringe of the trees watches
> a black bear
>   (BN, 71–72)

In a sense, we see here the same embrace as earlier in the "The Bear,"
but an embrace worked out quite consciously now in full awareness
of its grounds and limitations. Third, Kinnell's acceptance of the posi-

tive effects of emptiness are summarized: as contentedly standing near an echoing cliffside, fully conscious of the fact that the next step brings one to the point "where the voice calling from stone / no longer answers, / turns into stone, and nothing comes back" (BN, 72–73); and as the number of this last poem, "one / and zero / walk[ing] off together, / . . . one creature / walking side by side with the emptiness" (BN, 73). And finally, the book's opening image—Kinnell's cupped, empty hands—is returned to by way of a concert violinist who "puts the irreversible sorrow of his face / into the opened palm / of the wood" and produces, in a shower of rosin, "the sexual wail / of the back-alleys and blood strings we have lived." The violinist's wail, now holding an entire concert hall captive in its power, is a final refiguring of the poet's opening "howl"; that howl, made as it has been out of Kinnell's sense of a division within himself and potentially within Whitman, overcoming his fear then giving into it again, in first one voice then another, has become, in its widest sense, a concert: a "concert of one / divided among himself" (BN, 75). What is most notable about the last poem of the sequence is that there is no longer a struggle. Kinnell has passed through his confrontation with human emptiness, as he is sure Whitman must have, but in full view, and he has transformed what he sees as the unstated sense of loss in "Song of Myself" back into its obvious sense of power, splintered and brief, but directed outward toward the world.

NOTES

1. Galway Kinnell, *Mortal Acts, Mortal Words* (Boston: Houghton Mifflin, 1980), p. 39. Cited in the text as MA. Other Kinnell texts referred to are: BR, *Body Rags* (Boston: Houghton Mifflin, 1968); BN, *The Book of Nightmares* (Boston: Houghton Mifflin, 1971); WDS, *Walking Down the Stairs: Selections from Interviews* (Ann Arbor: University of Michigan Press, 1978); WIW, "Whitman's Indicative Words," in *Walt Whitman: The Measure of His Song*, ed. Jim Pearlman, Ed Folsom, and Dan Campion (Minneapolis: Holy Cow! Press, 1981).

2. See my "Introduction" for a full discussion of these issues. Paul Zweig, in his recent biography *Walt Whitman: The Making of the Poet* (New York: Basic Books, 1984) makes a similar point: "Whitman would not make poetry out of the argument with himself. Instead, he would pour ecstasies of hope and anticipation into a dream of self-making, of self-transcendence, of which the fundamental discipline would be the making of poems. These poems would not be monologues of inward conflict and resolution. They would leap cleanly, with a tone of casual conviction, into a vision of expanded being" (p. 195). Lee Zimmerman, in the useful *Intricate and Simple Things: The Poetry of Galway Kinnell* (Urbana: University of Illinois Press, 1987), takes up this

issue as well. Quite properly aware that for Kinnell "pain and death . . . have
an insistent and tragic presence that he wants not to denigrate," Zimmerman
writes: "Kinnell doesn't directly accuse Whitman of a too-quick-and-easy
Tennysonian consolation or of letting his transcendentalism eclipse a proper
confrontation with pain and death, but he does feel that Whitman hides his
own human effort to accommodate them, to his poetic detriment" (pp. 11–12).
However, Zimmerman leaves Kinnell's criticisms there, not continuing, as I
do, to his statement that Whitman *did*, although outside the stated program
of his poetry, work through just such a confrontation. Accordingly, Zimmerman finds Kinnell's early "The Avenue Bearing the Initial of Christ into the
New World" to be "the most Whitmanesque of Kinnell's poems"—not only
because of the way the poem accumulates detail, but also because it "remain[s] relatively free of struggle" (p. 49), thereby covering over where "Kinnell's poetics depart from Whitman's, [in] incorporating a truer sense of
tragedy" (p. 12). Although I read this book after completing my chapter, the
entire argument I make here—that struggle and a confrontation with death
are exactly what Kinnell finds present and generative in Whitman—could be
seen as a response to such a reading.

   3. For other remarks by Kinnell on his use of Whitman, see his essay "The
Poetics of the Physical World," *Iowa Review* 2, no. 3 (1971): 113–16. On the
importance of this movement in Kinnell's work as a whole, see, for example,
Alan Williamson, *Introspection and Contemporary Poetry* (Cambridge: Harvard
University Press, 1984), pp. 87–89.

   4. The most important essay to date on this poem, Cary Nelson's "Eccle-
siastical Whitman" in *Our Last First Poets: Vision and History in Contemporary
American Poetry* (Urbana: University of Illinois Press, 1981), pp. 63–96, examines a similar relationship between Kinnell and Whitman. Nelson makes a
historical argument (pp. 63–64): that Kinnell has set himself up to compete
for Whitman's "prophetic voice," to speak for his entire country, but has
found "his effectiveness as a visionary speaker . . . undercut by the brute
reality of American history." Thus, in contrast to Whitman, Kinnell's poem
can claim only a formal resolution which, because it "cannot transform the
national history it acknowledges," testifies to its own failure to embrace the
world (pp. 94–96). In the following pages, I make a different argument: that
the difference between the two poets is best understood in personal terms,
with Kinnell competing for and modifying Whitman's more limited stance as
a self-portraitist, not a prophet. In these terms, I will argue, the reality of
such an experience as the Vietnam War needs only to be acknowledged, not
transformed.

   5. Kinnell has commented in an interview: "the poem deals with various
creatures and things with whom I have an affinity. You can really write only
about things you identify with, to some degree. Each creature or thing you
write about brings out some aspect of yourself." Thomas Gardner, "An Interview with Galway Kinnell," *Contemporary Literature* 20 (1979): 428–29. Two
useful examinations of empathy in Kinnell are Charles Molesworth, "The
Poetry of Galway Kinnell" in his *The Fierce Embrace: A Study of Contemporary*

American Poetry (Columbia: University of Missouri Press, [1979]), particularly pp. 104–9, and Robert Langbaum, "On Galway Kinnell's *Book of Nightmares,*" *American Poetry Review* 8, no. 2 (1979): 30–31. Zimmerman (*Intricate and Simple Things*, pp. 110–27), has a strong discussion of these two poems and the question of empathy, rightly stressing the struggle involved in Kinnell's version of this act: "even as his presumption of kinship aligns him with Whitman and the others, his ingrained sense of the difficulty of this kinship distinguishes him from many of them" (p. 119).

6. In *Walking Down the Stairs*, Kinnell comments: "Children live with death almost as animals do. This natural trust in life's rhythms, infantile as it is, provides the model for the trust they may struggle to learn later on" (p. 46).

7. In *Walking Down the Stairs*, Kinnell remarks: " 'The Hen Flower' was the first poem I finished of the sequence. It expresses the dread that is the poem's starting point. It addresses the protagonist before he begins the journey of the poem, instructing him to let go, to surrender to existence" (p. 47).

8. Nelson (*Our Last First Poets*, p. 94) makes a very important point about what he rightly calls the "incredibly elaborate" system of textual repetition and variation in this poem. But what he sees as an attempt to overcome history in "the self-referential perfection of the book's formal development," I see as an acknowledgment of struggle. Each repetition is a reminder of where he has been; the mistakes and successes of the previous poems are carried forward as public testimony to the stages of the journey, demonstrating—perhaps too insistently—his distance from Whitman's "unavowed" struggle.

9. Kinnell has referred more than once to the way Dickinson's "I heard a Fly buzz—when I died" uses the fly to capture the heightened feeling one might have for the world at the moment of death. See, for example, *Walking Down the Stairs* (p. 23) and "The Poetics of the Physical World" (p. 120).

10. See also his essay "Poetry, Personality, and Death," *Field* 4 (Spring 1971): 61: "The more we conquer nature, the more nature becomes our enemy, and since we are, like it or not, creatures of nature, the more we make an enemy of the very life within us."

11. Nelson (*Our Last First Poets*, pp. 94–96) argues that this Vietnam poem subverts the book's "perfection" because Kinnell has not been able to absorb it into his "verbal matrix." As I have just tried to demonstrate, however, the poem forms a significant part of the emptiness-embrace pattern.

12. Kinnell, "The Poetics of the Physical World," p. 125.

13. See Gardner, "An Interview with Galway Kinnell," p. 428: "When I was writing that, I was, of course, thinking of some sort of sympathetic and permanent linking of my life and the life of all things on earth."

CHAPTER 3

❖　❖　❖

FAR FROM THE CRASH OF THE LONG SWELL

Theodore Roethke's "North American Sequence"

Theodore Roethke shares with Berryman and Kinnell a commitment to Whitman's embrace as a means of singing forth what is "in me" but "without name." "It is paradoxical," he writes in an essay on "establishing a personal identity," "that a very sharp sense of the being, the identity of some other being—and in some instances, even an inanimate thing—brings a corresponding heightening and awareness of one's own self . . . ."[1] For Roethke as well, that increased awareness is the result of gaining or developing a language. What Kinnell describes as filling out the "languished alphabet" of another, and Berryman pictures as dressing "up & up" in different costumes, Roethke understands as the act of expanding another's "terms"—as in this early response to the work of Leonie Adams: "I loved her so much, her poetry, that I just had to become, for a brief moment, a part of her world. For it is her world, and I had filled myself with it, and I had to create something that would honor her in her own terms. . . . That poem is a true release in its way. I was too clumsy and stupid to articulate my own emotions" (OPC, 66). Unlike Berryman and Kinnell, however, what complicates and limits the embrace for Roethke—what needs to be acknowledged and worked with before any "release" of the spirit into articulation occurs—is the "sharp sense" of difference between "one's own self" and "some other being."[2] Where Kinnell and Berryman assumed that the embrace was disrupted by problems with the perceiver—and that its reformulation thus depended on the poet's clarity in examining his own personal struggles—Roethke sees a more fundamental disruption or gap, one more usefully addressed by asking about technique. As he puts it: "The human problem is to find out what one really is: whether one exists, whether existence is possible. But how?" (OPC, 20). If self and medium are separate, Roethke's struggle, like Whitman's in sections 30–38 of "Song of Myself," is to work out what sort of indirect approach might yet prompt the "flights of a fluid and swallowing soul."

The problematic nature of making contact with another and thereby singing the self has, of course, been central to Roethke's work throughout his career, although perhaps only his extended "North American Sequence" works out and puts into practice all of the implications of that process. The two "Cuttings" poems from his early greenhouse sequence, however, quite dramatically frame Roethke's approach to the problem. The first poem points to the occurrence of a progressively deeper embrace—and thus "a corresponding heightening and awareness of . . . [the] self"—by tracing the movements of the poet's eye. We see the just-reviving cuttings from a distance as "Sticks-in-a-drowse," then are brought close enough to notice their "intricate stem-fur," moved inside to notice how the "small cells bulge" as water is gradually absorbed, and finally are brought to rest under the soil—face up against "one nub of growth" that actively "nudges a sand-crumb loose" (CP, 37). Two things happen: the poet struggles through to a fuller, more participatory way of seeing, and the cutting comes back to life.

What this parallel implies but never states is that the struggle with medium—the struggle to see it, use it, enter it—has led to growth in the perceiver as well as in the cutting. If that was so, the next poem speculates, turning to the same cuttings "(later)," what sort of poetic implications would follow? Roethke is of two minds in answering. His first try is the traditional one: ignoring his own struggle to see, he turns the slips into tortured, reviving saints, declaring his own distance from them to be a non-issue: "This urge, wrestle, resurrection of dry sticks, / Cut stems struggling to put down feet, / What saint strained so much, / Rose on such lopped limbs to a new life?" Then he revises himself: if that distance *was* the issue, then what those changes in seeing accomplished was the spurt of his own new beginning:

> I can hear, underground, that sucking and sobbing,
> In my veins, in my bones I feel it,—
> The small waters seeping upward,
> The tight grains parting at last.
> When sprouts break out,
> Slippery as fish,
> I quail, lean to beginnings, sheath-wet.
>
> (CP, 37)

Rather than stepping back from the problem of distance, this second attempt insists that in acknowledging the gap between himself and the cuttings, then working by observation and imagination to cut that separation down, his initial response had suggested a new way of speaking. That these two opposing responses to what is "sharp" and vibrant in something other are simply juxtaposed here suggests that Roethke hasn't yet explored the full implications of embracing and working with a medium. But, as the following reading of "North American Sequence," his strongest work, argues, the techniques developed near the end of his career to weave himself into something external are quite similar to what is proposed in the last stanza of "Cuttings (later)."

"The Longing," first poem of the sequence, presents a blasted landscape that functions as an obvious correlative for the initial condition of Roethke's consciousness. Like the drowsing cuttings, all is asleep or decaying, slowed to a decidedly uneasy rest with no "balm" or promise anywhere apparent: "A kingdom of stinks and sighs, / Fetor of cockroaches, dead fish, petroleum, / . . . The slag-heaps fume at the edge of the raw cities: / The gulls wheel over their singular garbage" (CP, 187). The longing of the poem's title is touched on by suggestions that an earlier state has exhausted itself, leaving only memories of a once-vibrant world: "The great trees no longer shimmer; / Not even the soot dances" (CP, 187). In parallel fashion, Roethke notes that his own spirit—fatigued by sterile lust, drained by unfulfilled dreams of contact—is also unable now to engage the world actively: "Less and less the illuminated lips, / Hands active, eyes cherished; / Happiness left to dogs and children—" (CP, 187). Without the possibility of embracing this landscape, his spirit cannot develop and takes on the shape of a slug—a creature Roethke has described in another poem as simply "the cold slime come into being" (CP, 151): "And the spirit fails to move forward, / But shrinks into a half-life, less than itself, / Falls back, a slug, a loose worm / Ready for any crevice, / An eyeless starer" (CP, 187). As Richard Blessing notes, Roethke's pun on "eyeless" is quite important, for without the eyes actively responding to the world, the poet's internal "I" must always be less than itself.[3] Unable to touch another and so approximate its inner world, the spirit is simply asleep, deep within a crevice.

The memory of shimmering landscape and responsive soul in the poem's first section and the prediction of that state regained in the second section ("How comprehensive that felicity! . . . / A body with the motion of a soul. / . . . The light cries out, and I am there to hear—" [CP, 188]) suggest that exhaustion and waking of the spirit are joined cyclically. In fact, the shock of finding oneself inarticulate and being forced to gain speech again seems, in Roethke, to be a necessary condition for an increase in consciousness: "Are not some experiences so powerful and profound (I am not speaking of the merely compulsive) that they repeat themselves, thrust themselves upon us, again and again, with variation and change, each time bringing us closer to our own most particular (and thus most universal) reality? We go, as Yeats said, from exhaustion to exhaustion. To begin from the depths and come out—that is difficult; for few know where the depths are or can recognize them; or, if they do, are afraid."[4] Continually lifting himself from the depths and giving body to what was shapeless gives Roethke the opportunity, through the "variation and change" of each new act of formation, to unfold more and more of his own "most particular . . . reality." In this opening poem, Roethke finds himself stalled and the impulse to embrace exhausted. As the sequence continues, he will continually drop back to this state, often by raising new questions and fears about the embrace itself, in order to give himself an opportunity to work himself out of the mire once again. Repeatedly made shapeless, repeatedly forced to confront his "wretched" inability to take in the world, he will both define a self and think through the act of definition by flowering, petal after petal: "To this extent I'm a stalk. / —How free; how all alone. / Out of these nothings / —All beginnings come" (CP, 188).

The first movement out of emptiness that comes is a detailed expression of longing for the embrace's return:

> I would with the fish, the blackening salmon, and the
>   mad lemmings,
> The children dancing, the flowers widening.
> Who sighs from far away?
> I would unlearn the lingo of exasperation, all the
>   distortions of malice and hatred;
> I would believe my pain: and the eye quiet on the growing
>   rose;
> I would delight in my hands, the branch singing,
>   altering the excessive bird;
> I long for the imperishable quiet at the heart of form;
> I would be a stream, winding between great striated rocks
>   in late summer;
> A leaf, I would love the leaves, delighting in the
>   redolent disorder of this mortal life,
>
> (CP, 188)

The "imperishable quiet" that Roethke longs for here seems to be a core of identity—an imperishable core known only as it manifests itself in perishable ("mortal") form. As in section 5 of "Song of Myself," Roethke links an intuition of the soul's boundlessness with its possible approximation in the world external to it. By moving with the fish, dancing with the children, or widening with the flowers; by becoming a stream or a drifting leaf, part of the "disorder of this mortal life," the unformulated heart, Roethke proposes, will be made to take on shape.⁵ A "body" will be created which, indirectly, moves like the "soul." The image of the "eye quiet on the growing rose," with another pun on "eye," is a statement of the wish to move with the growing rose in order to become aware of the "I's" own quiet places. As we will see, that longing to again embrace the world is put into play in the next five poems, each of which is identically set "where the sea and fresh water meet." In the last poem of the sequence, Roethke describes this setting as "the place of my desire"—a landscape, almost a laboratory, where his desire, in all of its inescapable complication, might be acted upon, and his sleeping spirit be awakened.⁶

"Meditation at Oyster River" begins with Roethke sitting on a rock at the edge of a bay, the mouth of a river at his back. Although the world around him steadily increases in activity, he seems as weary and tentative as at the beginning of "The Longing." The "first tide-ripples" slowly move toward where he waits, protected by "a barrier of small stones" and a "sunken log" (CP, 190). When he is surrounded by water and "one long undulant ripple" has broken through, he responds: "I dabble my toes in the brackish foam sliding forward, / Then retire to a rock higher up on the cliff-side" (CP, 190). In short, he refuses the embrace, and in a deliberate manner that calls attention to his refusal. Cary Nelson observes that, "The decision is a partial rejection. He resists the natural world even while reaffirming his need for it."⁷ This twin rejection and reaffirmation insists that the problem—what he longs to do, he cannot—must be dealt with before there can be any movement of the spirit. The problem is made clear again a few lines later when the world outside comes back to life ("The dew revives on the beach-grass; / The salt-soaked wood of a fire crackles" [CP, 190]) while the poet remains unmoving. Eventually, in a pattern that will be repeated throughout the sequence, the problem of the failed embrace triggers an unstated question—why am I refusing contact?—that the second section of the poem begins to investigate:

> The self persists like a dying star,
> In sleep, afraid. Death's face rises afresh,
> Among the shy beasts, the deer at the salt-lick,
> The doe with its sloped shoulders loping across the highway,

The young snake, poised in green leaves, waiting for its fly,
The hummingbird, whirring from quince-blossom to
    morning-glory—
With these I would be.

(CP, 190)

The problem expressed, anticipated by the "disorder of this mortal life" in "The Longing," is fundamental to the poem: although Roethke would be part of the "loping," "whirring" world surrounding him, he is unable to break away from a persistent awareness of himself. To relax his attention on his own boundaries and become totally absorbed in something other is, he fears, to risk the dissolution of what makes him a self. Thus, "death's face" insistently includes itself in the catalog of animals Roethke would be with. As James McMichael writes, "What he desires is outside him, outside the self. But this desire is blunted by the unavoidable awareness and fear that to be lured out of the confines of the self is to court death, the absolute loss of self."[8]

What the structure of the sequence suggests is that such a confrontation with "the absolute loss of self" must have occurred before "The Longing" began—the no longer "illuminated" lips and sterile "dreams" of that poem marking a near total retreat from an overreaching attempt at full absorption in an other. A way to think about this would be to recall the experimental overimmersion Whitman risked in sections 26 and 28 of "Song of Myself." Where Whitman was whirled wide by the "orbic flex" of an orchestra which, when too fully embraced, wrenched such previously hidden "ardors" from him that he was left puzzled and silent, "throttled in fakes of death" by his own self-betrayal ("I talk wildly, I have lost my wits, I and nobody else am the greatest traitor, / I went myself first to the headland, my own hands carried me there" [SM, 28]), so Roethke, reacting to just such a confrontation with the "death's face" of his own boundlessness, insistently holds on to the "dying star" of his established self even when listing the shy beasts he longs to embrace. Just as Kinnell and Berryman began their poems by declaring the impossibility of such a full embrace, then, so too does Roethke.

How to move beyond this fear? As Whitman did in sections 29 and 38, Roethke silently reformulates the manner in which one embraces in more indirect, and thus more limited, terms. Rather than turning on himself and addressing his fear of immersion, as Kinnell might have in this situation, Roethke uses his awareness that he cannot give himself fully to the sea as a prompt in developing a new means of contact. Playfully, and at a distance, he muses about water. "I shift on my rock, and I think," he writes: first, of a "trembling . . . Michigan brook in April, / Over a lip of stone, the tiny rivulet," then of a "wrist-thick cascade tumbling from a cleft rock," and finally of the Tittebawasee River, poised, "between winter and spring, / When the ice melts along the edges in early afternoon. / And the midchannel begins cracking and heaving from the pressure beneath, / The ice piling high against the iron-bound spiles, / Gleaming, freezing hard again, creaking at midnight—" (CP, 191). As with the "Cuttings" poems, these increasingly powerful images testify to Roethke's growing ability to work with the moving tide; acknowledging by his fear that he can't be the same as the swirling currents, he yet develops a way of speaking and moving:

> And I long for the blast of dynamite,
> The sudden sucking roar as the culvert loosens its
>   debris of branches and sticks,
> Welter of tin cans, pails, old bird nests, a child's
>   shoe riding a log,
> As the piled ice breaks away from the battered spiles,
> And the whole river begins to move forward, its bridges
>   shaking.
>
> (CP, 191)

The longing is so precisely rendered that both reader and poet do experience, momentarily, a movement forward. By becoming aware through the failed embrace of the distinction between himself and the sea and creating a series of metaphors in response to that tension, Roethke has also enabled himself to become more a part of the seaside setting. That is, working with an aspect of this landscape "small enough to be taken in, embraced, by two arms," he has avoided a dissolving of boundaries while yet opening himself to that world. As will be seen throughout the sequence, each such increase in consciousness is signalled by an increasing ability to join with ocean. Here, he records a steady rocking of the spirit ("I rock with the motion of morning") as he leans to move forward then pulls himself back, finally "lull[ing]" himself into a "half-sleep" (CP, 191). He is in between, no longer sealed off by his barrier of rocks, but quite careful to claim only a "small" embrace of his surroundings: "And the spirit runs, intermittently, / In and out of the small waves, / Runs with the intrepid shorebirds— / How graceful the small before danger!" (CP, 192).

The next poem in the sequence, "Journey to the Interior," takes place later in the evening, in "the moonlight," and uses the word "rehearse" ("I rehearse myself for this: / The stand at the stretch in the face of death" [CP, 194]) to describe the weave of memory and speculation that Roethke constructs in order to prepare to confront the sea without fully dissolving the boundaries of self.[9] Again, the structure is a response to the problem raised by the failed embrace; as with the rivulet-cascade-river memories of the previous poem, this is a rehearsal, a construct—not a direct approach to the landscape (which would be "death"), but an indirect unfolding of one of its problematic implications. The poem begins by comparing the movement out of the self and toward the world to a journey, one constantly interrupted by dangerous, "raw places" that send the self off on long, circuitous detours:[10]

> In the long journey out of the self,
> There are many detours, washed-out interrupted raw places
> Where the shale slides dangerously
> And the back wheels hang almost over the edge
> At the sudden veering, the moment of turning.
>
> (CP, 193)

What has caused *his* "sudden veering" away from what one might have thought would be a simple and direct "journey" from self to something other, Roethke goes on to suggest, are two problems of which he is now "wary." The first is the risk of violent, surging expansion: "The arroyo cracking the road, the wind-bitten buttes, the canyons, / Creeks swollen in midsummer from the flash-flood roaring into the narrow valley" (CP, 193). The second is the risk of reduction and annihilation:

> —Or the path narrowing,
> Winding upward toward the stream with its sharp stones,
> The upland of alder and birchtrees,
> Through the swamp alive with quicksand,
> The way blocked at last by a fallen fir-tree,
> The thickets darkening,
> The ravines ugly.
>
> (CP, 193)

Both threats might usefully be compared to the risks of overpowering contact Whitman imagines in sections 26 and 28—the sudden expansion of being whirled "wider than Uranus flies" followed by his "windpipe [being] throttled."

Roethke counterbalances this fear of annihilation by recounting a long, circuitous journey that, he remembers, gently led him out of himself. The journey—successfully taking Roethke from self-absorption to union with the external—is a rehearsal for the present decision to make or refuse contact with the sea: a rehearsal, or (as we learn only after thirty-four absolutely convincing lines), a "detour"— an indirect, long way around which, avoiding the "raw places" of direct contact with the other, works out a way to eventually allow the "journey out of the self" to proceed. Emphasis is given first to the remembered dangers of the road ("dangerous down-hill places, where the wheels whined beyond eighty—"), then to the boy's sense of pride at his mastery of the terrain:

> The trick was to throw the car sideways and charge over
>   the hill, full of the throttle.
> Grinding up and over the narrow road, spitting and
>   roaring.
> A chance? Perhaps. But the road was part of me, and
>   its ditches,
> And the dust lay thick on my eyelids,—Who ever wore
>   goggles?—
>
> (CP, 193)

Gradually, the speaker disappears, and the landscape, a blur of small towns and discarded objects, takes over: "An old bridge below with a buckled iron railing, broken by some idiot plunger; / Underneath, the sluggish water running between weeds, broken wheels, tires, stones" (CP, 194). This is the sort of exhausted landscape that Roethke had turned away from in "The Longing." Now, however, transfixed by the rhythm of the speeding car, he begins to lose himself to the flashing scenery. He seems to be still, with the world flowing by ("The floating hawks, the jackrabbits, the grazing cattle— / I am not moving but they are") until, finally forgetting himself, he becomes a part of his surroundings, both still and moving: "I rise and fall in the slow sea of a grassy plain, / The wind veering the car slightly to the right, / Whipping the line of white laundry, bending the cottonwoods apart" (CP, 194). With the same wind moving the car and the cottonwoods, inside and outside are joined. Although the memory itself is quite powerful, the reference to the "slow sea" reminds the reader that this journey is being recounted and worked with as a way around Roethke's current failure to embrace the waves around him.

The memory concludes with what Roethke has called "the first stage in mystical illumination":

> I rise and fall, and time folds
> Into a long moment;

> And I hear the lichen speak,
> And the ivy advance with its white lizard feet—
> On the shimmering road,
> On the dusty detour.
>
> (CP, 194)

Although several commentators have cited this passage as a mystical culmination to the sequence, the word "detour" is a reminder that this moment of union in which "all is one and one is all" is only one of several possible results of the journey out of the self (OPC, 26). Roethke is investigating the problem of whether one can move out of the self and not be destroyed, not simply describing the possibility of illumination. This memory serves as a demonstration that the journey might be made safely if indirectly and round-aboutly. That is, as the tense change reminiscent of that in Whitman's gradual participation in his grandmother's father's sea fight (SM, 35–36)—from past ("the road was part of me") to present ("And all flows past")—suggests, working with the memory has led the poet to experience a similar union with a greatly enlarged world here, beside the ocean: "I see the flower of all water, above and below me, the never receding, / Moving, unmoving in a parched land, white in the moonlight" (CP, 194). By making his way down this detour, skirting the "raw places" it seeks to avoid, Roethke has increased his technical resources and brought himself to a point where he can make a decision about moving beyond the soul's "still-stand" (CP, 194). What is the result? Here in the present, claiming only a blind man's intuition, Roethke changes position, moving away from his fear of death and, with his "body thinking," out toward the world:

> As a blind man, lifting a curtain, knows it is morning,
> I know this change:
> On the one side of silence there is no smile;
> But when I breathe with the birds,
> The spirit of wrath becomes the spirit of blessing,
> And the dead begin from their dark to sing in my sleep
>
> (CP, 195)

From a position of silence and immobility, Roethke has gazed at the disastrous, unsmiling face of the journey out of the self ("the spirit of wrath"), then at the breathing, singing aspect of the journey, and has chosen to risk contact. And it is this rehearsal, which has indeed "made something" out of his first contact with the sea, that has made possible that greater, although indirect, embrace.

Roethke, by continually raising new questions about his ability to embrace this world directly, repeatedly gives himself opportunities to struggle out of the mire by refining his ability to work with it indirectly, as a medium different from him. Once again, "The Long Waters," the next poem in the sequence, opens with an acknowledgment of fearfulness—Roethke again retreating from the "advancing and retreating waters" he is drawn to make contact with. He begins by suggesting that the senses, as demonstrated by innumerable small creatures, seem to provide both contact and a means of making and expressing newly-discovered distinctions: "Whether the bees have thoughts, we cannot say, / But the hind part of the worm wiggles the most, / Minnows can hear, and butterflies, yellow and blue, / Rejoice in the language of smells and dancing" (CP, 196). It seems to Roethke that the languages (wiggling, dancing) employed by these creatures illustrate a kind of thinking that he might use himself. Roethke has pursued this idea further in an essay in which he speculates that for the poet who "thinks with his body: an idea for him can be as real as the smell of a flower or a blow on the head. And those so lucky as to bring their whole sensory equipment to bear on the process of thought grow faster, jump more frequently from one plateau to another . . ." (OPC, 27). The senses then, he proposes, might provide an entrance into the external world and a language to give his ideas shape—make them "real." To choose this manner of thinking is to choose not to rely on those extraordinary insights into our world or those intuitions of some other world beyond the range of the senses:

> Therefore I reject the world of the dog
> Though he hear a note higher than C
> And the thrush stopped in the middle of his song.
> And I acknowledge my foolishness with God,
> My desire for the peaks, the black ravines, the rolling
>   mists
> Changing with every twist of the wind,
> The unsinging fields where no lungs breathe,
> Where light is stone.
>
>   (CP, 196)

Instead, he situates himself at that place of his desire, a world full of potential where the senses might be fully engaged:

> I return where fire has been,
> To the charred edge of the sea
> Where the yellowish prongs of grass poke through the
>   blackened ash,
> And the bunched logs peel in the afternoon sunlight,
> Where the fresh and salt waters meet,

> And the sea-winds move through the pine trees,
> A country of bays and inlets, and small streams flowing
>   seaward.
>
>   (CP, 196)

This is a complete world where the four elements—fire, water, earth, wind—all meet and interpenetrate. Grass pokes "through" the fire's ash, winds "move through" the pines, fire touches the sea, fresh waters meet salt. In short, this is a universe no longer immediately threatening, as in "Oyster River," but open to the senses' penetration.

Characteristically, however, Roethke immediately retreats from this decision to immerse himself in the sea-edge world. Discovering a familiar problem implicit in his description of the charred, reviving landscape, he thrusts himself away, back into the depths, and gives himself another opportunity to climb out. Addressing Mnetha, Blake's guardian of two "perpetual infants" who are kept forever innocent, he acknowledges his fear of the flurry of change and new birth that the natural world offers him.[11] He reaches back, in fact, to the language-bearing worm and butterfly of the opening lines of the poem and sees them again, now as examples of disorder and retreat: "Mnetha, Mother of Har, protect me / From the worm's advance and retreat, from the butterfly's havoc, / From the slow sinking of the island peninsula, the coral efflorescence, / The dubious sea-change, the heaving sands, and my tentacled sea-cousins" (CP, 196). Once articulated, however, these fears of the flowering ("coral efflorescence"), changing, and self-dissolving world can be countered. Roethke does so by calling attention to another, unnamed deity who might intensify and shape that about-to-dissolve world rather than free him from it:

> But what of her?—
> Who magnifies the morning with her eyes,
> The star winking beyond itself,
> The cricket-voice deep in the midnight field,
> The blue jay rasping from the stunted pine.
>   (CP, 196)

Magnifying the morning—these examples indicate—involves adding the presence of the viewer to an otherwise unmarked world, that of night sky, "midnight field," and "stunted pine." Her presence, voicing the world while not being overwhelmed by it, seems to be a stand-in for the poet, for Roethke immediately turns to his own faculties of imagination and memory that might intersect the changing world and magnify its potential. A remembered "pleasure," he argues in the next stanza, dies slowly; it lasts like a "dry bloom" still holding its battered shape under the coming "first snow of the year," and in doing so gives depth and richness to his present contact with the world: "Feeling, I still delight in my last fall" (CP, 197). This opening expression of doubt, then, forcing Roethke to acknowledge the havoc of the sensual world, has also led him to assert the role of human memory and imagination in deepening, and thus rendering nonthreatening, the order of that world. In a sense, he has spelled out, in the image of memory as a magnifier, what the indirect contact of the two previous poems simply demonstrated.

The final three sections of "The Long Waters" investigate this combined use of memory and the senses in contacting the world, and do so with a similar pattern of statement, challenge, and a deepened restatement. Roethke begins by repeating his commitment to enter the "rich desolation of wind and water" stretching before him (CP, 197). To move toward that world, he reminds himself, is to enter the advancing and retreating world of time:

> *In time* when the trout and young salmon leap for the
>   low-flying insects,
> And the ivy-branch, cast to the ground, puts down roots
>   into the sawdust,
> And the pine, whole with its roots, sinks into the estuary,
> Where it leans, tilted east, a perch for the osprey,
> And a fisherman dawdles over a wooden bridge,
> These waves, in the sun, remind me of flowers:
>   (CP, 197, emphasis mine)

In the world of time, advance is cyclically linked to decline; trout leap as insects fly low; a newly cast down branch roots itself while established roots are pried out whole; as a pine tree sinks, an osprey uses its perch to lift itself. Previously, this "dubious" movement would have inspired retreat; now the poet realizes that this cyclical pattern also lifts human memory out of worlds cast down. The presence of his memory, then, "magnifying" the sea's waves into the familiar shapes of lilies and morning-glories, helps him to engage his senses and, "Blessed by the lips of a low wind," come forward to enter this "rich desolation." Once again, however, this insight must be tested. The blessing is followed by a quivering moment of doubt where, as another "long swell, burnished, almost oily" washes toward him, he fearfully erects a barrier and uses memory not to deepen his response to water but to find an emblem for his feelings of vulnerability at loosening his boundaries. What would it be like to enter this world without the tools of memory and desire to reshape it?

> I remember a stone breaking the eddying current,
> Neither white nor red, in the dead middle way,
> Where impulse no longer dictates, nor the darkening shadow,
> A vulnerable place,
> Surrounded by sand, broken shells, the wreckage of water.
>
> (CP, 197)

Immediately though, as if his momentary tendency to remain inert and stonelike "in the dead middle way" proved no match for the combination of slowly dying memory and the whispering sea, Roethke finds himself awakened again:

> As a fire, seemingly long dead, flares up from a downdraft
>   of air in a chimney,
> Or a breeze moves over the knees from a low hill,
> So the sea wind wakes desire.
> My body shimmers with a light flame.
>
> (CP, 198)

And wonderfully, now that his senses are in contact with the world, his spirit is able to awake, move, and (reaching back to "The Longing" for the term) shimmer. The awakening of desire—the method Roethke has developed for entering and shaping the world through memory—has been a slow process bringing him to a union that has been doubted, lost, and won several times over.

Interestingly, Roethke chooses to end "The Long Waters" not with these striking lines, but with a passage that Cary Nelson rightly characterizes as "mere posturing."[12] Roethke concludes by claiming that, set loose from his fear of dissolution, he is able to "Become another thing," disperse himself to the gathering waters, and "embrace the world" (CP, 198). This progression neatly completes the sequence's major themes, but the strikingly pat presentation contrasts noticeably with the painstaking advance and retreat we have just followed. This manner of presentation seems to be a deliberate signal of another intensification of the problem, a signal supported by an additional claim that although he senses in the sea's waves a "shape" that corresponds to an aspect of his sleeping spirit, Roethke is unable to label it clearly. That is, he signals his inability, at this stage, to make more than a striking pose out of his union with the waves.

> I see in the advancing and retreating waters
> The shape that came from my sleep, weeping:
> The eternal one, the child, the swaying vine branch,

The numinous ring around the opening flower,
The friend that runs before me on the windy headlands,
Neither voice nor vision.

(CP, 198)

The last line is particularly telling. To see the shape as a montage of traditional images—alternately the "one," a child, a branch, a numinous ring, a friend running—is deliberately to "conceive too much of articulation," suggesting that although a union has been established, there has not yet been a proper assessment of its limits. To achieve "Neither voice nor vision" is to have put nothing into useful form and to indicate both a temporary end to one poem and the need for further meditation.

"The Far Field" attempts to think through the necessary limits to embracing "the advancing and retreating waters" by linking the sea of the previous poems with the far field of eternity in order more forcefully to bring to awareness the problem of "immensity." This is Robert Duncan's concern as well. Is it too much to claim that a single individual might comprehend and articulate such an expanse? The poem begins, as has become customary, by answering that unspoken question with an expression of fear that temporarily negates the previous union and provides the poet with another opportunity to remake his answer to that problem. Roethke imagines driving out a "long peninsula," alone, in a frightening thrust away from the mainland and out toward the sea: "Ending at last in a hopeless sand-rut, / Where the car stalls, / Churning in a snowdrift / Until the headlights darken" (CP, 199). Roethke responds to the fear of what "Journey to the Interior" called those "interrupted raw places" where one could be overwhelmed and diminished by remembering a series of equivalent "ends" he experienced as a child: a culvert at the end of a field; a pile of discarded cans and tires; the decayed face of a dead rat; the entrails of a cat, blasted by a night watchman. The images parallel the stalled car, but, by placing them in a larger context of constantly changing shapes, Roethke understands why, as a child, his "grief was not excessive": the field's end was also the "nesting-place of the field-mouse"; and both the flower dump and the "twittering restless cloud" of an elm tree insisted that the world was "ever-changing" (CP, 199). In a similar manner, he also "learned of [his own place in] the eternal" through viewing his own body in that larger context. Lying "naked in the sand," "fingering a shell," sinking "down to the hips in a mossy quagmire," or sitting with bare knees "astride a wet log" were all ways of indirectly "thinking" himself into contact with an older world by reliving his earlier shapes:[13] "Once I was something like this, mindless, / Or perhaps with another mind, less peculiar" (CP, 200). As a child, then, he reminds himself, he "learned not to fear infinity, / . . . The sprawl of the wave, / The on-coming water" by developing an artistic, sensual means of thinking about, and thereby indirectly participating in, the constant movement of time and shapes. He learned to give himself to "infinity" in a way that "was not excessive."

This reminder—this rehearsal—frees him from his opening fear of being overwhelmed; now able to entertain imaginatively and indirectly the "thought of my death" and his subsequent connection with "earth and air" as the simple loosing of the scents of a garden or fire to the air, he is "renewed by death" and experiences a forward movement of the spirit: "I feel a weightless change, a moving forward / As of water quickening before a narrowing channel / When banks converge, and the wide river whitens" (CP, 200). This forward movement is made possible by the poet teaching himself again how to think about the broad, surrounding expanses. Roethke returns to the combination of stillness and movement first introduced in "The Longing" in order to explain this manner of participating without being dissolved:

> I have come to a still, but not a deep center,
> A point outside the glittering current;
> My eyes stare at the bottom of a river,
> At the irregular stones, iridescent sandgrains,
> My mind moves in more than one place,
> In a country half-land, half-water.
>
> (CP, 201)

Holding himself out of the force of the main current, Roethke insists that he is able to join it by looking at it ("my eyes stare") and, most importantly, by flexibly thinking about it ("my mind moves in more than one place").[14] That outward movement, or embrace, has made possible, in turn, an insight into what "The Longing" called "the imperishable quiet at the heart of form"—an insight now carefully qualified, however, as an approach to "a still, but not a deep center." Full insight, for both Whitman and Roethke, is an overpowering deepness—an approach to an "infinity" beyond words and articulation.

The quiet tone of these lines is convincing and prepares the reader for a second, and more limited, attempt to define the shape discovered in the union between the individual and the long waters: "The lost self changes, / Turning toward the sea, / A sea-shape turning

around,—" (CP, 201). The lost self, the self that has loosened its hold
on its original boundaries, turns toward the sea and, identifying with
the waves it faces but also remaining a thinking creature, becomes
both a man and a "sea-shape turning around." To realize that one has
the potential to merge with such an expanse is to awaken to one's
own immensity without being overwhelmed by it: "A man faced with
his own immensity / Wakes all the waves, all their loose wandering
fire" (CP, 201). He wakes these waves within himself, but, because he
has approached them indirectly, through "finite things [which] reveal
infinitude" without themselves carrying the infinite's full weight, he
finds himself no longer threatened by "The murmur of the absolute";
it simply "fails on his naked ears." So, Roethke can claim that, as a
single man, he is, through such a merger, also an "old man" in the
sea's "robes of green" or, more abstractly, "the end of things, the final
man" (CP, 201). Touching those long waters, working with them without fully embracing them, his work is a limited thrust into immensity:
"A ripple widening from a single stone / Winding around the waters
of the world" (CP, 201).

The final poem of the sequence, "The Rose," is both a summary
of the sequence's overall movement and a demonstration of what
Roethke has learned about how to embrace the other. Its central image is a wild rose blowing in the sea wind, a figure, as Nelson remarks, "for a self exceeding the limits of time and space, yet supremely flowering in its place."[15] Indeed, the sea rose, which "Stays
in its true place," "Rooted in stone," yet also unfolds its petals, extends its tendrils, and drops down to the waves—"struggling out of
the white embrace of the morning-glory," "Moving with the waves,
the undulating driftwood"—is a completed version of the spirit that
has been given struggling form in the sequence (CP, 205, 203). The
rose functions as an ideal image (unlike the poet, it is bound by no
limitations and thus embraces "the whole of light," all of "sound and
silence") to which Roethke may compare himself, and thus assess
where his poem has arrived. In a sense, the ideal rose and *his* apparent distance from its fully realized potential are the problems that
spur both the meditation and demonstration of this poem and of the
entire sequence.

The poem begins with a long description of "this place, where
sea and fresh water meet" (CP, 202). Everything is in movement:
hawks sway in the wind, eagles sail, gulls cry, the tide rises, birds
flash and sing. In time, as the poet watches and listens, this motion
gradually diminishes until "The old log subsides with the lessening
waves, / And there is silence." Summarizing his carefully developed

abilities to join with this world, Roethke writes: "I sway outside my-self / Into the darkening currents, / Into the small spillage of drift-wood, / The waters swirling past the tiny headlands" (CP, 202). Delib-erately, this embrace, in effect the entire sequence, is described in quite modest terms. Both the limited context for the movement—"small spillage," "tiny headlands"—and the contrast, in the next lines, to a grander, remembered union complete with a "crown of birds," place this embrace in carefully limited perspective, exactly that developed by the many discussions of such a connection through-out the sequence. Through "change and variation," that is, the em-brace has been refined.

The next two sections focus on this modest union with "the dark-ening currents"—demonstrating and assessing the technique that has made this connection possible. This is done quite precisely. Com-paring the spirit's constantly adjusting sense of itself to the move-ment of a ship ("rolling slightly sideways, / The stern high, dipping like a child's boat in a pond—/ Our motion continues" [CP, 203]), Roethke immediately juxtaposes that rolling, piecemeal sense of de-velopment to that of the ideal rose that "Stays, / Stays in its true place" and knows itself whole. How is that human, non-ideal move-ment achieved? Like Whitman in section 33 calling deliberate atten-tion to the act of flinging his fancies out toward an arctic world, Roethke returns to the gradually silenced world of section 1 and quite consciously shows us *how* that connection was accomplished. "What do they tell us, sound and silence?" he writes—that is, what does this observed distinction give him that might be worked with or "used?" How might memory or desire or other forms of indirect par-ticipation "magnify," and thus make accessible, that aspect of this potentially overpowering landscape? "I think of American sounds in this silence: / On the banks of the Tombstone, the wind-harps having their say, / The thrush singing alone, that easy bird, / The killdeer whistling away from me" (CP, 204). A long, Whitmanesque catalog follows in which Roethke demonstrates how one fills silence with sound, seasons, and occupations. He moves outward, as he has learned to do in the course of this poem, through use of his full men-tal powers: enumeration ("I think of American sounds"), memory ("the catbird / Down in the corner of the garden"), and the careful discrimination and patterning of the various sounds. Magnifying and working a problem posed by the distinctness of the other is how a poet, in contrast to a rose, embraces, however indirectly, the world. Interestingly, as Roethke completes this demonstration and returns to the darkening "place of my desire," he once again distinguishes his achievement—approximating the "single sound" at the "heart of form" with a "twittering" of multiple movements—from an impossibly removed ideal:

> I return to the twittering of swallows above water,
> And that sound, that single sound,
> When the mind remembers all,
> And gently the light enters the sleeping soul,
> A sound so thin it could not woo a bird.
>
> (CP, 204)

This distinction is referred to again in the sequence's conclusion, where Roethke celebrates "the place of my desire," the place where his desire has been focused and given form:

> I live with the rocks, their weeds,
> Their filmy fringes of green, their harsh
> Edges, their holes
> Cut by the sea-slime, far from the crash
> Of the long swell,
> The oily, tar-laden walls
> Of the toppling waves,
>
> (CP, 205)

By living "with the rocks," Roethke points to the way he has, like the Indian of "The Longing," become absorbed by this particular setting in the course of the sequence, but he also insists, in using that phrase, that his proper place is at the edge of the sea, rather than in the middle of crashing swells. He has been out in those waves, of course, but in a way that needs to be carefully set forth:

> Near this rose, in this grove of sun-parched, wind-warped
>   madronas,
> Among the half-dead trees, I came upon the true ease
>   of myself,
> As if another man appeared out of the depths of my being,
> And I stood outside myself,
> Beyond becoming and perishing,
> A something wholly other,
> As if I swayed out on the wildest wave alive,
> And yet was still.
>
> (CP, 205)

Once, Roethke writes, "near this rose," he had an insight into "the true ease" of himself. But like Whitman's full contact with his soul in section 5, that was in the past: "once we lay such a transparent summer morning." And if—again like Whitman in that section—that full insight into the "depths of my being" seemed *"as if"* he had realized his connections with the full range of created things (Roethke with "the wildest wave alive," far on the horizon; Whitman with "all the men ever born"), now Roethke lives at the edge of the sea, "far from the crash of the long swell," working out a series of more limited and more indirect contacts with those waves and his "being." If, then, what is in him remains "something wholly other," Roethke has, at the same time, worked out a way to bring us "nearer" to it (SM, 42).

NOTES

1. Theodore Roethke, "On Identity," in *On the Poet and His Craft: Selected Prose of Theodore Roethke*, ed. Ralph J. Mills, Jr. (Seattle: University of Washington Press, 1968), p. 25; Cited in the text as OPC. Roethke's poems, from *The Collected Poems of Theodore Roethke* (Garden City: Doubleday, 1966), will be cited as CP.

2. For more on the role of the other in Roethke, see Stephen Spender, "The Objective Ego" in *Theodore Roethke: Essays on the Poetry*, ed. Arnold Stein (Seattle: University of Washington Press, 1965), p. 9, who writes, "In Roethke the not-I—the things ouside him—seem to become him, or he to become them." In the same book, John Wain (p. 60) argues, "the starting-point of Roethke's work is certainly this intensely felt impulse to merge, to identify himself, to participate in the naked processes of life itself," while Ralph J. Mills (p. 118) adds, "The spirit retains its central position and yet seems to step outside itself, to merge with things other than itself." More recently, Cary Nelson in his valuable *Our Last First Poets: Vision and History in Contemporary American Poetry* (Urbana: University of Illinois Press, 1981), p. 35, writes, "Roethke's whole career moves toward . . . a textuality extending the body's privacy to an immense landscape and, at the same time, harboring the world within the body's space."

3. Richard Blessing, *Theodore Roethke's Dynamic Vision* (Bloomington: Indiana University Press, 1974), p. 139.

4. Theodore Roethke, "Open Letter" in *On the Poet and His Craft*, ed. Mills, pp. 39–40.

5. Both Harry Williams, *"The Edge Is What I Have: Theodore Roethke and After* (Lewisburg, Pa.: Bucknell University Press, 1977), p. 106, and Blessing, *Dynamic Vision*, p. 140, offer discussions of the way this line about stillness is juxtaposed to other lines referring to movement.

6. For an excellent discussion of the importance of the sea in this poem, see James McMichael, "Roethke's North America," *Northwest Review* 11 (Summer 1971): 155–56. He writes: "I find it hard to resist describing the sequence to this point as a very specifically developed journey, one that begins with a longing for water and proceeds both literally and figuratively toward the sea. . . . But only now and then is the soul able to do what it should. Only

now and then is the self where it needs to be in relation to all that's outside of it."

7. Nelson, *Our Last First Poets*, p. 40. See also Nelson's valuable discussion of Roethke's deliberate alternation between "self-exploration" and "kaleidoscopic description of nature," p. 39.

8. McMichael, "Roethke's North America," p. 150.

9. Nelson, *Our Last First Poets*, pp. 45–46, points out the use of this word.

10. McMichael, "Roethke's North America," pp. 150–52, has a valuable discussion of the metaphor of the journey.

11. Harold Bloom, "Commentary" in *The Poetry and Prose of William Blake*, ed. David Eardman (New York: Doubleday, 1970), p. 863.

12. Nelson, *Our Last First Poets*, p. 54.

13. For more on the eternal as process, see Blessing, *Dynamic Vision*, pp. 151–52, and Williams, *The Edge Is What I Have*, p. 113.

14. The idea of being both still and moving runs throughout Roethke's poetry. See, for example, "A Light Breather," CP, p. 101. Two sources for the phrasing are Whitman in section 11 of "Song of Myself" ("Where are you off to, lady? for I see you, / You splash in water there, yet stay stock still in your room"), T. S. Eliot in *Four Quartets* ("We must be still and still moving / Into another intensity"), *Collected Poems 1909–1962* (New York: Harcourt, Brace and World, 1970), pp. 189–90. For discussions of Roethke's use of Eliot in this poem, see Jenijoy LaBelle, *The Echoing Wood of Theodore Roethke* (Princeton: Princeton University Press, 1976), p. 154, and Rosemary Sullivan, *Theodore Roethke: The Garden Master* (Seattle: University of Washington Press, 1975), p. 150.

15. Nelson, *Our Last First Poets*, pp. 58–59.

CHAPTER 4

❖   ❖   ❖

WHERE WE ARE

Robert Duncan's "Passages"

> Our consciousness, and the poem as a supreme effort of
> consciousness, comes in a dancing organization between
> personal and cosmic identity.[1]

If Theodore Roethke's work can be said to think through and extend
Whitman's development of indirect ways of embracing the world—a
world not fully graspable, not the same as he—then Robert Duncan's
poetry can be said to work out the implications of Whitman's next
step: approximating the self's intuited fullness by, as Whitman suggests in sections 5 and 6 of "Song of Myself," sketching in an apparently boundless network of such indirect, intersecting readings.[2] For
both Duncan and Whitman, the hum of the soul's "valvèd voice"
is approached only through what Duncan calls "the resonances of
the totality" (CP, 174); "there is no being heard," he writes, "except as we hear how we sound in the community around us" (CP,
199). Where Roethke struggles with *how* such detours or soundings
might be accomplished, Duncan goes on to ask how they might be
linked in a series—in a sense, thinking through the "solution" to self-
portraiture offered in Whitman's catalogs by slowly demonstrating
and testing the complexity of his own "dancing organization."

Poetry, for Robert Duncan, has always been an art of self-realization—a process of discovery in which his inner nature is brought
from "latency into awareness" (H.D.:II, 4, 42). A poem is "a source
of feeling and thought," he writes in his introduction to *The Years as
Catches*. "By my eighteenth year, I recognized in poetry my sole and
ruling vocation. Only in this art—at once a dramatic projection and
at the same time a magic ritual in which a poet was to come into
being—only in this art, it seemd to me, could my inner nature unfold.
I had no idea what that nature was, it was to be created in my work"
(Y, i). Speaking of that same recognition in his *H.D. Book*, Duncan
reports an early understanding of this created self as a showing forth
of "fullness." Responding to the work of H.D., Woolf, and Law-
rence—writers who "intensely showed what they are" (H.D.:I, 1,

12)—the young writer decided: "My work in life must be likewise to reveal inner forces, to make articulate what pulse, nerve, and breath knew. . . . Where truth is the root of the art, to come to fullness means to unfold at last the full flower of what one was, the truth of what one felt and thought—a flowering of corruptions and rage, of bile and intestines, as well as of sense and light, of glands and growth" (H.D.:I, 2, 32).

That flowering, it has become increasingly clear as Duncan's work has evolved, takes as its basic mechanism the same response to the world external to the self that I have examined throughout this study—a response in which the poet "recognizes in the world about him those contentions he feels within" (H.D.:II, 5, 344). As might be expected, Duncan's use of this device is characterized by a remarkably broad range of areas in which he insists it is possible to "discover the hidden features of our own emotional and mental processes" (H.D.:I, 6, 6). "We find our company in Euripedes, Plato, Moses of Leon, Faure or Freud, searching out keys to our inner being in the rites of the Aranda and in the painting processes of Cezanne" (H.D.:I, 6, 62). As with Whitman, the expansiveness of this drive to participate in *all* aspects of the "larger language where minds and spirits awaken sympathies in me, a commune of members in which myself seems everywhere translated" (H.D.:II, 9, 60) is, finally, what potentially makes possible a sense of fullness in articulating the latent self: "[The poet] individualizes himself, deriving his individuality from the ideas and possibilities at large of manhood in a community that includes all that we know of what man is ('Grandeur, horror!' Victor Hugo cries out in his vision of that Leviathan). And the desire to know more of what man is, extending the idea of man beyond the limitations of particular nationalities, races, civilizations, the taking of self in the species, or in the life force, or in the cosmos, is the need for self beyond what can be granted by whatever known community, the need for a manhood big enough to live freely in" (H.D.:II, 5, 344). As discussed previously, Duncan claims as an inheritance from Whitman "an urge that seeks to scatter itself abroad, to send rootlets out into a variety of resources in deriving itself" (CP, 175). For Whitman, of course, those various resources were the throngs moving through Manhattan or crowded together in ferries—a shifting, vibrant ground from which his "grandly conceived personality" (CP, 178) could be derived. Although Duncan's understanding of "community" dramatically extends our sense of possible resources available for such self-derivation, the core impulse of his work is clearly Whitmanic. "In the very place where often contemporary individualism finds identity most lost," Duncan writes, "Whitman takes the ground of his identity and person: in the 'particulars and details magnificently moving in vast masses'" (CP, 191).

That idea that such a body of shifting particulars provides an adequate medium through which to read the "hidden" self, Duncan painstakingly shows, was founded on Whitman's understanding of the universe as a force gradually realizing itself through the creation and mutation of individual events, its various aspects, in Whitman's words, "necessary sides and unfoldings, different steps or links, in the endless process of Creative thought, which, amid numberless apparent failures and contradictions, is held together by central and never-broken unity—not contradictions or failures at all, but radiations of one consistent and eternal purpose."[3] We are each an immediate aspect of that unfolding "ensemble of created and creating forms" (CP, 167)—each the site where one possibility of the universe's evolving "law" is worked out: "Law is hidden in us, for it—our share of the Law—is what we must create as we create ourselves. . . . In all, the very nature of the mass is flowered forth in individualities, new events force new comprehensions of the law" (CP, 172–73).[4] As "an immediate apprehension of or sense of locality in . . . the grand ensemble" (CP, 168), then, each individual part is potentially linked to, "co-inherent" (CP, 189) with, all other parts of that hidden, "never broken unity."[5] Each part has an almost infinite series of possible connections and identities within the ensemble—"each part in every other having, if we could see it, its condition—its opposite or contender, and its satisfaction or twin" (Y, x) another essay puts it—and as each part is "awakened" or "inspired," it becomes more fully aware of those possible connections. For Whitman, then, Duncan writes, unfolding the theory behind Whitman's movement from an intuition of the soul's presence to contact with the "limitless . . . leaves" of creation in section 5 of "Song of Myself," "Self is most intensely experienced in the individual's unique identity as part of the universe at large" (CP, 172). As the self responds to the "particulars and details moving in vast masses," it becomes conscious of, as fully and deeply as possible, its own unique "network of associations" (IE, xiii), and thus its sense of locality, within that moving universe.

Of course, as I have suggested earlier, because that medium is not fully graspable—it is both too immense and, even if it were not, still in the process of unfolding itself—a complete connection is never possible. Whitman's poetry, for Duncan, working its way through a network of partial embraces, grows "as a man grows, composed and recomposed, in each phase immediate and complete, but unsatisfied." When Duncan puts these principles to work in his poem-in-process "Passages," his own "intense / area of self creation" (BB, 15), what he finds is that developing a technique flexible enough to record adequately the intersecting pulses of composition and recomposition, caused by the incomplete nature of any single sounding of himself, is an amazingly complex task. Extending Whitman not only by shifting the community to be embraced from crowds on the streets to the associations possible within the "ground of man's imagination of what he is" (TL, 8), but also by struggling with the technical and political implications of such a form of self-reading, Duncan finds that giving full shape to "where we are"—"our own configuration entering and belonging to a configuration being born of what 'we' means" (BB, ii)—is a process almost infinitely generative of meaning.[6]

The poem began, Duncan has remarked, in response to two passages copied into a notebook from Julian's neo-Platonic *Hymn to the Mother of the Gods*. According to Julian, Attis, son and lover of Cybele, mother of the gods, broke away from the "defined and uniform" heavens and fell to earth—the world of matter, unending generation, and endless struggle.[7] Attis is associated with the sun; through "his union with that which was subject to passion and change," he gave certain bounds and a sense of order to the boundless earth, only to be eventually checked and recalled to the heavens. As the editor of the volume from which Duncan copied the two passages comments, "Julian expresses the Neo-Platonic dread and dislike of matter, of the variable, the plural and unlimited." Indeed, Julian sees the tale as a cautionary one, speaking to all mortals of the risk of generation: "For what could be more blessed, what more joyful than a soul which has escaped from limitlessness and generation and inward storm, and has been translated up to the very gods?"[8] Duncan reads the story quite differently; *he* is drawn to the first half of the tale—to Attis creating a world within the boundless "ensemble of created and creating forms":

> And Attis encircles the heavens like a tiara, and thence sets out as
> though to descend to earth.
>
> •
>
> For the even is bounded, but the uneven is without bounds and there
> is no way through or out of it.

(BB, 9)

For Duncan, Attis's creation within the evolving ensemble offers confirmation of his own Whitmanesque "poetics in which the poem is thought of as a process of participation in a reality larger than my own—the reality of man's experience in the terms of language and literature—a community of meanings and forms in which my work would be at once derivative and creative."[9] The copied-out passages, he has remarked, encouraged his own dreams of a self-created world that would approximate his sense of the self's fullness by entering and reordering the boundless world of humanity's made things: "To set out 'as though to descend to earth' upon the life of a poetry 'without bounds,' having no bounds, being out of bounds—these two passages as I came upon them rang in my spirit as the announcement of a world leading into a world I had long yearned for" (P, 53). And as with Whitman's created self, composed through working out a network of associations within the ensemble, Duncan understood that a similar participatory notion of form would direct his "entrance" into that larger, evolving world: "The principle of form for this poem, for all my poetry and works in the light of this poem, its originality, was posited not in my own works but in the great ground of forms created in Man's Poetry, in the realm of his Made-Things, and, beyond, in the ground of all forms as apprehensions of the Real, in the physical and spiritual reality of the Universe as a present creation, a Self-making in process" (P, 53).

In the early sections of the poem, Duncan works out the formal or "poetic" implications that follow from his response to Attis's descent by "listen[ing] to the reverberations of [his] first thought in the reservoir of communal meanings" (OU, 219). As he weaves together various contributions from "the storehouse of human experience in words" (OU, 219) that seem linked to Julian's story, he comes to understand the formal principles, or poetics, of working within the ensemble and begins to work out the "network of associations" of his own self-flowering. "Passages 1" opens with a dedication of the work that is to follow to "Her-Without-Bounds"—a figure for the boundless world of matter entered by Attis, addressed, in a projected form, as a completely fulfilled totality:

> And to Her-Without-Bounds I send,
>   wherever She wanders,   by what
>   campfire at evening,
>
> among tribes setting each the City where
>   we Her people are
> at the end of a day's reaches   here
>   the Eternal
> lamps lit, here   the wavering human
>   sparks of heat and light
> glimmer, go out, and reappear.
>   (BB, 9)

That whole, like Duncan's version of Whitman's ensemble, is in motion; She "wanders" through the individual manifestations of her
presence—here, the flickering pinpoints of light that are at once the
"Eternal lamps" of her nature and "wavering human / sparks" that
flare and then fail. Like Attis, the dedication suggests confidently, we
are active within that boundless whole. Making what was dark visible, we establish a portion of that evolving city "*where / we* Her
people *are*"—or as Duncan has it in "Structure of Rime XXIV": we
make "a station of the way to the hidden city in the rooms where we
are" (BB, 36). The first formal implication that follows is that the "I"
who dedicates the poem is part of the "we" engaged in manifesting
the whole. Creation is a communal task; whatever else we may be
about, we are necessarily members of what Duncan calls "the company of the living, of all the forms Life Itself, the primal wave of it,
writing itself out in evolution, proposes" (BB, iii–iv). The poet is no
oracle, then, able to embrace fully that moving world. He creates his
household, rather, from within—at the heart of the evolving whole:[10]

> For this is the company of the living
> and the poet's voice speaks from no
> crevice in the ground between
> mid-earth and underworld
> breathing fumes of what is deadly to know,
> news larvae in tombs
> and twists of time do feed upon,
>
> but from the hearth stone, the lamp light,
> the heart of the matter where the
>
> house is held   •
>
> yet here, the warning light at the edge of town!
>
> (BB, 9)

The last line quoted here is particularly interesting; in the act of
accentuating his centrality in the ensemble's self-revelation, Duncan
catches himself in mid-thought, marks that hesitation with a bullet
mark, and then revises himself to say that the individual is also potentially the site of a disordering of the whole—"a new crisis in the
equilibration of the whole" (H.D.:I, 6, 26). Both roles are present
within a company. The second potential is not developed any further—in a sense, it remains an unspoken problem through these
early "Passages," returned to when the poet has gained confidence
in his method—but the hesitation is enough to change the direction
of the poem, acknowledging the introduction of an element of doubt
in the poet's initial self-confident description of working out his place

within the ensemble. The ideas of crisis and struggle lead Duncan back, in a kind of retreat, to reimagine "Her-Without-Bounds" *before* she was in motion. What was it like before Attis broke away—or in Duncan's case, before he awoke and consciously engaged the world?

> Mnemosyne, they named her, the
>   Mother with the whispering
>   feather'd wings.   Memory,
> the great speckled bird who broods over the
>   nest of souls, and her egg,
>   the dream in which all things are living,
> I return to, leaving my self.
>
> I am beside myself with this
>   thought of the One in the World-Egg,
> enclosed,   in a shell of murmurings,
>
>   rimed round,
>   sound-chamberd child.
>
> It's that first!
>
>   (BB, 10)

Before time, Duncan speculates, all was one in a world-egg brooded over by a great mother—an idea, "Passages 14" indicates, drawn from the accounts of the origins of the universe attributed to Orpheus. "All things" were latent within that egg, safely enclosed. When that egg was broken, the universe was suddenly in time, its previously hidden potential becoming manifest in a grand unfolding Duncan describes as a "drama in which the One is in many acts enacting Himself" (H.D.:I, 3, 97), or as an intricate creative struggle in which each of us is at work "restoring, re-membering, the Mother" (H.D.:I, 2, 27)—the two conditions pictured in the first half of this poem. Now, however, in the same gesture of retreat that Berryman and Roethke employ following similar confrontations with core problems, Duncan seems interested in "leaving my self" and its difficult world of conscious activity and slipping back into the egg. In contrast to Attis—"the forth-going to be" who, joining with the world of matter, makes a world that "bursts into green as the spring / winds blow watery from the south / and the sun returns north" (BB, 10)—Duncan momentarily prefers inactivity.[11] Reading these passages from Julian and sensing the challenge "racing out of the zone of dark and storm / towards us," he retreats: "I sleep in the afternoon, retreating from work, / reading and dropping away from the reading, / as if I were only a seed of myself, / unawakend,   unwilling / to sleep or wake" (BB, 10).

The manner in which Duncan links "work" and "reading" is important, as is the result of their cessation—the seed of the self lying dormant and unawakened. As did Roethke's retreat from the sea in "Oyster River," the retreat of "Passages 1" forces Duncan, in the following poems, to define exactly how it is that he will work to awaken himself within the ensemble, forces him to struggle for a detailed understanding of what was, at first, too easily asserted. What he needs to develop, then, is a *method* of actively working within or embracing the evolving whole: "The artist's conscience lies in the depth and wholeness of his involvement in the work where it is. There is a profound change in poetry between the pre-literate art of Homer and the literate art of our own day. Our knowledge of Homer enlarges our apprehension of the world, but our work in that apprehension of the world . . . remains" (OS, 231). More precisely—because, as several commentators have noted, the two are linked [12]—he needs to develop a flexible way of reading that will work out the entire range of connections between himself and the evolving whole he exists within, thereby awakening himself to a deeper sense of his identity, where he is: "All that we can know of Man's engagement with Self and World, what we can read from the wall paintings of the Ice Age as well as what we can read from Darwin and Lyell, must be acknowledged and redeemed in our own feeling of Self and World. . . . The stars, the dark depths of space beyond, the light streaming from the sun, speak to us; the earth, the waves and winds, the twittering of birds and the glances of animals, speak to us. The fall of a rock, the shifting of sands can be read and, in one way of reading, the story of the earth is revealed, in another way of reading, elusive apprehensions of our own inner fate or identity in process emerge" (OS, 236). Although the objects are different—in Roethke the sea, in Whitman crowds on the street—the task is, by now, a familiar one.

Duncan discovers a model for such active reading in a passage from Canto 39 where Pound, acknowledging a personal resonance in Homer, touches his own desolation in the present through an intuition of himself as Odysseus remembering Circe's loom:

> Desolate is the roof where the cat sat,
> Desolate is the iron rail that he walked
> And the corner post whence he greeted the sunrise.
> In hill path: "thkk, thgk"
>   of the loom
> "Thgk, thkk" and the sharp sound of a song
>   under olives

> When I lay in the ingle of Circe
> I heard a song of that kind.[13]

Duncan opens "Passages 2" by wondering what it was that led Pound to make that association; perhaps, he muses, Pound noticed a shared sound, hearing in the longed-for purr of the absent cat the undertone of the whirring loom: "A cat's purr / in the hwirr thkk '*thgk, thkk*' / of Kirke's loom on Pound's Cantos / '*I heard a song of that kind . . .* '" (BB, 11). Whether this was in fact Pound's mental arc, what is important is what Duncan finds useful here: that in sensing himself in the earlier story (literally tracing a sound present in both worlds) and in "translating" Homer into his own text, Pound was able to grasp his own experience. ("To experience is to read," Duncan writes, "to be aware involves at once the senses and the translation into language of our own" [H.D.:II, 4, 28]). Pound, that is, became aware of an aspect of himself through locating himself in the ensemble.

What this means, Duncan tells himself, obediently picking up and "translating" the image of the loom, is that when he reads in a like manner, confusing himself with the various forms of humanity's imaginings, he is taking on the roles of an Attis or a city-builder, active within the boundless whole:

> my mind a shuttle among
>   set strings of the music
> lets a weft of dream grow in the day time
>   an increment of associations,
>   luminous soft threads,
> the thrown glamour, crossing and recrossing,
>   the twisted sinews underlying the work.
>
> Back of the images, the few cords that bind
>   meaning in the word-flow,
>   the rivering web
>   rises among wits and senses
> gathering the wool into its full cloth.
>
> The secret!   the secret!   It's hid
>   in its showing forth.
>
>   (BB, 11)

This new image—a tapestry of many threads rather than evolving city, company of many members, or boundless world of matter— continues to stress the individual's active role within the whole. The "twisted sinews" of a tapestry form its warp, the "set strings" of humanity's made things that the poet's mind moves in and out of, while the "luminous soft threads" of his attention, "crossing and recrossing" those underlying cords and gathering together "an increment of associations," work to creates its weft. (This last quoted phrase is Pound's out of Douglas, but one that Duncan often uses in his own prose. For example: "The meaning and intent of what it is to be a man, and, among men, to be a poet, I owe to the workings of myth in my spirit, both the increment of associations gathered in my continuing study of mythological lore and my own apprehension of what my life is at work there" [TL, 7–8]). As the poet's *own* images, made from those gathered associations, "bind" his meaning to the "word-flow" of that evolving tapestry, the tapestry's "full cloth" or "rivering web" gradually appears. That totality is the "secret" whose completed form is "hidden" in its shown-forth manifestations—hidden, as we have seen in previous uses of the ensemble-individual configuration, in each individual's work, his created world "one articulated cell of a larger fabric" (H.D.:II, 9, 60).

What the image of the loom helps Duncan bring to the surface is the importance of craft in making something out of those potentially shared connections. As Roethke learned in weaving together memory and observation, craft arouses and binds the poet's thoughts and feelings to those already visible forms to which he, at some deep level, ultimately belongs. In doing so, it brings those thoughts and feelings into consciousness—it literally *makes* them real. "Threads are spun out and are woven, from event into event," Duncan writes in his *H.D. Book.* "Hands work the dancing shuttles of a close net to make things real, to realize what is happening" (H.D.:II, 1, 133). Without that aroused dance, apprehensions touched on in reading are allowed to vanish, sounded once and let slip from consciousness:[14] "Why, even in the room *where we are*, / reading to ourselves, or I am reading aloud, / sounding the music, / the stuff / vanishes upon the air, / line after line thrown" (BB, 11–12; emphasis mine). The problem, then, is to find a way to hear and then to make music out of "the clack of the shuttle flying / forward and back" (BB, 12)—music being a coherent bringing together of those particulars: "The power of the poet is to translate experience from daily time where the world and ourselves pass away as we go into the future . . . into a melodic coherence in which words—sounds, meanings, images, voices—do not pass away or exist by themselves, but are kept by rime to exist everywhere in the consciousness of the poem" (H.D.:I, 6, 21).

"Passages 2" does not work out the shape of such a crafted coherence, but it does offer a striking example of how one might begin the act of sounding: "warp, *wearp, varp: 'cast of a net, a laying of eggs'* /

from *warp- 'to throw'* // the threads twisted for strength / that can be a warp of the will" (BB, 12). As this history of "warp," drawn from the *Oxford English Dictionary* demonstrates, what Duncan proposes is a poetry which, seeking to realize all possible co-extensive "rimes" within a single intuited connection, continually splinters what is to be embraced into its constitutive parts. Not unlike Roethke's "magnifying" and indirectly working with distinctions posed by the landscape he would enter, Duncan's "tender use" of this word is *his* version of Whitman's translation of the grass's "many uttering tongues." Actively tracing out the word's lifetime of uses, he would draw those other meanings into the fabric of his poem as well, making possible, when their connections with his work are more fully worked out, a greater resonance for his own poem *and* a more permanent binding of himself to the evolving "word-flow." Duncan goes no further at this point, simply suggesting that the word has had sharply opposed uses, but he has clearly begun to think through some of the practical poetic implications of the individual-ensemble model.

One notable characteristic of "Passages" is its constant testing and revising of itself. Because no embrace of the ensemble is full, each new proposition is itself potentially shatterable, the ground for a movement backward as well as forward. A striking example of that rethinking occurs in "Passages 4–6" where Duncan challenges the very core of the loom metaphor—the poet's dependency on the "fixed strings" of an already existent work. Might he cut himself free from the "twisted sinews" of his ancestors and weave his portion of the grand poem on his own, relieved of the necessity of consciously sounding out the echoing patterns of his responses? "I'd cut the warp / to weave that web / in the air / and here / let image perish in image" (BB, 15). Duncan considers the possibility seriously. Perhaps his work, freed by virtue of its insignificance, might gain thereby a kind of self-concentration and focused intensity: "Statistically insignificant as a locus of creation / I have in this   my own / intense / area of self creation" (BB, 15). His relationship to the boundless, then, could be said to be that of a mirror to the sun, rather than a thread within a tapestry: "a mirror,   an / iridescence,   an ocean / which I hold in the palm of my hand" (BB, 15). But he immediately backs off, as if the image of an ocean within his hand made him realize his overestimation of one poet's power:

> as if I could handle • this pearl • that touches
>
> upon every imagination of what
>
> I am •

wrong about the web,   the

reflection,   the lure of the world

I love.

(BB, 16)

Hesitantly, as the bullet marks indicate, Duncan revises himself: to think that he, as a solitary web-spinner, could handle this reflecting "pearl" on his own—that, like Roethke embracing the world or Whitman being whirled "wider than Uranus flies," he could grasp fully, "every imagination of what I am"—is to misunderstand both the "lure of the world" of created things and, more deeply, the very nature of reflection itself. But what the mistake does is generate a new image for understanding the poetic principles Duncan is working out.[15] Wrong about the reflection in "Passages 4," Duncan reapproaches the notion in "Passages 5" through a meditation on a larger, more fluid reflector—the moon. "Partially / disclosed," with "the light of their faces,   the / light of their eyes" a reflection of "the sun at the source of light" (BB, 17–18), the moon is described as a lord and lady over us. "My Lord-and-Lady Moon," like its earlier equivalents the "company of the living" and the woven, evolving tapestry of creation, is a partially disclosed reflection of an unseen whole in which an individual may participate—his work "Passages of moonlight upon a floor" (BB, 23)—but not master or fully embrace. More important, though, the moon as an image of the ensemble suggests for the first time that larger field's power over us. The moon initiates an action—drawing up the tide, releasing dreams—that the individual follows.[16]

The moon seems to have disappeared when we turn to "Passages 6" and find the poet struggling with a work turned overcomplicated and static: "(I mean to force up emblems again into these passages of a poetry, passages made conglomerate, the pyramid that dense, a mountain, immovable . . .)" (BB, 19). In sexual terms—still another image for the part-whole relation—Duncan describes the ensemble ("the language, the sea" [BB, 20]) as aroused and desiring union with the poet: "the mouth of the cave or temple growing moist / shining, to allow   the neophyte / full entrance" (BB, 19). The problem is that the poet, struggling with his work and caught up in a kind of sterile play with the poem-body metaphor itself, is unable to respond. Instead of "the body of the poem, aroused" (BB, 19), he is left with his own questions. Does a poem in fact resemble a body? It seems not; or, it seems that this poem cannot. Its body "is soft, and / as far as I get in the play / runs down" (BB, 20). (Several meanings are compressed here, all signifying impotence: this is as far as he "gets in," as far as he gets "in the play," and—because of his failure—"the play runs down" as the initial impulse is exhausted.) The poem is broken off at this point, but when Duncan returns to it—apparently days later because he dates his new addition to the poem—he allows himself to be taken over, no longer "forcing" entrance on his own terms. Now the whole "runs away with me / and I enter the wave of it" (BB, 20). And now, strikingly, the moon returns; sensing the aroused body of his poem "rising above / sleep," Duncan credits the moon—the ensemble in its active role—with his awakening:

> the moon taking over tides of the mind,
>
> pulling back
>   whatever cover love had
>
> until the reefs upon which we lie are exposed,
>
>   the green water going out over
>
>   the rock ledges,
>
> body upon body
>
>   turning keys as the tide turns
>
> and reaching up into . . .
>   (BB, 21)

That is, the moon, "pulling back" the tides over rock ledges, exposes the poet and makes possible the desired union of "body upon body." It is the moon, or to return to "Passages 4," the totality of humanity's boundless reflections, which is first active, "turning keys" in the individual's locked and inactive world. Without the moon's long pull, poet and poem remain "dense, . . . immovable."

With this arc of doubt completed, we return, in "Passages 8 and 9," to the question of how to make a household within the ensemble. Duncan begins "Passages 8" by recalling his initial inability to be aroused by Attis "racing out of the zone of dark and storm / towards us," but adds to that situation now what he has discovered about the ensemble's initiating and persistent activity: "the ones of the old days / • / will not be done with us / but come to mind" (BB, 24). The "ones of the old days" are what Duncan calls "ancestors—those who have contributed to the association of man" (H.D.:I, 6, 64): the loom's fixed strings, the ongoing company of the living, the changing faces of the moon. In response to their continual presence, he continues, the mind at first designs "chariots and horizons"; that is, it creates a way to understand them that emphasizes their "distance" from us, both in time (chariot) and in space (at the horizon of our consciousness). The problem that "Passages 8" addresses is how to respond when they near "where we are" (BB, 24)—or to put it another way, how to respond so *that* they near where we are, the horizon of our attention merging with the horizon of their presence. As "Passages 2" suggested, this merger is a question of "design" or craft— what Whitman called "use"; Duncan must devise a way to translate these multiple "ancestral echoes" (BB, 25) into his own created world.

Duncan discovers a lead for such a creation in Jacob Sessler's account of one Count von Zinzendorf, founder of the renewed Moravian brotherhood. He writes of Zinzendorf in *The H.D. Book*:

> Count von Zinzendorf not only was patron of the renewed Church but he created rituals and wrote hymns in which a new religious language emerged that brought out the associations of sexual and spiritual images. The spear, the wound, and the flow of blood from Christ's side were deliberately related to the penis, the vagina, and the menstrual flow. Sessler in his study of the Moravian movement tells us "It is said that a niche covered with red cloth was built into the wall of the church, into which children were placed to symbolize their lying in Christ's Side-Wound, and that Christian Renatus, Zinzendorf's son, built a *Side-Wound* through which the congregation marched"—called "the true Matrix." (H.D.:II, 9, 65)

Zinzendorf speaks to Duncan's intuition of what is needed in his own work: drawn to two different sorts of imagery—sexual and spiritual—he devised, through their combination, "a new religious language" that "brought out . . . associations" of that language that were potential but never before realized. Putting into play the same impulse as that behind Duncan's desire to include in his embrace the multiple uses of the word "warp," Zinzendorf "created rituals" that successfully worked out, through the juxtaposition of two different worlds, an aspect of the ensemble's self-creative, constantly "renewed" unfolding. Not able to grasp the whole in its entirety, he worked out a part of the ensemble *where he was*. And Zinzendorf's rituals—children placed in a red-covered niche to symbolize new life, or the congregation marched through Christ's wound—so echo Duncan's earlier images for entering or binding himself to the evolving whole ("The life door, the cunt" of "Passages 6," the "word-flow" of "Passages 2") that he senses there an answer to the problem of how *he* might enter and speak:

I am

at the lips   before speech,   at life's

labia,   Her   crack of a door opening,

her cunt   a wound now

the gash in His side

from which monthly   blood flows   •

so Zinzendorf saw

(BB, 24)

Juxtaposing quotations from Sessler's study with a reference to the
"ancestral" echoes with which he must link himself, Duncan ends
"Passages 8" with the assertion that a responsive awakening to the
flowing ensemble—"the mothering language in which our psyche is
continually reborn, the matrix of meanings, of evolving thought and
feeling" (H.D.:II, 9, 88)—involves the creation of a new household
whose most intimate rituals are involved with the folding together of
what had been distant in time and space:

"To be born again from the wound in His side"

From the horizon   ancestral

echoes ring   •

In the streams of the wound they
*"want to have little beds, and tables,
and everything else."*

(BB, 25)

Duncan finds a floor-plan for that household from, of all things, in
"Passages 9," a 1909 architecture study. The poem is an intricate col-
lage in which Duncan, "reading while the music playd / curld up
among the ornamental cushions" (BB, 27), isolates structural principles from passages of that manual, then tests them out against details
from the room in which he works. The first quotation suggests that
to build within that ever-developing stream the individual must create a form that is itself a not-fully-seen whole: "it must have recesses.
There is a great charm in a room broken up in plan, where that slight
feeling of mystery is given to it which arises when you cannot see the
whole room from any one place . . . when there is always something
around the corner" (BB, 26). Such a structure—a room broken by
alcoves so that its fullness is sensed but not seen—is, by virtue of that
many-sidedness, open to further and more elaborate "readings" of
the space it encloses. And as Duncan discovers, searching out the

"recesses" of his own room, these tucked-away places hold the potential for expansion because they are possible entrances for, or sites of engagement with, that flowing, outside world: "from the bookcases   the glimmering titles arrayd   keys / Hesiod   •   Heraklitus   •   *The Secret Books of the Egyptian Gnostics . . .*" (BB, 26). As a key line repeated from "Passages 8" suggests, the "light beyond," the "distant intoxications" of records and the "glimmering titles" of books, echo *"in the distance"* but, through these deliberately nonexploited openings or niches, might in time come near to "where we are." The problem, then, is to create a structure that not only keeps the light beyond potentially accessible but is also responsive to those distant and external "keys" as they become available—a structure, that is, able to make visible what is recessed and not yet acknowledged in the creating self.

The architecture text, as Duncan continues to read, gives him a lead: "instead of being hidden away," the seams or joints of a structure might be emphasized. Calling attention to the passages between one area and another—French doors between living room and porch, porch between house and garden, stairway between the social part of the house and the upper, individual part—such a building style confirms what we saw with Zinzendorf: that what was recessed can be made visible through a structure that makes "prominent" the act of making connections, in all its beauty, audacity, or dailiness. The text suggests the act of creating a household is, in fact, the act of bringing together, into an expanding but coherent structure, things that had been separate and distant. Signalling the usefulness of this structural principle, Duncan remembers an actual incident, in the recesses of his own linked house and garden, where what was dark was embraced and brought into the light, where an aspect of the "mystery" of the whole was unfolded into active complication: "Below the house   in the dark of the peppertree / stript to the moonlight   embraced / for the mystery's sake   mounting / thru us   •   the garden's recesses" (BB, 27).

In "Passages 12," a section based primarily on a poem by Baudelaire, Duncan begins to put these principles into action. Baudelaire tells a story of a Spanish guitarist—"the genius, the sorcerer"—who, in a strange city to give a concert, discovers a fellow Spaniard working as a marble-cutter. Drinking together one night, they forget about a concert; when forced to perform, the drunk guitarist insists that his companion play as well. He does, terribly, on a violin—in these lines, given here in English, which Duncan works into his poem:

"Begin," said the guitarist to the marble-cutter. It is impossible to describe the kind of sound that issued from the drunken violin; the sound
of a delirious Bacchus cutting stone with a saw. What did he play or try
to play? It mattered little, after the first tune was heard. Suddenly, a
melody at once soft, lively, whimsical, surrounded the noisy din, sup-
pressing it, smothering it, concealing it. The guitar was singing so loud
that the voice could no longer be heard. And yet it was indeed the tune,
the very same wine-soaked tune that the marble-cutter had bitten into.

The guitar expressed itself with enormous resonance; it babbled, it
sang, it declaimed, with alarming spirit, the unheard-of sureness and
purity of diction. The guitar was improvising a variation on the violin's
theme. It was letting the theme guide it, while it garbed the slender
nudity of its sound with splendor and maternal tenderness.[17]

The situation described is exactly the one Duncan has been examining, with the individual's part taken by the clumsy marble-cutter and
that of the company, the ancestors, the reflections of the moon, or the
rising word flow taken by the guitarist. The violinist plays as though
he were attacking stone with a saw, but the "slender nudity of his
song," encouraged and extended by the "enormous resonance" of
the more talented figure, is given fullness and intensity—a vision, of
course, of the individual participating in the ensemble, and a recessed, as yet unrealized "rime" for Duncan to respond to and translate into his text.

This poem, then, as Duncan dramatizes (or makes "prominent")
that act of translation, is an example of his "working the dancing
shuttles" in order to become fully conscious of the multiple associations between Baudelaire's poem and his own evolving self-creation:

> *"Commence," dit le guitariste au marbrier.*
>
> He draws the sounds forth from his drunken violin
> Bacchus in delirium cuts from the stone with a saw.
>
> What does he play?   What does he   attempt to play?
> It makes no difference,   the first ayre comes,
>
> and suddenly,
>
> an energy, a melody   suave, capricious   •
>
> all the time   encircles me,
>
> stifles the cry in my mouth, stops the beat
> of my heart, conceals the rage of the child squalling,
>
> until I lie at the edge
>
> (BB, 34)

The first line, still caught in its original French, presents Baudelaire as an "ancestral echo," sounding from a horizon distant and foreign to the poet. Duncan translates accordingly, his words and sensibility simply a neutral medium for Baudelaire's lines to pass through and—if we remember "Passages 2"—"vanish upon the air." After six translated lines, however, Duncan breaks the movement with a spaced period—makes the break "prominent"—then begins to indicate a connection between his own situation and that of the drunken violinist. He continues to render Baudelaire more or less faithfully, but senses a union as the commanding music "encircles me" and "stifles the cry in my mouth." Baudelaire's lines, no longer simply "distant intoxications," seem to be actively "nearing / where we are": "at the edge" of entrance into the ensemble.

Another bullet mark follows; then Duncan begins to work with that connection, "reading" it in what Michael Davidson calls a "charged, participatory" manner that "instead of hermeneutically recovering a text in an act that leaves it essentially unchanged, . . . translates its terms into a new text.[18] Or as "Passages" has put it, sensing a connection, Duncan sounds out the resonances between his own position to date—wanting to unfold the "full flower" of his created self by binding it to the ensemble—and this new ancestral voice.

> all the time, I have been   at the edge of this
> avidity, this din.   *La guitare chante.*
> He lies in wait   for the passing glance, the aroused
> glitter,   the sullen
> change in the light of this   •   hard-on the music presses
> its rime   *que le violon*
> *ne s'entend plus*   but gives itself over to the need,
> the guitar's imperative.   Release,
> I sing, without sound: Release the thunders
> from this cloud   that gathers   impending
> song.   The threatening air,
> the drunken air,   that has broken thru,   I sing
> without sound   to take over   the
> aroused marbler.
> The guitar takes over, takes the voice
> its sound enormous.
>
> (BB, 34–35)

Like Pound and Homer, or Whitman's mournful taking over of the "sea-fight" narrative in section 36 of "Song of Myself," or even Roethke bringing his memories of rivers to the threatening ocean, the words are primarily Duncan's now, woven around traces of Baudelaire's. Baudelaire, resonating in several contexts, confirms that the individual is always "at the edge" of the ensemble; more than that, that the ensemble's recessed members must "lie in wait" for a spark of arousal in the individual, then, in a kind of sexual by-play, bring forth their potential resonances. Just as the violin "gives itself over to the need" of that beautiful "impending" music, so Duncan would have the cloud that gathers near him "release its thunders" and give fullness and intensity to his aroused silence—would have it "take the voice" that now "sings without sound." And, in fact, although articulated fully here for the first time, that is just what *has* happened throughout these early poems. Duncan has released the thunder of the ensemble and given resonance to his own struggles with the poetics of self-creation by giving himself over to, and working out his connections with, various members of the company of the living present "where we are."

If, following Whitman, Duncan has, in these early poems, worked out a manner of reading that should permit an active engagement with the elements of a not fully graspable, evolving whole—that "larger language where minds and spirits awaken sympathies in me, a commune of members in which myself seems everywhere translated"—what still remains unconfronted is the problem temporarily sidestepped in "Passages 1": that one's actions within the ensemble, translating oneself and thereby creating a strange, new "language" of previously unconnected elements, also involve the forcing and dissolving of old boundaries. An active reader, who can be seen from one perspective as "the lamp light, / [at] the heart of the matter," must also be seen, from another, as "the warning light at the edge of town" (BB, 9). Zinzendorf, for example, working out a personal attraction to the imagery of religion and of sexuality and thereby creating a new religious language, can be seen as both a figure generating new structures *and*, to those entrusted with maintaining the old language, a renegade working his distortions "at the edge" of what is acceptable. Duncan's use of Baudelaire—weaving that work into a series of contexts never anticipated by the author—might equally be greeted, if the responses to Pound's translations are a reliable guide, as a distortion, doing violence to its "intended" use. To enter Attis's boundless world of "unending struggle," Duncan comes to see in these later poems, creating as it does a sense of "endless struggle" and "inward storm" not fully apparent in Whitman's "average unending procession," involves developing a method of reading responsive even to those elements of the community arrayed against his work. In fact, what Duncan eventually learns is that his own struggle against opposing aspects of the ensemble is another potential "stairway" or joint which, in being made prominent, might hold in readiness his eventual deeper engagement with the community. Signalling his inability to embrace fully, in time confrontation becomes a passage to increased openness. In this second group of "Passages," then, Duncan applies the poetics sketched out in the first poems—active reading, making prominent the struggle to link co-extensive elements of the ensemble while acknowledging that the full, "redeemed" form is, as yet, nowhere visible—but applying that new understanding of Whitman's catalog to a quite specific crisis involved in reading himself.[19]

Duncan frames this problem quite simply. To speak of the various manifestations of the universe, in Whitman's words, as "necessary sides and unfoldings, different steps or links, in the endless process of Creative thought, which, amid numberless apparent failures and contradictions, is held together by central and never-broken unity—not contradictions or failures at all, but radiations of one consistent and eternal purpose" is to envision creation as an ensemble, or a "field of meanings" (TL, 68), in which "all parts belong, no member is to be dismissed as trivial or mistaken" (TL, 63). Further, it is to envision corresponding social and political structures in which—because "contradictions" are only apparent, all members being part of that "never-broken unity"—"the authority of the individual response or impulse [is recognized] within a community of differing responses" (H.D.:II, 5, 34). Because "a new order is a contention in the heart of existing orders" (OS, 229), modifying, deepening, even overthrowing an apparently settled ordering of elements, this vision becomes complicated when the individual response is greeted not with the ready acceptance Duncan at first envisions—"this is the creative strife that Heraclitus praised, breaking up, away from what you know how to do into something you didn't know, breaking up the orders I belong to in order to come into alien orders, marches upon a larger order" (OS, 230)—but with jeers, resistance, even violence. How does one read a position in the ensemble under those conditions?

> I thought to come into an open room
> where in the south light of afternoon
> one I was improvised
> passages of changing dark and light

a music dream and passion would have playd
to illustrate concords of order in order,
a contrapuntal communion of all things   •

    but Schubert is gone,
        the genius of his melody
has passt, and all the lovely marrd sentiment
disownd I thought to come to

                          (BB, 78)

This problem is introduced at the end of "Passages 2" where, after discovering both the opening of a net *and* the twisting tight of individual will in the history of use contained in the word "warp," Duncan goes on to sound out the background of the word "shuttle" (an image, in that context, for the individual's mind moving "forward and back" in its reworking of the fixed strings, or warp, of tradition), and finds there another acknowledgment of strife: "And the shuttle carrying the woof I find / was *skutill* '*harpoon*' —a dart, an arrow, / or a little ship" (BB, 12). He works with that discovery by calling up an ideal version of contention in which elements or "harpoons" jostle but are held together in a single "field." "The battle I saw / was on a wide plain," he writes:

        each side

    facing its foe for the sake of
        the alliance,
    allegiance, the legion, that the
        vow that makes a nation
    one body not be broken.
            (BB, 12)

But this is a vow, Duncan reluctantly admits, that seems to be forgotten, time after time, as one or another member insists on the priority of its own partial and thus "mistaken" vision of the whole, turning the field into a site of mayhem:

    Yet it is all, we know, a mêlée,

        a medley of mistaken themes
        grown dreadful and surmounting dread,

    so that Achilles may have his wrath
        and throw down
        the heroic Hektor who raised
    that reflection of the heroic

        in his shield . . .
           (BB, 12–13)

The problem Duncan struggles with, then, is how to sing in a culture which, like Achilles, has grown monstrous in its rage against the song by which it is challenged, thereby denying its deepest nature as a participant in a larger, not-yet-visible body. In his "Introduction" to *Bending the Bow*, Duncan offers an account of a Vietnam-era protest that provides a parable of the situation: "We enter again and again the last days of our own history, for everywhere living productive forms in the evolution of forms fail, weaken, or grow monstrous, destroying the terms of their existence. . . . Standing before the advancing line of men on guard, it seemd futile at first to speak to them. They were under a command that meant to overcome us or to terrify us, a force aroused in the refusal to give even the beginnings of a hearing. This is the nature of all dying orders, a death so strong we are deadend to the life-lines. Encircled, it seems as if only we few standing here had life still striving in us. We must begin where we are. Our own configuration entering and belonging to a configuration being born of what 'we' means" (BB, i–ii). How, then, to begin an entry into that continually-being-born ensemble when "where we are" seems to have all of its energies marshalled, in these "last days," against that very entry?[20]

Duncan's full engagement with this problem begins in "Passages 13," where, juxtaposing two blocks of words that function as ideograms, he refigures the battle scenes of "Passages 2." Duncan calls the first block an "ideogram of a childhood memory"—"a dawn-of-man scene, with its play of leaf-boats and sand harbors in a mountain stream, close and cool with shadow and sunlight . . ." (TL, 45). Like the battle of "Passages 2" where opposing forces were held within a single body—or, more accurately, like the nostalgic dream of "passages of changing dark and light" with which I began this section—the words are separate, even opposites, but, at the same time, shimmering in a kind of Edenic simplicity and newness, united as elements of a single harmonious order:

jump	stone	hand	leaf	shadow	sun
day	plash	coin	light	downstream	fish
first	loosen	under	boat	harbor	circle
old	earth	bronze	dark	wall	waver
new	smell	purl	close	wet	green
now	rise	foot	warm	hold	cool

(BB, 40)

This block of words is followed by a second grouping—an ideogram of what Duncan has called the "Last Day" in which the sun of the first scene, glinting richly among shadows and coins of light, has become a blood-red, apocalyptic disk filling the horizon.[21]

> blood   disk
>
> horizon   flame

Taken together, the two ideograms reframe the problem of "Passages 2": sensing his first dream of individual, counterpointed creation given over to an approaching apocalypse of collapsing and distorted forms, what is the poet to create or sing? How is he to read?

Duncan begins to sketch an answer by meditating on two contrasting paintings—Piero di Cosimo's *A Forest Fire* and Bosch's *Christ Bearing the Cross*—dating from the same period (1490–1500) but combining the threat of "flaming rage" and the dream of "pastoral stillness" in quite different ways. As Duncan's introductory self-query suggests—"Do you know the old language? / I do not know the old language" (BB, 40)—both paintings suggest responses which, although different, go beyond an impossible nostalgic retreat to the safety of "the language of the old belief." *A Forest Fire* pictures a disaster from which animals are fleeing—a "panic" in which, "as if in Eden," "lion and lamb lie down" together. Di Cosimo has envisioned a new world in which Eden lost has, in response to the threat of fire, been regained. The frightened animals at the edge of the burning wood are in a world in which the "old language" of contrasting but united elements has been made anew. But, although lion and lamb, gentle beasts and furies, are held together again in a single "charmd field," there is a difference. This is not the first Eden where opposites played together harmlessly, but a world in which their various natures are opposed and yet, momentarily, united. Di Cosimo's "field" is an unfolding of that first field. It is an original melody sounded anew, under the insistent pressure of disorder, in a higher harmony:

> featherd, furrd, leafy
>
> boundaries where   even the Furies are birds
>
> and blur   in higher harmonies Eumenides;
>
> whose animals, entering a charmd field
>
> in the light of his vision, a stillness,
>
> have their dreamy glades and pastures.
>
> The flames, the smoke.
>
>   (BB, 42)

Di Cosimo, then, offers Duncan a model for an artist faced with a world destroying itself who is thereby prompted to see "apparent contradictions and failures . . . held together by central and never-broken unity." In this, he stands for the many artists who stubbornly have pointed to the breaking and rebinding of individual elements within the ensemble:

> magic Pletho, Ficino, Pico della Mirandola prepared,
>
> reviving in David's song,
>
> Saul in his flaming rage heard,   music
>
> Orpheus first playd,
>
> chords and melodies of the spell that binds
>
> the many in conflict in contrasts of one mind
> (BB, 41–42)

If di Cosimo offers one response to the problem, Bosch's Christ marching to Calvary, his "sweet music" almost completely overcome by the "opposing music" of the crowd raging against his "harmonies," offers another:

> The Christ closes His eyes,   bearing the Cross
>   as if dreaming.   Is His Kingdom
> not of this world, but a dream of the Anima Mundi,
>   the World-Ensouling?
> The painter's *sfumato* gives His face
>   pastoral stillness amidst terror,   sorrow
> that has an echo in the stag's face we saw before.
> About, Him, as if to drown   sweet music out,
>   Satan looks forth from
>   men's faces
>   (BB, 43)

As the echoes between the paintings suggest, Bosch's Christ shares with di Cosimo the still, pastoral vision of a harmony beyond "this vain sound," but he finds himself within a world in which the old boundaries, instead of destroying themselves and prompting the birth of new forms, cling tenaciously to their power. Linking "the faces of evil" (BB, 43) in Bosch's painting with the "glints of the evil that one sees in the power of this world" (BB, 44), translating the crowd's rage into that of "Princes, Popes, Prime Usurers, Presidents" who "meet to conspire, to coerce, to cut down" the threatening rise of individual expression, Duncan finds in the painting a vision of the contemporary artist as an isolated solitary, imprisoned in a world grown rigid, with his deepest allegiances "not of this world." Duncan elaborates in an essay: "We then live in a world that is 'theirs,' in 'their' power, in which a deeper reality, our own, is imprisoned. Our life is hidden in our hearts, a secret allegiance, at odds with the World, the Flesh, and the Devil, and the true kingdom is 'not of this World.' . . . Not only gnostics and pacifists but artists and poets, those who live by an inner reality or world, having a prior adherence to the heart's truth or wish, appear as heretics or traitors to those who lead or conform to the dominations of the day" (H.D.:II, 4, 47).

What the structure of "Passages 13" suggests, then—juxtaposing the first and last ideograms, moving first to di Cosimo's vision of a reordering of the elements of apocalypse in a new Eden, then to Bosch's account of that expansive vision reduced to a solitary loyalty, hidden and virtually overcome—is that Bosch's vision seems, at least by this present accounting, to be inevitable. We seem "disownd," that is, from Whitman's dream of fully coexisting with all elements of this world. It can't be embraced. Interestingly, Duncan concludes "Passages 13" by throwing his lot in with neither painter. Instead, bringing di Cosimo's fire up to date by linking it with the "improverisht, swollen," modern city—"They are burning the woods, the brush-lands, the / grassy fields razed;   their / profitable suburbs spread" (BB, 44)—he retreats into the "old language" of the first ideogram. That is, thinking through the two options but unwilling or unready yet to act on either, he reintroduces the language of the old ideo-gram—rows turned into columns but otherwise untouched by the burning woods juxtaposed to it—to call attention to the present in-adequacy of *his* vision. In unsettled words that recall Roethke's man-ner of keeping a problem alive, he concludes the poem with a scene "that barely holds" (TL, 45).[22]

"Passages 16," framed as a response to Duncan's translation of Ver-laine's "Saint Graal," continues to keep those difficult options sus-pended in order to attempt a return to the old language. Verlaine also describes his day as a "time of evil" in which even "the strongest, giving way to mortal terror, / abase themselves to the law without honor," a time in which authority has grown monstrous, insisting on its dominance through "death-chambers and instruments / of inter-rogation" (BB, 55). Like di Cosimo, Verlaine sees that the violence of his condition—"dying of the period in which we live" (BB, 55)— makes possible the vision of a larger field in which these elements can be reordered. Verlaine's image for the opening out of that larger world is the sudden presence of "the blood of Christ stream[ing] down from everything," the old world made new in a forceful, "Torrent of love" (BB, 55). Duncan responds by retreating to the old dawn-of-man language, creating an alternative scene out of key words from that first ideogram:

> No, Verlaine, I thirst for *cool* water, for the
> cool of the shade tree,   I would
>
> drink in the *green* of the *leafy* shade,
>
> for the sweet water that wells up from *under*
> the rock ledge,   the mossy *shadows*
>
> the *coins* of *light*,   shaken down
> drifting, dreaming in the ever-running
>
> *stream* of bright water pouring over
> rocks gleaming admist the cold
>
> current, s   •   words
>   (BB, 58, italics mine)

The rest of "Passages 16" traces, by means of scattered, dated entries, the course of a love relationship that serves as an example of how one might drink from that cool, dappled spring—recreating an Eden as yet untouched by "the period in which we live." Early in September, for example, we read: "At dawn, your breath stirs   first light / auras of the cool line of hill-horizons / ringing,   your eyes closed,   sweet smile / bitter smile" (BB, 58). The "cool hills," "first light," and mixture of sweet and bitter all pick up elements of that contrasting but harmonious ideogram. The connection is further elaborated later in September when, noting that "his time / that was forever has slipt away" (BB, 59), Duncan imagines that loss as "clear light and shadow on the moving water," the darkness of separation not overwhelming but simply an element of passion's "continual song": "   •   a heavy bough of darkness above / mirrord   depth-dark below   • / sparks of sun-light   There must be / breaks in the first-thought-solid shade" (BB, 59). The language and delicacy of this lyric are quite remarkable—and thus show a more thoughtful attempt to revive the old language than at the close of "Passages 13"—and yet Duncan again concludes with a acknowledgment that such a dream of individual passion seems to "barely hold" when held up against the darker context of the entire ensemble, the world "where we are": "The soldier in a dirty corner of the war / finding his lover,   the youth   sending roots of innocence / into the criminal ground   striking   a light that illumines / the dark belly" (BB, 59).

With "Passages 19," Duncan begins a movement away from such an apparently inevitable retreat.[23] The poem opens with three brief

images of ways of "abiding in the Mind of the Universe," images with
which Duncan's dissatisfaction gradually becomes clear. The first of
these describes reading as a version of the "drifting, dreaming in the
ever-running / stream of bright water" (BB, 58) that Duncan had re-
treated to earlier. To read, in this sense, is simply to lose hold of this
world in order to awaken to new aspects of oneself: "Incidents of
me   the eye sees / a leaf among many leaves   turning upon the
stream, the screen, / the words upon the page   flow away into   no
hold I have" (BB, 66). Such an act, he reads in Jacob Boehme, allows
the self to be shaped and driven into form by contact with the ensemble of already-formed figures—what he has called earlier ancestors or eternal ones: "for the stars have their kingdom in the veins of
the body which are cunning passages (and the sun has designed the
arteries)   where they drive forth the form, shape and condition of
man" (BB, 66). But, Duncan begins to speculate, juxtaposing a third
passage from Hesiod's *Works and Days*, to be shaped in that way is to
throw one's lot in with what the earlier poet called "the divine race
of heroes"—predecessors who, when their time had passed, Zeus
settled at the ends of the earth:[24]

> They live in a place apart from men,
>
>> at the ends of the earth
>
> along the shores of the deep roaring Ocean   their campfires
>
>> their circles of great stones   their gold crowns of hair
>
>> untoucht by sorrow
>
>>> having no guilt.
>>>   (BB, 66)

What Duncan comes to see in juxtaposing these three passages is that
there must be a connection between his work in the ensemble, his
form driven forth by contact with its members, and the world in
which he now exists—for all aspects of creation, even this current
"time of evil," are ultimately part of Whitman's "bond of unity."
Separation from *this* world, whether forced on the poet or welcomed
as a retreat, is finally a mistake. It is no embrace, no self-reading, at
all. If the act of reading, at least as it appears to function now, pulls
the poet away from this world, then it needs to be revised. "What
shall we have to do with them then?" he asks of those heroes, stars,
eternal ones he had been flowing away into: "For those who love
us   must be heavy with sorrow / We ourselves can know no good
apart / from the good of all men" (BB, 66).

It is one thing, of course, to commit oneself to a course of action, quite another to work out all the steps necessary to get to that new manner of reading. At this point, Duncan is able to see only far enough to sense that taking part in the "good of all men" means risking violent, personal change—developing "another face / breaking into changes of agony and submission" (BB, 67). He captures his own inner debate about risking such submission in the second part of "Passages 19" by working with a few lines from Kipling's "The Knife and the Naked Chalk." In Kipling's story, two children wander onto the chalk downs of England, meet an old shepherd, then fall asleep as he explains his craft to them. Dreaming, they overhear a conversation between another shepherd and the sprite Puck about how the wolf was driven from the English countryside. The shepherd explains that the wolf roamed freely until the development of powerful iron knives by the woods-dwelling Children of the Night. The problem, and here the shepherd narrates the voices of his own inner conflict *and* Duncan's, was that to go into the woods and ask for those knives was to risk change: "One voice said, 'If you go among the Trees, the Children of the Night will change your spirit. Eat and sleep here.' The other voice said, 'Ask for the Knife.' I listened to that voice. . . . I said to my Mother in the morning, 'I go away to find a thing for my people, but I do not know whether I shall return in my own shape.'"

Although the remainder of the story is not given in the poem—the shepherd is given the knife, but in return allows his right eye to be plucked out—Duncan shows his awareness of the risk inherent in his own decision by closing the poem with a set of nostalgic lines from Hesiod that indicate what would be given up ("let me have a seat in the shade some rock casts, / with water and good wine") and a final comment from Kipling's shepherd, uttered *after* his change: "She answered, 'Whether you live or die, or are made different, I am your Mother.'"[25] In Duncan's terms, this is an assurance, however frightening, that his work will continue to be an aspect of the evolving universe of created and creating things, that "Mother," no matter what direction he is forced toward.

In "Passages 21" and following, Duncan, like Kipling's shepherd, begins to "go among the Trees" for the sake of his people—in his case, the trees are American political events of the middle and late sixties. Although some of the early sections here are quite hesitant and reveal traces of the same struggle we have been examining, the movement is for the most part toward greater involvement with *all* aspects of the world "where we are." "Passages 21" is an account of the Berkeley Free Speech Movement, which Duncan renders as a version of Bosch's painting with those in authority bearing the "false faces" (BB, 70) of the hydra of established power. "Raging against the lawful demand / for right reason" of those few "concernd / about freedom of speech" (BB 70, 72), the authorities are seen as defenders of decayed forms, frightened by new expression and driven by the self-perpetuating power of "office." What should be possible even in this world, Duncan asserts (although he doesn't yet demonstrate), is for those dying forms to be made anew into a larger form, aching to be born. That work is to be the poet's, the creator, who, recalling the juxtaposed ideograms of "Passages 13" and the architecture manual of "Passages 9," is able to see the "door" that opens out from forms grown wrong:

> Each day   the last day;   each day   the
>   beginning   the first word
>   door of the day or law awakening we create,
>   vowels sung in a field in mid-morning
>   awakening the heart from its oppressions.
>   (BB, 72)

The next poem—not "Passage 22" but, significantly, "In the Place of a Passage 22"—slips back into fear, but in doing so, as often is the case in Duncan, comes to a key realization—in this case, how it is the poet must sing within this smoky, fire-razed field. In a sense, Duncan, in marking his fear, also marks a place of potential engagement. The poem begins with another statement of an ideal—Schubert's world, or that of the first day ideogram, in which an individual's self-creation and his contribution to the evolving ensemble struggle against no imposed boundaries:

> The seed I am knows only the green law of the tree into which
> it sends out its roots, life and branches,
>   unhinderd,   the vast universe
>   showing only its boundaries we imagine.
>   (BB, 74)

We see immediately why Duncan uses such a hesitant title when he follows this dream with an account of what that green tree has come to. Let me sleep, he says, recalling the end of "Passages 1" and the opening of *The Waste Land*: "Grant me passages from winter's way, / and in the cold let me enclose my / self in sleep.   The tree is   as if dead   each / naked twig shakes in the wind" (BB, 74). But what he comes to, after using Victor Hugo's Leviathan (*"harsh, enormous in his wild ugliness, his stupidity, / his heaviness . . ."* [BB, 75]) to get at his fears about the dying order in which he finds himself, is another reassurance from the Mother of "Passages 19" that whatever the change forced in his singing, he will still be sounding out the core of his identity and will contribute to the World Tree's gradual development:

> Grand Mother of Images,   matrix
> genetrix,   quickening in rays
>   from the first days of the cosmos,
>
> turning my poet's mind in tides of
> solitude, seductive reveries, fears, resolves, outrage
>   yet
> having this certain specific agent I am,
>
>   the shadow of a tree wavering and yet staying
>
>   deep in it
>   (BB, 75)

This is significant, for the point here—that Duncan's earlier flirtations with "solitude," his "reveries" of childhood regained, and the fear he has just articulated are *all* aspects of his self-unfolding— releases him from the confining simplicity of singing only "vowels in mid-morning" and marks a crucial addition to the notion of the embrace. In a move that is repeated in Ashbery, Duncan sees that his position within Whitman's ensemble is marked by, and is thus to be read in terms of, an entire range of responses to its potentially coextensive elements. In fact, as the following "Passages" demonstrate, working with—weaving connections generated by—such forbidden emotions is just what is needed for him to achieve di Cosimo's vision of an Eden regained under pressure of the red disk of apocalypse.

"Passages 24," then, allows the "matrix genetrix" (the moon of "Passages 6") to begin turning Duncan's mind "in tides of / . . . fears, resolves, outrage"—these the responses coming most readily in the political climate of the time. He argues, quoting Dante and summarizing much of the struggle with the temptation of isolation dealt with earlier, that such responses are more than Bosch's displays of personal grief. The responses are in service to the ensemble:

> For the Good,
>
> il ben dello intelletto,   the good of the people,
>   the soul's good.
>
>   I put aside
>
> whatever I once served of the poet, master
> of enchanting words and magics,

> not to disown the old mysteries, sweet
> muthos   our mouth's telling
>
> and I will tell the beads, in the fearsome
> street I see glimpses of
>
> (BB, 77)

This is put carefully, in the manner of a proposition: Duncan will put aside the cool, shadowy waters of childhood *in order* "not to disown the old mysteries," in order, that is, to find a way to sing them again. By "tell[ing] the beads" of what is fearsome, he argues, he will help release what Dante calls "the good of the intellect"—or in Duncan's gloss of the phrase, "the fulfillment of their humanity, . . . the good of the whole population of man" (CP, 171–72).

How? How can such a prayer such as—"Mothering angels, hold my sight steady / and I will look this time as you bid me   to see / the dirty papers, moneys, laws, orders / and corpses of people and people-shit" (BB, 77)—lead him to the old mysteries? Duncan suggests that in our rage or dismay at "living productive forms . . . destroying the terms of their existence" (BB, i), we are forced to see them clearly—forced, in fact, to imagine the fullest expression of their selfhood, the "terms" that they have distorted or denied or from which they have drifted away. Because, for Duncan, that fullest expression involves both "utter individuality" and a series of possible relationships within the ensemble, imagining that nondistorted form as it might exist in today's troubled world involves Duncan in imagining, momentarily, that larger vision where "nothing circumscribed the flowering of being into its particular forms."[26] He puts it this way in an essay: "the 'we' who find ourselves on the brink of the destruction of the World Order are also, wherever we have sought to imagine the nature of freedom and of our commonality, the meaning of living for one's own true sake and of the multiplicity of freedoms necessary for the fulfillment of the whole of Man's potentiality, we are also on the brink of our own vision of World Order" (OS, 235). So then, he can argue in this poem that "rage, / grief, dismay" are "transports of beauty" (BB, 79) because they drive him to see the "good of self" that has been betrayed by the failure or weakening of what was potentially a healthy form. Seeing clearly the mistaken, too-narrow notion of "self-interest" that has brought about such actions, Duncan is then prompted to envision a larger notion of that same selfhood:[27]

> There is no
>
> good a man has in his own things except

it be in the community of every thing;

no nature he has

but in his nature hidden in the heart of the living,

in the great household.

(BB, 79)

Like di Cosimo, then, Duncan has taken the occasion of a world grown apocalyptic to come to a vision of that same world made new again, convinced as he is that any wrong action can somehow be fitted, if only as an opposition that generates a vision of its opposite, within the ensemble's bond of unity, because "The cosmos will not / dissolve its orders at man's evil" (BB, 79). That reenvisioning of the world is as much an "embrace" as his earlier reworking of Baudelaire.

A specific example of such an embrace arising from outrage occurs in the sustained condemnation of "the bloody verse America writes over Asia" (BB, 113) found in "Passages 25 and 26" where, as Duncan notes in an essay, "riding the wave of my outrage I saw Johnson as the demotic leader, unleashing into action and moved by the secret evil of the American karma" (OS, 242). Johnson, "drawing from the underbelly of the nation / such blood and dreams as swell the idiot psyche / out of its courses into an elemental thing" (BB, 81), is seen as prompting the nation's growth out of its proper "courses" toward "something terrible, gone beyond bounds" (BB, 81), in which a too-narrow notion of self-interest betrays the original dream of America:

in the line of duty, for the might and enduring fame
of Johnson, for the victory of American will over its victims,
releasing his store of destruction over the enemy,
in terror and hatred of all communal things, of communion,
of communism •

(BB, 81)

Such actions, Duncan writes, are "unacknowledged, unrepented crimes" (BB 83), but his outburst against them offers a first stage in an expansion of that "ensemble" we label America: "an acknowledgment and potential repentance . . . of what America means" (OS, 247). We see the second step in "Passages 26," where, proposing that, like our soldiers, he must "in the slaughter of man's hope / distil the divine potion, forbidden hallucínogen / that stirs sight of the hidden / order of orders" (BB, 112), Duncan adopts the "hatred [that] the maimd and bereft must hold / against the bloody verse America writes over Asia" (BB, 113), then develops what that hatred had stirred him to see concerning our self-protective fear of "communal things" into a larger vision of America which, he asserts, "we must recall to hold" (BB, 113) against this now-grown-monstrous version.

Duncan gets at that larger vision, in "Passages 26," by working with a passage from Whitman's 1855 Preface to *Leaves of Grass* which, in a kind of object lesson, he reads first as a nearly obscene boast about American's importance, then reads again, in the light of his outrage, as something quite different. That is, driven by outrage, Duncan "uses" Whitman to get to a vision of what seems denied in his prose, then reads Whitman in the light of that expansion as a contributing, co-extensive voice. Pushed by outrage, he is able to successfully "weave" that boast into an evolving form, adding another room to his expanding household. Initially, he comments in an essay, Whitman's lines had seemed an earlier version of the "secret entity of America's hatred of Europe, of Africa, of Asia" (BB, 82) made plain now by Johnson:

> Is it the deadly boast of the Chauvinist, the patriotic zeal of a spiritual imperialism, that fires Whitman's "The Americans of all nations at any time upon the earth have probably the fullest poetical nature. The United States themselves are essentially the greatest poem?" Presidents, congresses, armed forces, industrialists, governors, police forces, have rendered the meaning of "America" and "the United States" so fearful—causing fear and filled with fear—in our time that no nationalistic inspiration comes innocent of the greed and ruthless extension of power to exploit the peoples and natural resources of the world that has spread terror, misery, and devastation wherever it has gone (CP, 169).

But, his outrage at that boast having prompted him to articulate an opposing vision of an America not driven by a self-interested will to power, Duncan now discovers that very vision in Whitman. "Writing the poem 'The Soldiers,'" he remarks, "I came to read Whitman's lines . . . in a new inspiration":

> the "United States" appeared to me as the states of being or of Man united, all one's states of mind brought together in one governance; and "the Americans of all nations at any time upon the earth" meant clearly that "America" and being "American" was a community that was from the beginning of Man and everywhere in the world. . . . underlying these United States and this America, comes a mystery of "America" that belongs to dream and desire and the reawakening of earliest oneness with all peoples—at last, the nation of Mankind at large. It is this that informs Whitman's enthusiasm for America (CP, 170).[28]

Such a coming to "a new inspiration"—reading these lines in a new and consequently expansive context—is just what Zinzendorf, com-

bining two different ways of speaking, or any other figure active in
the ensemble, does. It is how one reads oneself through the medium
of the community of humanity. And just as, in the light of that "new
inspiration" prompted by the intensity of his negative response,
Whitman's "America" was seen again as a dream of community
traced under an apparently narrow boast, so our own struggle in
Vietnam against communism, seen first as "hatred of all communal
things," prompts Duncan to a larger view of that potential form that
had been betrayed—"the idea of an America latent and at work" (CP,
166), yet to be fully seen, which we had been "removed therefrom by
habit" (BB, 114):

> "*The United States themselves are essentially the greatest poem*"?
>
> Then America, the secret union of all states of Man,
>
> waits, hidden and challenging, in the hearts of the Viet Cong.
>
> "*The Americans of all nations at any time upon the earth,*"
>
> Whitman says—the libertarians of the spirit, the
>
> devotées of Man's commonality.
>
> (BB, 113)

Our struggle in Vietnam, then, if Johnson were a better poet and
shared such a view, would be, as in "Passages 2," the coming together of contrasting but finally united elements "on [the] wide
plain" of a new notion of America rather than the wrathful domination of one element by another.

Of course Johnson doesn't share such a view, so the poet has work
to do, as the discussion of the role of the artist in "Passages 27" indicates. The poem begins with a reference to other poets who have
acted on that larger vision of commonality generated by, but at odds
with, "the period in which we live." Like those others who, although
"estranged from all but a few about them, . . . made a new dimension in which eternal companions appeared" (H.D.:I, 6, 134), Duncan would also take up the challenge:

> In the War they made a celestial cave.
>
> In the War now I make
>
> a celestial cave,   a tent of the Night
>
> (the Sun, no longer striking day upon the Earth,
>
> but light-years away   a diamond spark in the host of stars
>   sparkling net   bejewelld wave of dark   over us
>   distant coruscations

> "play of light or of intellectual brilliancy"
>
> in which I pretend   a convocation of powers
>
> (BB, 120)

The poem is best read as two statements: a short sentence about earlier artists, and a longer sentence about making a cave or tent in which the poet "pretend[s] a convocation of powers," that sentence broken by an open parenthetical comment about the darkness in which such activity becomes possible. The point is that because of the darkness of this continuing war, as "Passages 25 and 26" have demonstrated, it has become possible for Duncan to see and work with the larger "sparkling net," the "distant coruscations" of the ensemble of which we are a part.[29]

"Passages 29" is built around two examples of such an imaginative convocation of powers, points in history where, in response to an established form grown rigid and corrupt, heretics "made a new dimension in which eternal companions appeared." Both movements, as Duncan encourages himself to do, take shape as contending elements within an established form, drawing on an energy generated by that opposition and transforming that energy into a larger, inclusive music—that of the "Grand Symphony" or ensemble. Through contention rather than the "lovely marrd sentiment" from which we have been "disownd," these oppositions generate Schubert's "contrapuntal communion of all things." The first counterpointed element is the Caodist movement of Vietnam, a reformed Buddhism that as Gabriel Gobron notes in his *History and Philosophy of Caodism*, one of Duncan's sources for this poem, was an attempt, sparked by intolerance, to draw opposing religious visions into a larger pattern: "a synthesis of the three great Oriental religions: Buddhism, Confucianism, and Taoism, which united with Christianity and the worship of genii, represent the five great ways that Cao-Dai (The Supreme Being) opened to humanity for their development and spiritual evolution."[30] Working with Gobron's history, Duncan describes the movement as the unfolding of a new law from the restrictions of an old one, his language echoing earlier sections of the poem, Verlaine's refreshing river of fire among them:

> First from the Father   glance that lit
>
> New Love in Liberty   whose law
>
> dissolves in its coruscations
> (rainbow) (lapis lazuli)
>
> the chains of Eros and the Old Law!

Christmas Eve, 1925. The Spirit descended
to bring the Truth to Viet-Nam

Réjouissez-vous de cette fête,

anniversary of my coming to the West
to give my Sign

that certain hearts tremble
and pour out from their reserves

enduring Love

(BB, 124)

Weaving his own commentary and expansion around the Spirit's first words—that its Christmas Eve speech in Vietnam came on the anniversary of its earlier manifestation in Bethlehem—Duncan takes pains to frame this movement as the awakening to vision of a few, those "certain hearts" lifted to contact with an "enduring" order.[31] Such an individual vision also dominates Duncan's quotation of portions of a Caodist poem, an awakening moving from the contemplation of a "cold and sad world," not unlike our own, to the expanse of all things: "I have contemplated the Regulator of the Stars, / Commissar of Invisible and Visible Worlds" (BB, 124, 126).

Duncan moves away from the Caodist sect for a moment—leaves its vision in the temporarily peaceful possession of "certain hearts" in Vietnam in 1926—in order to juxtapose it to an example of an earlier vision raised against another order grown rigid: the heretical Catharist church destroyed by Innocent III in the thirteenth-century Albigensian Crusade. In doing so, Duncan repeats the pattern of "Passages 2 and 13"—the seemingly inevitable slip from di Cosimo to Bosch, and from the "alliance" to the "mêlée"—but now with quite a different end in sight. The Cathars, or "pure ones," were dualists who saw the material world as standing in opposition to God and thus attempted to separate themselves from it. Their movement developed, in a pattern we have seen throughout these later "Passages," as a criticism and reversal of the Catholic church's increasingly corrupt involvement with the world. Recalling his own vision of his work as "the warning light at the edge of town," Duncan writes that it was a stirring "from the margins of Christendom," a stirring in which "from outside the Empire, from the margins where things mix, a Christ returns . . . who is now the verso [the reverse side] of the law of the established Church" (HD.:I, 3, 77). Duncan's use of the word "returns" is significant, suggesting that the new Catharist vision was a reestablishment of an earlier, since-grown-rigid form—

exactly the point made in "Passages 24." (Zoé Oldenbourg, in *Massacre at Montségur*, the volume Duncan used in preparing this section, supports this idea in his description of the Catharist church as, in some senses, a development of "a latent streak of Manichaeism" within catholicism. Oldenbourg writes that "Mediaeval Civilization, having been formed originally in a monastic mould, regarded the material world with undiluted loathing and contempt. It may not have actually claimed that matter was the work of the Devil, but it *behaved* exactly as though it thought so.")[32] Like Achilles or the crowd about Bosch's Christ, the Church responded violently to this threat to its power. The most striking example of that response, focused on by both Duncan and Oldenbourg, was the Crusaders' successful nine-month seige of the Catharist stronghold at Montségur, their victory marked by the execution of more than two hundred *perfecti*—a tiny minority of believers known as the "finished" or "completed" ones who had sacramentally died to this world and had embarked on a life of prayer, preaching, and good works. All of the *perfecti* refused to recant and were burned in a mass pyre. As Oldenbourg imagines it, "In a few hours' time, the two hundred living torches heaped inside the palisade were no more than a mass of raw, blackened, bleeding flesh, slowly burning to a cindered crisp, spreading a ghastly stench of burnt meat right down the valley, and up to the very walls of the fortress."[33] Apparently, they were destroyed by a grown-rigid ensemble that refused to acknowledge them.

Significantly, what Duncan chooses to work with from Oldenbourg's study is his closing account of seventeen of the defenders at Montségur who, during the fifteen-day truce after the surrender but before the Crusader's possession of the fortress, chose to undergo the *consolamentum* sacrament—deliberately accepting certain death in order to possess what they saw as a perfected state.[34] In a sense, the defenders function as Bosch's Christ no longer silent, Kipling's shepherd allowing himself to be changed, Duncan making a "celestial cave" in the war, for they sing their notes in counterpoint to the established order in full awareness of what will come. Holding their positions "until the name of the Roman Church with its heapt honors / stinks with the smell of their meat burning," their names "enter as notes of a sublime sweetness / the resounding chords of wrath and woe.   Grandeur!" (BB, 126). Finally, then, "Passages 29" is less a poem about the abuses of those in power—as the movement from the dream of the Caodists to the destruction of the Cathars might suggest—than it is a celebration of the opposing power of those free voices, singing out of a larger vision that both acknowl-

edges the failures of the established order ("its heapt honors / stink")
and transforms the existing structures of that world apparently grown
apocalyptic into contrasting elements of a larger structure. Offering
new "notes of sublime sweetness," the Cathars turn those apparently
overpowering "chords of woe" into the darker elements of a higher
harmony.[35] So then, Duncan can close "Passages 29" by circling back
to the Vietnamese spiritualists who, facing the inevitable opposition
of those in power—in this case, opposition by the American war machine by which Duncan is also overruled—can now be seen as deliberately counterpointing their sweet notes to that din and so creating
a fuller melody:

> At the Saint-Siège Caodaïste at Tay-Ninh,
>
>> in the roaring din of American planes
>> performing their daily missions to destroy
>> the Viet-Cong's strongholds of the Holy Spirit
>
> the prayers of the shaman-priests at the altar
>
>> rise / and in the crescendo of the War,
>
> exact the line of a melody / as if
>
>> the faith of Schubert would enter the Heraklitean truth,
>
>> the polemic
>
> father of all,   harsh necessity,
>
>> in the roar and fire-fall
>
> (BB, 126–27)

The Caodists, creating that melody in Duncan's own grown-mon-
strous time, offer him a last and convincing example for how the apparently "disownd" sentiment of Schubert can be made to resound
again in a larger, more inclusive setting—as *part* of the struggling
world of necessity. What remains, then, is for Duncan the ensemblist
to sing in this manner, sounding his opposing "faith" within the
"roar and fire-fall" and thereby himself giving shape to "sentences of
an inaudible bell" (BB, 127).

"Passages 30," last poem in *Bending the Bow*'s gathering of this sequence, offers a set of summary propositions—"Stage Directions"—
for Duncan's future work in bringing to speech that as-yet-inaudible
sentence. He remarks first, by means of Ezra Pound's despairing
"*It's not so, not strictly so, / that's the trouble*" (BB, 128) on the apparent wreckage of the *Cantos*, that he has finally put aside the dream
of a simple, strict truth and its corresponding theory of reading for
the creative strife of "the Heraklitean truth."[36] Where Pound was
troubled, Duncan is empowered: "For the poet, *It*, the form he obeys

in making form, the very revelation of Art, is not strictly so. Creativity, as I have suggested, means such a change in the meanings of every part in the creation of each part that every new strictness is also a charm undoing all previous strictnesses, at once an imperative and at the same time a change of imperative" (TL, 66). To be convinced that truth is multiple rather than strict, that each aspect of it contends with and helps create all other aspects, means, as Duncan has convincingly demonstrated, that for the "lonely, isolate melodic singer" to fully pour forth his "utter individuality" he must give up the dream of a peaceful childhood Eden and enter the field of contention in which "all times and intents of peaceful men / Reduce to an interim, a passing play / between surpassing / Crises of war" (BB, 128). Accepting this proposition and devising a way to read and sing that both confronts and draws energy from the individual's inevitable struggle with forms that refuse this multiple view has given the poet a way to sense and contribute to the "music / Orpheus first playd, / chords and melodies of the spell that binds / the many in conflict in contrasts of one mind" (BB, 41–42). Like di Cosimo's Eden established under the flames of apocalypse, Duncan has also come to envision the process by which opposing elements are united. His image for that vision, first introduced in "Passages 28," is the winged horse Pegasos and the warrier Chrysaor springing from the dying body of the beheaded Medusa. Pegasos, whose pounding hooves released the fountain where the muses drank their inspiration, is linked to art and poetry—in the language of this poem, to Schubert's free expansion: "that great horse Poetry,   Rider / we ride, who make up / the truth of What Is" (BB, 122). Chrysaor, "of the golden sword" (BB, 122), is linked to contention and strife—the Heraklitean truth. *Together*, they indicate Duncan's realization that the new law gradually arising from the dying Gorgon of America ("from the dying body of America I see, / or from my dying body" [BB, 132]) will be a complex one, its individual elements both at war with each other and yet part of "one body not [to] be broken."[37]

Finally, Duncan asserts, that vision will only be brought to realization by active participation in the form in which we find ourselves. Facing what we are in opposition to, acknowledging and dramatizing both outrage and ultimate unity (as the Albigensians did), we are reading ourselves as fully as possible—embracing what we can of a world still making itself and thereby "envisioning the greatest commonality, seeing as if with 'God's' eye a release of Man's fullest nature from its bonds. At once creatures, subject to the intent of the creation we belong to, and, seeing ourselves so, creators, participants in that intent" (OS, 235). In "Passages 30," Duncan describes such a creator as having a director's or dramatist's eye—an eye that assumes that because conflicting figures and actions are part of a single form whose full meaning, or plot, becomes clear only from the complete working out of all tensions, is trained to look for and tease out such complexities. Like Shakespeare (and unlike his character Macbeth), such a dramatist would seek to understand, as best he or she could, the entire plot ("Macbeth / so little knows he moves as / messenger of the myth, the / plot of the play" [BB, 132]), attempting to draw toward realization the dance that would order our burning world: "('*So foule and faire a day I have not seene,*' another / murderous heart declares, who from Medusa's head / expects that Burning Would—to echo Joyce's pun— / will never come to Dance Inane" (BB, 130). What this means, then, to return to Duncan's protest parable, is that, desiring to enter and belong to the larger "configuration being born of what 'we' means" but finding himself surrounded by those "that meant to overcome us," the individual creator must, through conscious opposition as well as through simple identification, seek to unfold that larger form from the ranks of its present manifestation: "In the confrontation, had we danced, taking the advance of the soldiers by the number in ranks into the choreography of the day, or, members of the dance, sat where we were, tensing the strings between the horns for the music's sake, the event the poem seeks might have emerged. The poet of the event senses the play of its moralities belongs to the configuration he cannot see but feels in terms of fittings that fix and fittings that release the design out of itself as he works to bring the necessary image to sight" (BB, iv). What we have observed in these poems is an example of that dance—drawing out and responding to the tensions inherent in the world where we are—by means of which Duncan has begun to release the larger design in which he senses his participation. In Whitman's terms, Duncan has given resonance to his individual song by releasing the pent-up "power *en masse* of the ensemble in which he sings." And he has done so by developing a new sort of Whitmanic catalog—one that calls attention to and exploits the struggles of translation as it both "uses" and is opposed by the world that it would enter—which is itself a deep form of homage to the catalog's originator.

NOTES

1. Robert Duncan, "Towards an Open Universe," in *The Poetics of the New American Poetry*, ed. Donald Allen and Warren Tallman (New York: Grove Press, 1973), p. 214. Cited in the text as OU. Other Duncan works are abbre-

viated in the text as follows: BB: *Bending the Bow* (New York: New Directions, 1968); IE: "Iconographical Extensions" in *Translations by Jess* (New York: Odyssia Gallery, 1971); OS: "Man's Fulfillment in Order and Strife," *Caterpillar* 8/9 (1969); P: "Preface to a Reading of Passages 1–22," *Maps* 6 (1974); TL: *The Truth and Life of Myth* (Fremont, Mich.: Sumac, 1968); Y: *The Years as Catches* (Berkeley: Oyez, 1966). Selections from *The H.D. Book* are cited in the text by part and chapter numbers, as follows: H.D.:I, 1: *Coyote's Journal* 5/6 (1966); H.D.:I, 2: *Coyote's Journal* 8 (1967); H.D.:I, 3: *TriQuarterly* 12 (1968); H.D.:I, 6: *Caterpillar* 1 (1967) and *Caterpillar* 2 (1968); H.D.:II, 1: *Sumac* 1 (1968); H.D.:II, 4: *Caterpillar* 7 (1969); H.D.:II, 5: *Stony Brook* 3/4 (1969); H.D.:II, 9: *Chicago Review* 30 (1979); H.D.:II, 10: *Ironwood* 11 (Fall 1983); H.D.:II, 11: *Montemora* 8 (1981).

2. I say "approximating the self's intuited fullness" because Duncan, like Whitman, is convinced only that a poem "nearer bring[s]" us to that fullness, not that it ever achieves that goal. For both, we create a "fiction" of that whole. Duncan writes, "The ensemble, alone the field of the complete, haunts the work of the artist who makes in the poem a fiction of the existence of the whole, a fictional ensemble in which we become aware of the existence of the ensemble." This remark can be found in "Changing Perspectives in Reading Whitman" in *Fictive Certainties* (New York: New Directions, 1985), p. 181. Cited in the text as CP. For a general discussion of Whitman's influence on Duncan, see Mark Johnson and Robert DeMott, "An Inheritance of Spirit: Robert Duncan and Walt Whitman" in *Scales of the Marvelous*, ed. Robert J. Bertholf and Ian W. Reid (New York: New Directions, 1979). Cary Nelson's chapter "Form and Dissolution in Robert Duncan's Aesthetic" in *Our Last First Poets: Vision and History in Contemporary American Poetry* (Urbana: University of Illinois Press, 1981) forcefully argues that such a derivation, following Whitman, "nearly destroys" Duncan's later work—a conclusion with which this essay differs.

3. Walt Whitman, "Carlyle from American Points of View," cited by Duncan, "Changing Perspectives," p. 167. Duncan links this passage with Whitehead (pp. 168–69): "Dreaming of the ensemble of created and creating forms, Whitman was the poet of primary intuitions, ancestor of Whitehead's *Process and Reality*, and of our own vision of creation where now we see all of life as unfoldings, the revelations of a field of potentialities and latencies toward species and individuals hidden in the DNA, a field of generations larger than our humanity." For useful accounts of Duncan's understanding of Whitehead, see Charles Altieri, *Enlarging the Temple: New Directions in American Poetry during the 1960s:* (Lewisburg, Pa.: Bucknell University Press, 1979), pp. 150–63; Michael Davidson, "A Book of First Things: *The Opening of the Field*" in *Scales of the Marvelous*, ed. Robert J. Bertholf and Ian W. Reid (New York: New Directions, 1979), pp. 56–84; and Mark Johnson, "Robert Duncan's 'Momentous Inclusions,'" *Sagetrieb* 2 (Summer-Fall 1983): 71–84.

4. For more on this notion, see Norman Finkelstein, "Robert Duncan, Poet of the Law," *Sagetrieb* 2 (Spring 1983): 75–88.

5. Duncan makes this point in a number of other places. In H.D.:II, 1, 105,

he writes: "individual works are jointures of a larger structure, not conclusions but functions. Each thing-in-itself is revealed anew as it is seen as the member of possible sequences"; in IE, iv: "In a field of interacting melodies a single note may belong to both ascending and descending figures, and yet again, to a sustaining chord or discord." For further discussion, see Nelson, *Our Last First Poets*, pp. 123–24.

6. Other readings of the poem include Mark Johnson, "'*Passages*': Cross-Sections of the Universe," *Ironwood* 23 (1983): 173–91, and Ian W. Reid, "The Plural Text: '*Passages*'" in *Scales of the Marvelous*, ed. Robert J. Bertholf and Ian W. Reid (New York: New Directions, 1979), pp. 161–80.

7. *The Works of the Emperor Julian* I, ed. T. E. Page and W. H. D. Rouse (New York: MacMillan, 1913), p. 473.

8. Julian. The last three quotations are from pp. 479, 440, and 473.

9. Robert Duncan, *Poetry/Audit* 4, no. 3 (1967): 48. Cited in Michael André Bernstein, "Bringing It all Back Home: Derivation and Quotation in Robert Duncan and the Poundian Tradition," *Sagetrieb* 1 (Fall 1982): 176–89.

10. Johnson, "'*Passages*': Cross-Sections of the Universe," p. 177, makes a similar comment and notes that when reading Duncan stresses the *h* sounds here to emphasize these words.

11. For more on "Passages 1," see Wendy MacIntyre, "Robert Duncan: The Actuality of Myth," *Open Letter*, second series, no. 4 (Spring 1973): 41–42. Reid, "The Plural Text," pp. 162–63, reads this "forth-going" figure as Phanes breaking from the world-egg—a legitimate connection developed in "Passages 14," but one that, in isolation, overlooks the imagery of storm and solstice that are normally linked to Attis.

12. The strongest essays on Duncan's "work" as a "reader" are Bernstein's "Bringing It All Back Home," and "Robert Duncan: Talent and the Individual Tradition," *Sagetrieb* 4 (Fall-Winter 1985): 177–90, and Michael Davidson "Cave of Resemblances, Cave of Rimes: Tradition and Repetition in Robert Duncan," *Ironwood* 22 (Fall 1983).

13. Ezra Pound, *The Cantos* (New York: New Directions, 1971), p. 193.

14. See also H.D.:I, 6, 68: "The crux for the poet is to make real what is only real in a heightened sense. Call it his personal feeling, or the communal reality, it exists only in its dance, only to its dancers. Outside the created excitement, what we call the inspiration of art, the things done . . . do not communicate."

15. Johnson, "'*Passages*' Cross-Sections of the Universe," pp. 178–80, reads this poem as a display of "inconclusiveness" rather than a "mistake." It seems to me that a mistake more usefully generates new understanding.

16. For a thoughtful discussion of "reflection" in Duncan, see Altieri, *Enlarging the Temple*, pp. 150–63.

17. Charles Baudelaire, *Artificial Paradise: On Hashish and Wine as Means of Expanding Identity*, trans. Ellen Fox (New York: Herder and Herder, 1971), pp. 13–14.

18. Michael Davidson, "Cave of Resemblances, Cave of Rimes," p. 38.

19. Cary Nelson's chapter "Form and Dissolution in Robert Duncan's Aesthetic" (*Our Last First Poets*) has been useful in framing this problem. Nelson examines Duncan's pursuit of an "innocent, Whitmanesque openness" (p. 99) in which the poet surrenders his "troubled individual isolated experiences to the communal consciousness" (Duncan's phrase) and concludes that in the "trial by history" (p. 143) of the sixties, finding "his poem's substance . . . equated with the substance of his society" (p. 143), Duncan "comes to an unexpected crisis" (p. 140). Nelson and I differ, as will become clear, in how we read Duncan's response to this crisis. Ian W. Reid's "The Plural Text" also offers a thoughtful discussion of Duncan's response to strife.

20. Such a crisis, in Duncan's understanding, continually recurs: "Our contemporary concern with World Order seems specially charged with a crisis in language and world, we are in apocalyptic times. But this crisis is not at some particular time or place; it is the condition of man and we find it wherever men have been awake to that condition. This feeling of coming to the end or the beginning of things never comes to an end and is always beginning" (OS, 231).

21. See H.D.: II, 11, 79–81 for Duncan's recounting of the dream he has labelled "Glimpses of the Last Day" from which this ideogram is drawn—an apocalyptic dream directing him to "redirect the spring . . . in the first direction."

22. Two other readings of "Passages 13" can be found in Robert C. Weber, "Robert Duncan and the Poem of Resonance," *Concerning Poetry* 11 (1978): 67–73 and Mark Johnson, "'Passages': Cross-Sections of the Universe." Weber offers a sound argument for how we might approach that first ideogram, although I am not convinced that spinning the ideogram indicates a reversal "from an essentially mythic sensibility to an essentially demonic one" (p. 69).

23. "Passages 17," a translation and expansion of Hermes' "Perfect Sermon," continues such a retreat, Duncan arguing that his ability to "unite Kore and Xristmas" forces him toward a position "not of this world." See G. R. S. Mead, *Thrice Greatest Hermes: Studies in Hellenistic Theosophy and Gnosis*, vol. 2, *Sermons* (London: Theosophical Publishing Society, 1906). Duncan, as is his usual practice, has reordered the material quoted from Hermes' sermon. Lines 1 and 2 are drawn from p. 351, lines 22–25 from pp. 331–32, lines 26–50 from pp. 352–56. This also suggests that the remarkable love poem "The Torso" ("Passages 18") that follows should be read as another fragile but limited moment of individual vision, separate from, even at odds with, the world. Nelson's excellent analysis of the violent and "disabling" transformation of the language of this poem by "darker purposes" later in the sequence supports this view of Duncan's "recognition that an historical environment of inexplicable murder and all-too-explicable guilt pervades both sexual privacy and poetic creation and makes their isolation impossible" (p. 138).

24. Hesiod, *Works and Days*, line 160. Duncan has drawn his lines 11–16 from Hesiod's 168–72; lines 21–22 from Hesiod's 580; lines 42–45 from He-

siod's 582–89; lines 46–49 from Hesiod's 824–25. This is Duncan's own translation. I have used *Hesiod*, edited and translated by Apostolos N. Athanassakis (Baltimore: Johns Hopkins University Press, 1983).

25. See Rudyard Kipling, *Rewards and Faries* (Garden City: Doubleday, 1910), pp. 133, 134, 142.

26. Robert Duncan, "From a Notebook," *The Black Mountain Review* 2, no. 5 (1955): 212. Cited by Nelson, in *Our Last First Poets*, p. 102.

27. Duncan often uses the terms *acknowledge* and *redeem* for the two stages of this action. He writes, for example, "The vital center of my vision of any World Order is that it must *redeem*, must be the redemption of, not the rising above, that burden of *acknowledged* crimes against humanity" (OS, 242). Likewise, in a letter to Denise Levertov about the Vietnam war, he writes of the need "to *face* and *contain* somehow this . . . spiritually destroying evidence of what human kind will do," Levertov, "Some Duncan Letters," *Scales of the Marvelous*, p. 110. "To redeem, to save or keep alive the wholeness of what we are alive" (H.D.:II, 11, 87) means to imagine a larger pattern of human behavior in which such crimes, instead of being dismissed as contradictory or disabling, are seen as contrasting with—and thus in relationship with—other, freer actions. For example, Duncan writes, "The War itself and the power of the State I dimly perceived were not only a power over me but also a power related to my own creative power but turnd to purposes of domination, exploitation, and destruction" (Y, viii). Nelson's reading of Duncan in *Our Last First Poets* stresses Duncan's acknowledgment of such crimes—the manner in which this perceived connection "undercuts his [lyric] vision by showing the field taken up in both antogonistic social interaction and the deadly communality of the battlefield" (p. 142)—without giving equal notice to Duncan's struggles to contribute to a pattern that would redeem such acts.

28. For further discussion of Duncan's response to this aspect of Whitman, see Mark Johnson and Robert DeMott, "'An Inheritance of Spirit': Robert Duncan and Walt Whitman," *Scales of the Marvelous*, pp. 231–33.

29. "Passages 7," in which Duncan notes that at night, when "the light of the sun is gone," we "can see the dark interstices / Day's lord erases" (BB, 22), and "Passages 23," where he notes that "we live in the darkness in back of / her [the sun's] rising" (BB, 76), have prepared the ground for this image. Duncan uses the word "pretend" here to indicate that his imagination of that not-yet-seen whole is, of course, not accurate—it is a constructed fiction: "The plot we are to follow, the great myth or work, is the fiction of what Man is" (H.D.:I, 3, 67).

30. Gabriel Gobron, *History and Philosophy of Caodaism: Reformed Buddhism, Vietnamese Spiritualism, New Religion in Eurasia*, trans. Pham-xuan-thai (Saigon, 1950), p. 52. For more on intolerance, see p. 30.

31. Duncan has read "actively" here. The first five lines quoted are his own, connecting this passage with earlier sections of the poem; the next two lines are a condensed version of Gobron's history, followed by the quotation of the spirit's first words, and concluding with Duncan's own rendering of that first message.

32. Zoé Oldenbourg, *Massacre at Montségur: A History of the Albigensian Crusade*, trans. Peter Green (New York: Pantheon, 1961), p. 39. I have made use of the entire second chapter, "Heresy and Heretics," in writing this section.

33. Oldenbourg, *Massacre at Montségur*, p. 364.

34. Oldenbourg, pp. 356–64. The entire final chapter, "The Seige at Montségur," provides valuable background information for understanding Duncan's thinking here.

35. They are examples for Duncan of how, in Whitehead's words, "Creativity achieves its supreme task of transforming disjoined multiplicity with its diversities in opposition, into concrescent unity, with its diversities in contrast" (H.D.:II, 10, 51).

36. Duncan writes of Pound: "The Ezra Pound who would set up the Stone-Classics of Confucius as a moral order, even as he acts to make our European 'Western' mind heterogeneous and complex, seeks to introduce a foundation of simplicity against what he sees as an intolerable history of increasingly polyphasic relations." See "Notes on the Structure of Rime," *Maps* 6 (1974): 49. Bernstein's "Robert Duncan: Talent and the Individual Tradition," particularly pp. 187–89, is a valuable contrast of Pound and Duncan on this issue.

37. This is a vision in which "there is no preestablished law, for every happening destroys the law before it, moving, as it does, towards the creation of a law that will be established only in the composition of the whole" (H.D.:II, 9, 39). The corresponding view of poetry is that "there is not only the dream of an order of orders in Poetry and the World, but there is a polemic of orders in the struggle for larger terms of order. Poetry charged with meaning to the utmost degree must be thought of as being charged with a conscience of order and disorder" (OS, 241).

CHAPTER 5

❖ ❖ ❖

A METAPHOR MADE TO INCLUDE US

John Ashbery's "Self-Portrait in a Convex Mirror"

> Only out of such "perfectly useless concentration" can emerge the one thing that is useful for us: our coming to know ourselves as the necessarily inaccurate transcribers of the life that is always on the point of coming into being.[1]

John Ashbery has consistently situated his work within Whitman's distinction between "the Me myself" ("*behind* all the faculties of the human being, as the sight, the other senses and even the emotions and the intellect, stands the real power, the mystical identity, the real I or Me or You") and the visible, material world that might, indirectly, serve to bring him nearer "To it."[2] Like Roethke and Duncan, Ashbery finds what Duncan calls the "central drive" of "Song of Myself"—"the tension between speaking oneself and the utter commonality of the language that must be the medium of that self"—to be a richly generative frustration.[3] Oddly, although perhaps farthest from Whitman in terms of the texture of his verse, Ashbery, of all the poets in this book, comes closest to capturing the "amused, complacent" tone of Whitman's response to this tension:

> Apart from the pulling and hauling stands what I am,
> Stands amused, complacent, compassionating, idle, unitary,
> Looks down, is erect, or bends an arm on an impalpable certain rest,
> Looking with side-curved head curious what will come next,
> Both in and out of the game and watching and wondering at it.
>
> (SM, 4)

Guided by Ashbery's exploration of the same subject in his "Self-Portrait in a Convex Mirror," this chapter will examine the act of evaluation that must, at some level, have made possible both writers' ready acceptance of this gap between self and portrait, between "the real I" and its "pulling and hauling" medium.

Ashbery has consistently framed this tension as a "sobering" distinction between the moment as it is lived through—a "shapeless blur" one poem has it, "a dimensionless area" that seems both full and empty[4]—and the moment as it is thought about: "There is that sound like the wind / Forgetting in the branches that means some-thing / Nobody can translate. And there is the sobering 'later on,' / When you consider what a thing meant, and put it down" (DDS, 20). For Ashbery, the act of translation replaces the moment with a rich, multiple unraveling: "When we experience a moment we feel perhaps a kind of emptiness, but when we look back at it there will be differ-ent aspects and the moment will separate itself into these aspects. We won't be sure what the dominant aspect was, and I guess that results in my sense of a permanent unraveling. This best describes how I experience life, as a unity constantly separating" (AM, 75). And what is true about the experience of a single moment—a movement from "the inner emptiness from which alone understanding can spring up, [to] the tree of contradictions, joyous and living, investing that hollow void with its complicated material self" (TP, 63)—is, by extension, true about our lives as well, a cascade of such moments. As Ashbery would have it, we produce—in those unravelings of that inner "hol-low void"—a kind of "dumb harvest" in which speechless "Passions are locked away, and states of creation are used instead, that is to say synonyms are used" (TCO, 57).[5]

Ashbery's indirect reading of himself—harvesting what was dumb in an ensemble of "synonyms"—is a version of what we first saw in sections 5 and 6 of "Song of Myself" when Whitman suggested that the soul's intuited presence ("I mind . . . / How you settled your head athwart my hips and gently turn'd over upon me") could be approached through tenderly using the world's "many uttering tongues." For Ashbery, as for the other writers in this book, making use of what Duncan calls that "larger language where minds and spir-its awaken sympathies in me, a commune of members in which my-self seems everywhere translated" produces not that dimensionless unity, but "a fictional ensemble in which we become aware of the existence of the whole." A difference between Ashbery and these other writers—although a logical outgrowth of the tradition—is that, for him, this "larger language," these "resonances of the totality," have already been absorbed and internalized.[6] Soaking in the pulling and hauling of the world's ways of speaking ("I don't have any idea of what my own voice is, if indeed I have one, and I'm usually listen-ing rather than talking and what I hear somehow gets written down" [S, 184]), Ashbery consistently calls attention to what he terms "the polyphony that goes on inside me" (PR, 50), the various "ways in which one finds oneself talking to oneself or to someone else." (NYQ, 128).) As can be seen in an even more extreme version in James Merrill's work, it is as if Roethke's sea or Duncan's made things had been internalized. These resonating, dissolving voices are not his dimensionless consciousness but the medium through which it is made visible; for Ashbery, "one's consciousness is surrounded by one's thoughts" (NYQ, 126). Helen Vendler has usefully described these voices as a kind of humming commentary: "Something—which we could call ruminativeness, speculation, a humming commentary— is going on unnoticed in us always, and is the seed-bed of creation: Keats called it a state of 'dim dreams,' full of 'stirring shades, and baffled beams.' We do not quite want to call these things 'thoughts.' They nonetheless go on."[7] It is *that* ensemble—internalized, but as with all the writers examined in this book, clearly "other" and apart from that unlocatable "hollow space"—that Ashbery would enter and draw from in rendering himself. What Duncan understands as the "continual song" or "ever-running / stream of bright water" (BB, 58–59) of humanity's made things, is, for Ashbery, "going on all the time inside, an underground stream. One can let down one's bucket and bring the poem back up" (PR, 51). When he says, then, that his poetry is an "attempt at mimesis of the way experience and knowl-edge come to me" (CS, 305), or that it is a version of "the way a hap-pening or experience filters through to me" (MQ, 245), the remarks should be seen as claims to imitate not the valveless hum of the mo-ment itself, but the various voices by which we handle and filter it.

As these remarks suggest, there is, in Ashbery, little trace of the struggle, central to both Roethke and Duncan, to develop a technique to "use" and link elements of that stream properly. Any number of devices—a title, "a collection of odd notations that have come out of conversations, dreams, overheard remarks on the street"—allow him "to be able to start concentrating attentively in order to pick up what-ever is in the air" (NYQ, 112, 113). If poetry, for Ashbery, involves a kind of unraveling of a dimensionless moment's "different aspects"— "sitting down to somehow elucidate a lot of almost invisible currents and knocking them into some sort of shape" (NYQ, 121)—then once "something fixes itself in the flow that is going on around one and seems to have significance" (PR, 54), the process of defining and com-bining the ensemble's hum of voices can begin almost effortlessly. The result is a poetry which, although quite different in texture, joins Duncan's in making Whitman's catalogs workable again. Asked, for example, about the types of diction that he was aware of incorporat-ing in his poems, Ashbery links his own interest in ways of speaking with Duncan's expansive goals. He responds: "As many kinds as I can think of. In 'The System,' for example, there's an almost pe-dantic, philosophical language, and a lecturing quality and the poetry keeps running afoul of cliches and pedestrian turns of phrase; again these are the result of my wish to reflect the maximum of my experience when I'm writing" (NYQ, 128). As with all the poets in this book, "at the end a person is somehow given an embodiment out of those proliferating reflections that are occurring in a generalized mind which eventually run together into the image of a specific person, 'he' or 'me,' who was not there when the poem began" (NYQ, 131–32).

Where the tension involved in such self-reading becomes apparent is in Ashbery's constant monitoring of the act of translation. A sort of wry doubleness marks virtually every one of his poems in which he both invests "that hollow space with its complicated material self" *and* steps back from the process in order to muse over the value of such a patently impossible act. In "Clepsydra," for example, he describes the "bounding from air to air" of his work within the ensemble as:

> a serpentine
> Gesture which hides the truth behind a congruent
> Message, the way air hides the sky, is, in fact,
> Tearing it limb from limb this very moment: but
> The sky has pleaded already and this is about
> As graceful a kind of non-absence as either
> Has a right to expect.
>
> (RM, 27)

The stepping back that interests me occurs after the colon: although the truth of a moment is hidden behind the serpentine unravelings of what we construe to be its "message"—a point, as one soon learns to expect in reading Ashbery, itself both explicated and hidden behind the distracting opposition of sky (that "has pleaded already") and air ("congruent" to the sky, a medium rendering it visible by "tearing it limb from limb" into color and depth)—although that invisible truth is hidden behind form, there is yet something "graceful" and of value in working it into "non-absence." A similar act of evaluation occurs late in the same poem, this time moving in reverse order from value to limitation:

> there was no statement
> At the beginning. There was only a breathless waste,
> A dumb cry shaping everything in projected
> After-effects orphaned by playing the part intended for them,
> Though one must not forget that the nature of this
> Emptiness, these previsions,
> Was that it could only happen here, on this page held

> Too close to be legible, sprouting erasures, except that they
> Ended everything in the transparent sphere of what was
> Intended only a moment ago, spiraling further out, its
> gesture finally dissolving in the weather.
>
> (RM, 29)

What was "breathless" and "dumb" is made to happen only here on the page, in "orphaned" "after-effects" to which we assent because the empty waste of these "previsions" is made usable; and to which we can never assent because the spiraling out of that explanatory gesture forever ends the "transparent" moment.[8]

It is precisely this problem—the impossibility of speaking for the moment—on which Ashbery's "Self-Portrait in a Convex Mirror" centers:

> we know it cannot be sandwiched
> Between two adjacent moments, that its windings
> Lead nowhere except to further tributaries
> And that these empty themselves into a vague
> Sense of something that can never be known
> Even though it seems likely that each of us
> Knows what it is and is capable of
> Communicating it to the other.
>
> (SP, 77)

Like Whitman, Ashbery acknowledges both the impossibility of grasping that dimensionless world by unwinding it into a network of talk *and* the never-exhausted, commonsense notion driving us down those tributaries: it should, nevertheless, be possible to say what we are. Because we "have been given no help whatever / In decoding our own man-size quotient," both writers would agree, we "must rely / On second-hand knowledge" (SP, 81–82), for the already formulated speech of the world surrounding us offers some help, however short-lived and fragmentary, in making visible what is in us: "we must learn to live in others, no matter how abortive or unfriendly their cold, piecemeal renderings of us: they create us" (TP, 13). "Self-Portrait" is, first, a deliberate attempt to learn how to live in something other. In the "winding" speculations initiated by his encounter with a puzzling mirror painting, Ashbery deliberately enters and weaves together the rich polyphony of ways of speaking that radiate from, and create something of, that moment. What is most significant is that this rich weave of voices, this elaborate detailing of the self, is brought about by what I have called Ashbery's self-monitoring or his doubleness. As he continually calls attention to the medium's distance from himself, he also gives himself a way in which to use it more forcefully. Just as Whitman had to acknowledge his distance from the stallion before "using" it—or Roethke's his from the sea, or Duncan's his from the ensemble—so Ashbery's doubleness enables him to step back from, and then more richly work, the medium through which he speaks.[9] And one can go even further, for although the medium being embraced through much of this poem is a single painting, we realize by the end of the work that what is true about the hold of Parmigianino's self-portrait on Ashbery is finally even more applicable to the more extensive medium of language itself.

As the poem begins, Ashbery, "The dreaming model / In the silence of the studio," is considering "Lifting the pencil to the self-portrait" (SP, 71). Parmigianino's painting seems to seize and focus those dreams by, at first, offering a positive example of how one might go about shaping and articulating that humming commentary.[10] What the painter did was very simple:

> Vasari says, "Francesco one day set himself
> To take his own portrait, looking at himself for that purpose
> In a convex mirror, such as is used by barbers . . .
> He accordingly caused a ball of wood to be made
> By a turner, and having divided it in half and
> Brought it to the size of the mirror, he set himself
> With great art to copy all that he saw in the glass,"
> Chiefly his reflection, of which the portrait
> Is the reflection once removed.
>
> (SP, 68)

Vasari's description emphasizes the artistic mastery of Parmigianino's attempt to look at himself: he "caused" the ball to be made, "divided it," "brought it to . . . size," and copied what was clearly labeled a reflection "with great art," the series of verbs suggesting a confidence in technique. When Ashbery muses in the poem's opening line that he might *embrace* a version of the painter's painstaking art and, "As Parmigianino did it" (SP, 68), develop a method to look at and copy his own reflections, he means to borrow that confident mastery.[11] The rounded surface of the mirror and the painter's pose before it ("we have surprised him / At work" [SP, 74]) create a distortion in which the face seems to peer out from deep within the wooden globe. This deliberately chosen method of representation seems, on a first reading, to be a signal of technique's ability to master flux. Both the hand in the foreground grasping the ball and the locked-together details of the studio's background ("a coral ring"—a reef) appear as signs of protection. In separating one aspect of the self from its constantly moving world, then, art preserves what would ordinarily dissolve by giving it boundaries:

>   the right hand
> Bigger than the head, thrust at the viewer
> And swerving easily away, as though to protect
> What it advertises. A few leaded panes, old beams,
> Fur, pleated muslin, a coral ring run together
> In a movement supporting the face, which swims
> Toward and away like the hand
> Except that it is in repose. It is what is
> Sequestered.
>
>   (SP, 68)

Because what it advertizes—what it attractively represents to us—is protected and separated, then, the face in the painting will always retain its qualities at that moment; it will remain luminous, alive, and whole: "The time of day or the density of the light / Adhering to the face keeps it / Lively and intact in a recurring wave / Of arrival. The soul establishes itself" (SP, 68).

However, as David Kalstone points out, this initial embrace is rapidly revised, the face's distance from the surface (a boundary seemingly marked by the hand) suggesting a second, and more disturbing, reading: [12]

>   The surface
> Of the mirror being convex, the distance increases
> Significantly; that is, enough to make the point
> That the soul is a captive, treated humanely, kept
> In suspension, unable to advance much farther
> Than your look as it intercepts the picture.
>
>   (SP, 68–69)

That this surface holds the face at a greater remove than a flat piece of glass suggests that, in protecting the soul, the painter has had to make it a captive, permanently sequestering it from the moving world of which it was a part. In order to study the face, Parmigianino has had to restrain it forcibly: "The soul has to stay where it is, / Even though restless, hearing raindrops at the pane, / The sighing of autumn leaves thrashed by the wind, / Longing to be free, outside, but it must stay / Posing in this place" (SP, 69). And if this is true, the "soul" represented is no soul at all; unchanging, motionless, cut off from the secret world that has nourished its pose, the painting is a diminished thing: "The secret is too plain. The pity of it smarts, /

Makes hot tears spurt: that the soul is not a soul, / Has no secret, is small, and it fits / Its hollow perfectly: its room, our moment of attention" (SP, 69). The hot tears are Ashbery's, for, having realized that in this painting "we see only postures of the dream" (SP, 69) and not those dimensionless stirrings of the dream itself, he now reads the foregrounded hand as a warning addressed to him:

> it is life englobed.
> One would like to stick one's hand
> Out of the globe, but its dimension,
> What carries it, will not allow it.
> No doubt it is this, not the reflex
> To hide something, which makes the hand loom large
> As it retreats slightly.
>
> (SP, 69)

The painter's hand seems to be pressing futilely against the surface of the globe, distorting under its attempt to get out. If so, the painting becomes a warning to other artists that the medium—"its dimension, / What carries it"—used to englobe a life so that it can be seen has also frozen and distorted it. To the poet, the painting no longer offers the promise that it is possible to isolate and protect experience, but rather that statement that there is no true reflection: "There is no way / To build it flat" (SP, 69).[13] As with the openings of all the poems we have been concerned with in this study, then, the promise of embracing one's experience directly is simply put aside.

Given the implications of this newly understood argument for his own task—if he creates "As Parmigianino did," he will have trapped himself within the distortion of his own reflective medium—it is not surprising that Ashbery's immediate response is a personal appeal to the painter to break loose from that threatening position: "Francesco, your hand is big enough / To wreck the sphere, and too big, / One would think, to weave delicate meshes / That only argue its further detention" (SP, 70). But then, shockingly, he realizes that there is no Francesco to address—there is only a painted surface, neither encouraging him to use its method as a model nor warning him of its dangers.[14] Separation from the viewer's concerns—otherness— seems, finally, to be what the distortion has been signalling:

> your eyes proclaim
> That everything is surface. The surface is what's there
> And nothing can exist except what's there.
> There are no recesses in the room, only alcoves,
> And the window doesn't matter much, or that

> Sliver of window or mirror on the right, even
> As a gauge of the weather, which in French is
> *Le temps*, the word for time
>
> (SP, 70)

By blurring the recesses behind the painter and declaring the movements of time and weather to be nonsignificant, the painting has eliminated reference to any world beyond its aesthetic surface. Because there is no depth, the notion of a "soul" inviting the poet in or straining to break free seems curiously irrelevant. If this is the case, Ashbery's previous "words for the surface," based as they were on the assumption that art makes a "core" of the self visible and can thus be interpreted in personal terms, become simply his own speculations. Like the mirror painting, his own unraveled words are equally distortions, abortive snatches at an illusive meaning: "The words are only speculation / (From the Latin *speculum*, mirror): / They seek and cannot find the meaning of the music." He is left with no guidance about how to shape his buzzing, drifting experience: "And just as there are no words for the surface, that is, / No words to say what it really is, that it is not / Superficial but a visible core, then there is / No way out of the problem of pathos vs. experience" (SP, 70). What he has learned is that the painting is "neither embrace nor warning," but a third thing that is separate from him—a neutral surface "which holds something of both in pure / Affirmation that doesn't affirm anything" (SP, 70).

Ashbery responds, in the second section of the poem, by firmly turning away from the painting—"The balloon pops, the attention / Turns dully away" (SP, 70)—emphasizing the difference between himself and its cold surface. If the face in the globe is untouched by others and untouched by time, Ashbery counters by reminding himself "of the friends / Who came to see me, of what yesterday / Was like" (SP, 71). He is an agglomerate of such outside influences:

> How many people came and stayed a certain time,
> Uttered light or dark speech that became part of you
> Like light behind windblown fog or sand,
> Filtered and influenced by it, until no part
> Remains that is surely you. Those voices in the dusk
> Have told you all and still the tale goes on
> In the form of memories deposited in irregular
> Clumps of crystals.
>
> (SP, 71).

Unlike the painter's representation, Ashbery possesses an inner life so made up of others that at times it seems a rich wavering light glimpsed through their drifting presences or, shifting the metaphor, an unending story, its telling sustained and redirected by their clustered, internalized memories. In the world outside of the painting's tiny world, he asserts, experience is continuous, and one's thoughts form and peel off like leaves in a rush of seasons:

> Whose curved hand controls,
> Francesco, the turning seasons and the thoughts
> That peel off and fly away at breathless speeds
> Like the last stubborn leaves ripped
> From wet branches? I see in this only the chaos
> Of your round mirror which organizes everything
> Around the polestar of your eyes which are empty,
> Knowing nothing, dream but reveal nothing.
>
> (SP, 71)

Although the ensemble of one's experience appears uncontrolled and formless, Ashbery insists instead that actual formlessness ("chaos") results from the imposition of this particular organization's blank, vacant surface on its stubborn, various world.

The poet's distancing of himself from the painting is completed when he imagines how, accepting Parmigianino's example, the surrounding, internalized world would be reduced to "a silver blur" (recalling the painting's "coral ring") and how his dimensionless inner core, dependent on that world for depth and movement and visibility, would be leveled and made uniform, his various interiors melted down to a single, featureless substance:

> I feel the carousel starting slowly
> And going faster and faster: desk, papers, books,
> Photographs of friends, the window and the trees
> Merging in one neutral band that surrounds
> Me on all sides, everywhere I look.
> And I cannot explain the action of leveling,
> Why it should all boil down to one
> Uniform substance, a magma of interiors.
>
> (SP, 71)

Rather than accept such a reduction and imprisonment, Ashbery uses this section to make clear to himself "the straight way out, / The distance between us" (SP, 71). Although at present he has no means to do so, he hopes to find a way to express his intuition that "The strewn evidence meant something, / The small accidents and pleasures / Of the day as it moved gracelessly on, / A housewife doing chores" (SP, 71–72). For it is just those graceless, ordinary, and accidental incidents that mark the movement of a life, and it is just those specific incidents that are not registered by the painting's perfected surface.

The "distance" established by the painting and now insisted upon by the poet has an interesting effect on Ashbery's response to the portrait in the third section. Because he can neither embrace nor take warning from the painting, Ashbery is free to view it in a more detached manner, curious about the artistic problems it raises. Treating the painting as a neutral surface not directly related to his own personal anxieties, foregrounding its nature as simply medium, Ashbery is provoked to broader inquiry about the issues raised by its construction.[15] This is *his* version of what Whitman understood as "using" elements of the ensemble, Roethke as "magnifying," and Duncan as "reading." The seemingly random nature of this "inquiry," of course, is Ashbery's alone. He begins by realizing that Parmigianino's distorted perspective is simply an obvious example of what everyone does:

> today is uncharted,
> Desolate, reluctant as any landscape
> To yield what are laws of perspective
> After all only to the painter's deep
> Mistrust, a weak instrument though
> Necessary.
>
> (SP, 72)

By insisting on his mirror's arbitrary perspective—calling attention, that is, to how *he* has had to think about this problem—Parmigianino has made Ashbery see that any artistic shaping is a necessarily limited slant on experience, and further, that such a limited view results from human inability to capture more of the world's rich complications, not from a desire to deny that world. Although "weak," perspective is "necessary" because it is the only tool available to use to attempt a description of "what is promised today, our / Landscape sweeping out from us to disappear / On the horizon" (SP, 72). Once formulated, this admission suggests a way out of the problem. Although art's stiff, polished surface is not our lived world, perhaps its shaping of one representative piece might remind us of that world and keep its disappearing "promises" potentially accessible, if untouched:

> Today enough of a cover burnishes
> To keep the supposition of promises together
> In one piece of surface, letting one ramble
> Back home from them so that these
> Even stronger possibilities can remain
> Whole without being tested.
>
> (SP, 72)

Positioned beneath the surface's polished, hypothetical description is another world—our real "home," protected and fluid, where, Ashbery proposes, the "possibilities" of our lives remain unshaped, untested, and whole. According to this idea, the surfaces we make both protect that unitary, supposed world and provide a means to "ramble back home"; they are cover and entrance, simultaneously.

Immediately, however, Ashbery retracts this proposition. "Actually," he continues, however delicate and tenuous that formal approximation of experience might seem, "The skin of the bubble-chamber's as tough as / Reptile eggs" (SP, 72). What was tenuous soon becomes stiff and reassuring, proclaiming by its visibility that all experience might be formulated similarly: "everything gets 'programmed' there / In due course" (SP, 72). Once we accept such a testimony and force more and more of our inner world into form, we dull ourselves to that world, distorting rather than keeping it protected and whole:

> more keeps getting included
> Without adding to the sum, and just as one
> Gets accustomed to a noise that
> Kept one awake but now no longer does,
> So the room contains this flow like an hourglass
> Without varying in climate or quality
>
> (SP, 72–73)

Rather than increasing the sum of our awareness, Ashbery reluctantly argues, form may block that of which we should be most aware. It contains without revealing; in fact, as we make material a particular aspect of our unspoken world, we drain that world. Filling in the outline of one visible dream, attempting to sketch in all of the various elements making up "one piece of surface," we draw from and eventually exhaust our deeper "home":

> What should be the vacuum of a dream
> Becomes continually replete as the source of dreams
> Is being tapped so that this one dream

May wax, flourish like a cabbage rose
Defying sumptuary laws, leaving us
To awake and try to begin living in what
Has now become a slum.

(SP, 73)

Rather than providing access to "the source of dreams," that polished surface becomes a monstrous growth, exfoliating beyond our initial intentions and so dominating that we are forced to live not in the home within us, but in the slum of art—in its decaying, hastily assembled, perhaps once proud forms.

Interestingly enough, after criticizing the notion that form keeps some deeper world safe and accessible, Ashbery makes one final turn and declares himself satisfied with art's weak instrument. "Why be unhappy with this arrangement," he writes; if not life itself, form is "something like living . . . , a movement / Out of the dream into its codification" (SP, 73). Although that codification is stiff and unyielding, in its very stiffness it shows us the importance of our fluid thoughts:

We notice the hole they [dreams] left. Now their importance
If not their meaning is plain. They were to nourish
A dream which includes them all, as they are
Finally reversed in the accumulating mirror.
They seemed strange because we couldn't actually see them.
And we realize this only at a point where they lapse
Like a wave breaking on a rock, giving up
Its shape in a gesture which expresses that shape.

(SP, 73)

Form takes what was "strange" because unseen and puts a codification in its place, a construct that "reverses" life's fluidity but makes its importance "plain" and noticeable. To accept art as weak but necessary, then, would mean to see in its shape not life itself, but a monument to it—the crash of a wave signalling, in its expressive gesture, the loss of power, not the promise of accessibility. We have arrived at a momentary point of rest. The point is, however, that, like Roethke's response to the sea or Duncan's to an architecture text, the entire weave of this doubling-back argument has been prompted and directed by the issues brought into focus by Parmigianino's commentary on his own work—on his work seen as work, not as the same as the poet.

To this point, the embrace has been refused in the poem's first section (the cold, silent surface will not respond in personal terms); that distance insisted upon in the second section (Parmigianino's approach, if accepted as a model, would "level" the poet's lively experience); and then, the attempt to embrace the painting put aside, the poet prompted to explore a disturbing series of questions about the nature of representation itself (art's necessary "slant"). As the fourth and fifth sections make clear, such a response, although not an empathic merger of two "souls," *is* a form of connection. In fact, it is precisely because of the force of the painting's self-complete otherness that Ashbery's personal concerns have been supplanted and he has been enabled to follow the painting's lead speculatively. What Ashbery proposes, in the next two sections of the poem, is that the advance and retreat of his attention to the painting's argument is a new sort of embrace, based on an acknowledgment of difference, in which the strict surface of the painting is not a hindrance, but the very grounds for union.

The fourth section tries two different tactics for discovering in otherness a reason for the painting's continuing attraction. First, reminded anew of the painting's difference from him ("It presents its stereotype again / But it is an *unfamiliar* stereotype"[SP, 73, my emphasis]), Ashbery uses Vasari's description of the face as "rather angel than man" to muse about angels and unfamiliarity:

> Perhaps an angel looks like everything
> We have forgotten, I mean forgotten
> Things that don't seem familiar when
> We meet them again, lost beyond telling,
> Which were ours once. This would be the point
> Of invading the privacy of this man . . .
>
> (SP, 74)

If an angel looks like aspects of ourselves that we have forgotten completely, Ashbery speculates, aspects "lost beyond telling," then perhaps this off-putting face is so fascinating because it is his angel—his forgotten, inaccessible likeness. This proposition doesn't go very far, but it does suggest a way to talk about unfamiliarity: although difference does not signal that something actually was "ours once" (our angel), difference is indeed a tool to recover things asleep or "lost beyond telling." Again, the painting serves as an example. Because of Parmigianino's "extreme care in rendering / The velleities of the rounded reflecting surface," the globe seems at first to be a mirror:

> you could be fooled for a moment
> Before you realize the reflection
> Isn't yours. You feel then like one of those

Hoffmann characters who have been deprived
Of a reflection, except that the whole of me
Is seen to be supplanted by the strict
Otherness of the painter in his
Other room.

(SP, 74)

As we have seen, Ashbery has been fooled into trying to see himself reflected in the painting (section 1), then has discovered his error and, darkly, felt "deprived" (section 2), only to realize the value of having his personal concerns temporarily "supplanted" by the painting's "strict / Otherness" (section 3). Instead of identifying with the painting, Ashbery has "seen" his speechless inner world focused and directed by it. He has watched himself using it. By virtue of its overpowering attractive difference—its unfamiliarity—the painting has supplanted, or substituted for, what Ashbery calls "the whole of me"—his fluid, whole, untested nature. And the poem to this point has been a record of that focused seeing, the poet calling attention to his discovery of one implication of the medium after another.

The fifth section of the poem, testifying to Ashbery's restlessness with any fixed proposition, immediately challenges the painting's power to supplant by testing it against what Ashbery calls "the shadow of the city"—that bustling, created world outside, "alive with filiations, shuttlings," where all of humanity's made things mix and compete (SP, 75). To the city, Ashbery speculates, this tiny created world is simply "another life," one of many expressions to be acknowledged, catalogued, and discarded: "it wants / To siphon off the life of the studio, deflate / Its mapped space to enactments, island it" (SP, 75). Ashbery fights this process by declaring that "that operation has been temporarily stalled"—stalled, one would suppose, because of the painting's hold over him, which, until it is broken, makes the "mapped space" come alive and keeps it from being merely an enactment. But there is always "a new preciosity / In the wind" promising newer objects to which to turn, and the painting's dominance is thus continually threatened: "Can you stand it, / Francesco? Are you strong enough for it?" (SP, 75). The city constantly flushes out old creations or interrogates them in such a way that they "are seen to be / Hastening out of style" (SP, 75–76). It is always on the lookout for something new and vital—some "unlikely / Challenger pounding on the gates of an amazed / Castle" (SP, 76). Against this particularly modern challenge, the painting does not seem as strong or permanent; in fact, recalling his earlier frustration at the painting's silence, Ashbery sees that refusal as a cause of the portrait's diminishment and gradual loss of power: "Your argument, Francesco / Has begun to grow stale as no answer / Or answers were forthcoming. If it dissolves now / Into dust, that only means its time had come / Some time ago" (SP, 76).

Such distancing, however, leads not to dimissal but, in a rhythm repeated throughout the poem, to a new evaluation of where the life of the painting actually is: "It may be that another life is stocked there / In recesses no one knew of; that it, / Not we, are the change; that we are in fact it / If we could get back to it, relive some of the way / It looked" (SP, 76). Contrary to section 1, there are recesses and depths to this neutral surface, not the recesses of space deep within the painting, but those complications we have observed being drawn out of the observer. As the surface engages us, we give it words and strength; the life "stocked there" is our own; as we respond to the painting's nudges and hints, we "live" in it, loosing its "unlikely challenger" to pound on gates:

> Since it is a metaphor
> Made to include us, we are part of it and
> Can live in it as in fact we have done,
> Only leaving our minds bare for questioning
> We now see will not take place at random
> But in an orderly way that means to menace
> Nobody—the normal way things are done,
> Like the concentric growing up of days
> Around a life: correctly, if you think about it.
>   (SP, 76)

Potentially, then, as we have also seen in Duncan and Roethke, any surface that engages our minds has recesses. Once we are rid of the insistence on seeing personal concerns displayed, the other will lead us through its pattern, spur new questions within us, and, by focusing our attention, give shape to an expanding series of reflections— what we referred to earlier as "the tree of contradictions, joyous and living, investing that hollow void with its complicated material self" (TP, 63). Those concentric responses are not life—it is whole and fluid—but, as in section 3, they are "like" life: they are the "orderly" expressions grown up around our lives. These responses are "correct" and "normal" because they are, in fact, what we must do in going about the business of shaping and communicating ourselves. What Ashbery has done in these first five sections, then, is explore and amplify Whitman's concept of the embrace by allowing himself to see that one "lives" in another not through naive personal identification, but by means of an acknowledgment of its strict otherness and a continual, concentric openness to its directions and prodding. He has acted out just such an embrace.

The final section of the poem is an examination of what has been brought to speech by Ashbery's reading of the painting. What he realizes, as he evaluates and dismisses his own reflective network, is that the same criticisms made about the painting's static, neutral surface must also be made about his own work.[16] He applies what he has learned in embracing the painting to the larger, daily activity of embracing ourselves through language. The sixth section begins with an irritated account of the painting's sudden reassertion of dominance: "A breeze like the turning of a page / Brings back your face: the moment / Takes such a big bite out of the haze / Of pleasant intuition it comes after" (SP, 76). Ashbery describes the focus or "bite" that the moment controlled by the painting gives to his hazy, wordless intuition as a "locking into place" not unlike "death itself," restating the artifact's power to supplant the observer in quite negative terms. Further, although only "exercise or tactic," the painting's crystalized dream now begins to seem like a cloth over a birdcage, something stubbornly there, dominating all attention:

> Mere forgetfulness cannot remove it
> Nor wishing bring it back, as long as it remains
> The white precipitate of its dream
> In the climate of sighs flung across our world,
> A cloth over a birdcage.
>
> (SP, 77)

The reason for such dark descriptions of the painting's hold on him becomes clear as Ashbery describes having his life "channeled into some form" in these terms: "I go on consulting / This mirror that is no longer mine / For as much brisk vacancy as is to be / My portion this time" (SP, 77). That the mirror is not his and yet may be consulted is a restatement of the poem's first five sections. More to the point is the description of the result of that consultation as "brisk vacancy"— a phrase suddenly seen as applicable to his poem as well as the painting. Briskness, of course, testifies to the clean, orderly pattern that Ashbery's thoughts have assumed on becoming visible; but vacancy suggests that the discovery of section 3—that form is a monument to the fluidity of dreams, "the hole they left"—must also be applied to Ashbery's codification of his own "pleasant intuition." The convex mirror speaks for all art: "The sample / One sees is not to be taken as / Merely that, but as everything as it / May be imagined outside time—not as a gesture / But as all, in the refined, assimilable state"

(SP, 77). Parmigianino's sample, then, stands in for all speech made "refined" and "assimilable" by being lifted "out of time" and being given permanent shape—Ashbery's included.

Ashbery's frustration is that when we "Push forward ignoring the apparent / Naïveté of the attempt"—as he has done in this poem— and try to say what is in us, we accomplish the opposite of what was intended: "the end / Of our dreaming, as we had never imagined / It would end, in worn daylight with the painted / Promise showing through as a gage, a bond" (SP, 78). We lose both dreams and daylight, replacing them with an inadequate, cheapened representation. That "worn" production, Ashbery suggests, can be compared to a fabric with the impossibility of its task showing through its bare spots. Just as Parmigianino's work emphasized its nature as a painted surface, so any form that reduces the vital promises of lived experience to something shaped and visible must acknowledge, in its use of medium, the debt it has agreed to pay—the "bond" given that admits that what is created is a codification and not life itself. And this is what Ashbery's style (the deliberately side-tracked "explanations"—sky versus air), and what I've called the doubleness of his constant self-evaluation, have been up to all along: they both emphasize his work's codified status. In a sense, Ashbery has made the same payment that Parmigianino did in selecting his convex mirror and thus calling attention to the "painted" nature of his work. Although he had intended to capture "this nondescript, never-to-be defined daytime" in which "one / Is always cresting into one's present" (SP, 78), he grudgingly admits that he too has created a painted surface. Accordingly, he offers one last reading of the enigmatic portrait:

> I think it is trying to say it is today
> And we must get out of it even as the public
> Is pushing through the museum now so as to
> Be out by closing time. You can't live there.
> The gray glaze of the past attacks all know-how:
> Secrets of wash and finish that took a lifetime
> To learn and are reduced to the status of
> Black-and-white illustrations in a book where colorplates
> Are rare.
>
> (SP, 79)

Despite the blurring "its" in the first two lines, which serve to insist that we are bound here to the necessarily inaccurate medium of words, the point seems clear: the painting reminds Ashbery of "its" difference from "today," and in doing so, urges him back to that mov-

ing, seamless world. As the museum comparison insists, one can't
live permanently in the other because to do so is to step out of time,
stopping the world in order to exhibit one of its aspects. Inevitably,
as the apparent promise of each new way of ordering becomes dated,
the "soul" is reduced to a series of illustrations, lifeless monuments
to itself. To say, then, that "our time gets to be veiled, compromised /
By the portrait's will to endure. It hints at / Our own, which we were
hoping to keep hidden" (SP, 79) is both to criticize and acknowledge
the inevitability of the painting's enduring gesture and "our own"
now-visible nature as language users that has been drawn out and
made permanent in concentric rings of response.[17] Such representation is the veil that we continually drop over the changing face of
our days.

Even as Ashbery abandons his poem, however, he slows down to
insist on its value:

> the "poetic," straw-colored space
> Of the long corridor that leads back to the painting,
> Its darkening opposite—is this
> Some figment of "art," not to be imagined
> As real, let alone special? Hasn't it too its lair
> In the present we are always escaping from
> And falling back into, as the waterwheel of days
> Pursues its uneventful, even serene course?

The intended answer here is that the poem's focused attention—the
"long corridor" established between the poet and his "opposite"—is
indeed real. Art is *not* a figment. Its created "space" is an actual lair
within the whirling, nameless present, a structured escape from that
serene waterwheel in which we pass from sensation to sensation
without word or marker. "Today has no margins," he continues, "the
event arrives / Flush with its edges, is of the same substance, / Indis-
tinguishable. 'Play' is something else; / It exists, in a society specifically / Organized as a demonstration of itself" (SP, 79). Although it
does do violence to what is represented, art's playful distortion, its
attempt to distinguish margins and edges, is also something that can
be seen. It is the game in which we have chosen to think about and
weigh our "way[s] of telling" ourselves about ourselves:

> *This* thing, the mute, undivided present,
> Has the justification of logic, which
> In this instance isn't a bad thing
> Or wouldn't be, if the way of telling
> Doesn't somehow intrude, twisting the end result

Into a caricature of itself. This always
Happens, as in the game where
A whispered phrase passed around the room
Ends up as something completely different.

(SP, 80)

That "the way of telling" always twists one's attempts to describe "the
mute, undivided present" is perhaps best illustrated in Ashbery's
own work by the playful way in which his pronouns and images shift,
dissolving references so that the reader is unsure if an earlier reading
of "it" or "surface" is applicable. Such devices are deliberately employed distorting mirrors. And yet, even as the poet's "whispered"
interpretations are passed from sentence to sentence, their meaning
twisting and untwisting in a deliberately acknowledged "caricature"
of truth, Ashbery also reminds us that it is all there is to be seen.
Although a "life-obstructing task," representation or language use—
in whatever form—is our only view of life:

Is there anything
To be serious about beyond this otherness
That gets included in the most ordinary
Forms of daily activity, changing everything
Slightly and profoundly, and tearing the matter
Of creation, any creation, not just artistic creation
Out of our hands, to install it on some monstrous, near
Peak, too close to ignore, too far
For one to intervene? This otherness, this
"Not-being-us" is all there is to look at
In the mirror, though no one can say
How it came to be this way.

(SP, 80–81)

And this is "all there is to look at" in any Ashbery poem as well: the
realization that although an act of attention gives us something real
to examine, it is not "us," *and* the assurance that, in playfully handling those acts, we might understand our "most ordinary / Forms of
daily activity." It is such handling that this poem both demonstrates,
as it works with the issues the painting raises, and encourages us to
employ in turn in our interpretive responses. Calling attention to the
full complexity of any specific engagement with a medium, this suggests, opens up all human activity.

With this last testimony, the embrace is broken off. The portrait's
ability to crystalize thought is a limited one ("You can't live there"),
and now "the fertile / Thought-associations that until now came / So
easily, appear no more, or rarely" (SP, 81). As time continues to

sweep us along, the painting and the ideas it has generated become monuments to something in the past, already accomplished:

> This past
> Is now here: the painter's
> Reflected face, in which we linger, receiving
> Dreams and inspirations on an unassigned
> Frequency, but the hues have turned metallic,
> The curves and edges are not so rich.
>
>   (SP, 81)

Although "once it had seemed so perfect," now that it has been made use of, the painting's surface must be regarded as "the first step only, . . . / . . . a frozen gesture of welcome etched / On the air materializing behind it, / A convention" (SP, 82). It has been used as a kind of "kindling"—bringing a flame into existence, then being quickly discarded—and must be seen only in those limited terms: "The sooner they are burnt up / The better for the roles we have to play" (SP, 82). Consequently, Ashbery's dismissal of the painting— "Therefore I beseech you, withdraw that hand, / Offer it no longer as shield or greeting" (SP, 82)—is less criticism of the work done and more a decision to move on.

Ashbery's tone in the poem's last lines, as he returns to his "waking dream" and gazes back over what he has created, is likewise calm and measured. What he has "uttered," although now behind him, is material and permanent:

> Its existence
> Was real, though troubled, and the ache
> Of this waking dream can never drown out
> The diagram still sketched on the wind,
> Chosen, meant for me and materialized
> In the disguising radiance of my room.
>
>   (SP, 82)

The diagrams and portraits made of our dreams are, as Whitman perhaps never anticipated, "the cold, syrupy flow / of a pageant" (SP, 83)—too confining to remain in long—and yet, they are all that speak for us. Because our hands, in themselves, hold no chalk with which to communicate, our lives simply fall away on the waterwheel of a continual present, broken only now and again by the cold, insufficient whispers of art:

> The hand holds no chalk
> And each part of the whole falls off
> And cannot know it knew, except

Here and there, in cold pockets
Of remembrance, whispers out of time.
(SP, 83)

What we have seen is how the other—"The utter commonality of the language that must be the medium of that self," unfriendly and second-hand—has given a shape to the "strewn evidence of our lives" and made such whispers possible. And, while dismissing his fragmentary self-portrait as a "pocket of remembrance," Ashbery has, at the same time, offered a detailed model for how one might enter and live in whatever kindling its cold suggestive surface provides. He has shown, then, that although our inner lives cannot be known fully, our codifications of them are rich, puzzling, and endlessly communicative.

Spelled out in this poem, implicit in the "amused, complacent" tone of much of Ashbery's work and implicit as well in the work of the other poets in this book, is an argument for what might be gained in Whitman's failure to provide more than "Outlines" of "what is in me." An awareness of a specific example of limitation, Ashbery suggests, yields an intimacy with all of its fruits: ". . . the word that everything hinged on is buried back there . . . It is doing the organizing, the guidelines radiate from its control; therefore it is good not to know what it is since its results can be known so intimately, appreciated for what they are; it is best then that the buried word remain buried for we were intended to appreciate only its fruits and not the secret principle activating them—to know this would be to know too much" (TP, 95).

And appreciating all of our medium-bound gestures "for what they are," Ashbery would argue, is what makes possible Whitman's dream of a flood of such forms used with enough delicacy that they might "leap beyond" their routine nature and bring us "nearer" to their buried source:

No words of routine this song of mine,
But abruptly to question, to leap beyond yet nearer bring;
This printed and bound book—but the printer and the
    printing-office boy?
(SM, 42)

To which list Ashbery would have us add, "The celluloid print—but the viewer, alive in the dark?":

But only focus on the past through the clear movie-theatre dark and you are a changed person, and can begin to live again. That is why we, snatched from sudden freedom, are able to communicate only through this celluloid vehicle that has immortalized and given a definitive shape to our formless gestures; we can live as though we had caught up with time and avoid the sickness of the present, a shapeless blur as meaningless as a carelessly exposed roll of film. There is hardness and density now, and our story takes on the clear, compact shape of the plot of a novel, with all its edges and inner passages laid bare for the reader, to be resumed and resumed over and over, that is taken up and put aside and taken up again.

(TP, 103)

NOTES

1. John Ashbery, "Second Presentation of Elizabeth Bishop," *World Literature Today* 51 (Winter 1977): 10.

2. Walt Whitman, *Notes and Fragments*, ed. R. M. Bucke (1899 repr., Folcroft, Pa.: Folcroft Library Editions, 1972), p. 60.

3. Robert Duncan, "The Adventure of Whitman's Line," in *Fictive Certainties* (New York: New Directions, 1985), p. 200. For a brief account of Ashbery's place within this tradition, see Stephen Fredman, *Poet's Prose: The Crisis in American Verse* (Cambridge: Cambridge University Press, 1983), pp. 114–15. Fredman writes: "Ashbery operates from the central American premise that the self is a shared entity, that through language, consciousness is both individual and collective."

4. John Ashbery, *Three Poems* (1972; reissued, New York: Penguin, 1977) p. 103; cited in the text as TP. Other Ashbery texts are abbreviated in the text as follows: DDS: *The Double Dream of Spring* (1970; reissued, New York: Ecco, 1976); RM: *Rivers and Mountains* (1966; reissued, New York: Ecco, 1977); SP: *Self-Portrait in a Convex Mirror* (New York: Viking, 1975); TCO: *The Tennis Court Oath* (Middletown, Conn.: Wesleyan University Press, 1962). In an interview, Ashbery speaks of wishing, in one poem, to "exemplify the fullness, or, if you wish, the emptiness, of life, or, at any rate, its dimensionless quality." See Peter Stitt, "The Art of Poetry," *Paris Review* 90 (Winter 1983): 46–47; cited in the text as PR. Other interviews referred to in this chapter are: AM: Richard Jackson, *Acts of Mind: Conversations with Contemporary Poets* (University: University of Alabama Press, 1983); CS: Piotr Sommer, "An Interview in Warsaw," in *Code of Signals*, ed. Michael Palmer (Berkeley: North Atlantic Books, 1983); MQ: Al Poulin, Jr., "The Experience of Experience," *Michigan Quarterly Review* 20 (Summer 1981); NYQ: *The Craft of Poetry: Interviews from the New York Quarterly*, ed. William Packard (Garden City: Doubleday, 1974); and S: John Koethe, "An Interview with John Ashbery," *Substance* 37/38 (1983).

5. Ashbery has been quite fortunate in the critics who have been attracted to his work, many of whom have thought carefully about just this distinction. I find myself most in sympathy with John Koethe's assertion that Ashbery works not from a "psychological concept of self" (as in Berryman, where the

self is "a real entity among other real entities") but from a notion of a "meta-physical subject," "positioned outside the temporal flux of thought and experience" and apparently "inhabit[ing] a durationless 'now.'" From this second viewpoint, "The subject and its 'wooden and external representation' occupy fundamentally different positions." See "The Metaphysical Subject of John Ashbery's Poetry" in *Beyond Amazement: New Essays on John Ashbery*, ed. David Lehman (Ithaca: Cornell University Press, 1980), pp. 87, 89, 92. Although confining Ashbery's work with this problem to the world of dreams rather than the full sweep of mental life, Marjorie Perloff's argument in "'Fragments of a Buried Life': John Ashbery's Dream Songs," in *Beyond Amazement* (pp. 66–85), that Ashbery's poems recreate the "logic" of a dream rather than its "content" is based on the same fundamental distinction between inaccessible subject and it representation. "Dream is thus regarded as the source of our energy, our élan, of life itself; and yet that life remains curiously 'unknowable.' This paradox is at the heart of Ashbery's poetry and accounts for his preoccupation with dream structure rather than dream content. Not *what* one dreams but *how*—this is the domain of Ashbery . . . ." I would oppose such views as that put forward by Alan Williamson in *Introspection and Contemporary Poetry* (Cambridge: Harvard University Press, 1984), pp. 116–48, who, working from a psychological conception of self, sees no opposition and reads the "joyous and living contradictions" in Ashbery as "verbal equivalents . . . of states of consciousness" (p. 117), techniques "through which he renders visible in-between spaces, uncertainty principles, in consciousness" (p. 147). Useful discussions of this tension can also be found in Andrew Ross, *The Failure of Modernism* (New York: Columbia University Press, 1986), pp. 184–91 and Fredman, *Poet's Prose*, pp. 101–7. Critics who have approached this gap from the problem it presents to the reader include David Lehman, "The Shield of a Greeting: The Function of Irony in John Ashbery's Poetry" in *Beyond Amazement*, ed. Lehman, and, most valuably, Helen Vendler, in "Understanding Ashbery," *The New Yorker*, March 16, 1981, and "Sociable Comets," *New York Review of Books*, July 10, 1981. She writes of this separation, in "Sociable Comets," "Ashbery's metaphors rarely connect with one another on a horizontal plane; instead, each radiates out from a central notion animating the lines" (p. 24).

6. In "Understanding Ashbery," Vendler writes (p. 134) that we sense in him Stevens's "crowd of voices"; there is "a pressure to speak in the voice of the many, with no portion of their language (whether the language of cliché, the language of media, the language of obscenity, or the language of technology) ruled out."

7. Ibid., p. 110.

8. Charles Altieri, in *Self and Sensibility in Contemporary American Poetry* (Cambridge: Cambridge University Press, 1984) forcefully examines this question of the value to be found in such "orphaned" "after-effects." Although he frames the question differently than I, his discussion is quite useful for thinking about this problem. Altieri sees in Ashbery not an unbridge-

able distinction between the "hollow space" of the self and its "complicated, material" rendering, but a distinction between an "empirical self," with its multiple desires and restrictions, and a "written self." We both agree, however, that Ashbery exploits this tension in order to reflect on what it means to enter into the "duplicities of discourse." For Altieri, "by rendering this complexity, Ashbery creates a dramatic field where he can explore the ironic combinations of creative freedom and existential pathos" (p. 149).

9. Although Parmigianino's work is, in a sense, an already internalized voice and Ashbery's patient unfolding of it simply an expanded version of what normally goes on in the internal "bounding from air to air" of all his poems, Ashbery's uncharacteristic focus on a single object's way of speaking helps the reader visualize the imaginative activity implied by his other work. Ashbery supports the idea that the painting can be considered an already internalized voice: "I had always meant to do something about that painting because it haunted me for so long." See *American Poetry Observed*, ed. Joe David Bellamy (Urbana: University of Illinois Press, 1986), p. 17. Altieri, *Self and Sensibility*, p. 115, also comments on the uniqueness of this poem's slow unfolding.

10. David Kalstone, in *Five Temperaments* (New York: Oxford University Press, 1977), writes: "The speaker in 'Self-Portrait' appears to 'happen' upon Parmigianino's painting as a solution to a problem pondered before the poem begins" (p. 176). Kalstone's reading of the poem's opening section is particularly strong.

11. Several critics have noted the connection between Parmigianino's reflection in the mirror and Ashbery's on the page. See, for example, Kalstone, *Five Temperaments*, p. 177.

12. Ibid., pp. 176–77. Accounting for the speaker's changing readings of the painting is a key interpretive decision in working with the poem, as studying the three strongest discussions of the poem will demonstrate. Kalstone and Richard Stamelman, "Critical Reflections: Poetry and Art Criticism in Ashbery's 'Self-Portrait in a Convex Mirror,'" *New Literary History* 15 (Spring 1984): 607–30, treat the painting as a celebration of the "powers of foreshortening and concentration" (Kalstone, p. 180) or an expression of "faith in the representability of world and self through art" (Stamelman, p. 611). The speaker's different readings, then, illustrate his struggles in accepting or, ultimately, rejecting this fixed view. Altieri sees in the painting "multiple contexts"—a variety of "expressive energies" that help prompt the "various ways the speaker sees himself in the painting," all of which are significant in Ashbery's explorations of the counterbalancing energies of "the processes of thinking" (p. 151). As my own reading will make clear, I also see the speaker's different readings as prompted, in at least some sense, by the painting's own metaphors.

13. I take this to be a statement Parmigianino was fully conscious of making in his initial choice of such an obviously distorted reflecting medium. That Parmigianino thus calls attention to the "difference" involved in his act of

self-representation makes it difficult to read this poem, as Stamelman does for example, as simply the author's "radical criticism of the illusions and deceptions inherent in forms of traditional representation"—with Parmigianino defending the accuracy of reflection. Nevertheless, I agree with him on the position the poem finally arrives at: that "painting and poetry can represent nothing other than their own difficult, often thwarted efforts at representation" (p. 611).

14. I was aided in seeing this by Helen Vendler's analysis of "Ode on a Grecian Urn," a poem that clearly stands behind Ashbery's. See *The Odes of John Keats* (Cambridge: Harvard University Press, 1983), pp. 116–52.

15. Vendler, in *The Odes of John Keats*, writes of a similar development in Keats's response to the urn: "Once we pass . . . beyond a wish for the explanatory factual truths of historical or cultural captions, and beyond the narcissistic stage of being interested only in 'lyric' art which we can see as a reflection of something in ourselves, we can confront art as it is in itself, in its ultimate formal anonymity and otherness" (pp. 123–24).

16. Harold Bloom, in "The Breaking of Form," in *Destruction and Criticism* (New York: Seabury Press, 1970), p. 36, describes the tone of this last section as "majestic in the aesthetic dignity of its mingled strength and sadness."

17. See Kalstone, *Five Temperaments*, p. 182.

CHAPTER 6

❖　❖　❖

IMBUED WITH OTHERNESS

James Merrill's *The Changing Light at Sandover*

James Merrill's three-volume *The Changing Light at Sandover*, a shaping of more than twenty years' worth of messages received by the poet (JM) and his companion David Jackson (DJ) at a ouija board, can be seen—once its initial strangeness has been adjusted to—as another exploration of the tension involved in translating the self that Whitman brought forward in "Song of Myself." Like Whitman in section 50 of that poem, Merrill finds himself embracing something different from the self—Whitman calls it "the creation"—in order to find words for its alien, unsayable depths: "Something it swings on more than the earth I swing on, / To it the creation is the friend whose embracing awakes me." Like Ashbery, Merrill is more likely to use the paired, writerly terms *see* and *render* for Whitman's bodily *embrace* and *awake*, but the need to work through an external medium is quite similar. Echoing the other writers in this book, Merrill remarks in an interview: "What I mean by the outside world are the things we see, our experiences, those around us, our friends, strangers. You can render yourself, see yourself reflected by these people and things so that you wouldn't know you had a self except through these surroundings."[1] And, again like all of the others, Merrill acknowledges that what we have called Whitman's poetics of self-translation involves an effacing of the core self—Ashbery's "wave breaking on a rock, giving up / Its shape in a gesture which expresses that shape"— as well as its substantial expression:

> But nothing's lost. Or else: all is translation
> And every bit of us is lost in it
> (Or found—I wander through the ruin of S
> Now and then, wondering at the peacefulness)
> And in that loss, a self-effacing tree,
> Color of context, imperceptibly
> Rustling with its angel, turns the waste
> To shade and fiber, milk and memory.[2]

Lost or found: what this long poem does is provide Merrill with a framework with which to demonstrate that replacing the imperceptible angel of the self with "shade and fiber" is tied directly to such a double-minded response to self-portraiture. Like Whitman and like Roethke, Duncan, and Ashbery, Merrill shows that an awareness of the tension involved in singing the self through a medium or an "otherness" is finally what generates the ability to "use" that medium. Although Whitman is not named directly in this poem, the remarkably detailed way in which Merrill drives us to "see" how one finds words for what is "in me" but "without name" might usefully conclude this study by demonstrating the continuing life of those problems and solutions originally framed by "Song of Myself." After having worked through Roethke's and Duncan's and Ashbery's Whitmanesque meditations on singing the self through embracing "A strangeness that was us, and was not," we should not be as surprised as we perhaps are in hearing Whitman's confrontation with his pulling and hauling medium beneath these lines from Merrill's trilogy:

> Feared and rejoiced in, chafed against, held cheap,
> A strangeness that was us, and was not, had
> All the same allowed for its description,
> And so brought at least me these spells of odd,
> *Self-effacing balance.* Better to stop
> While we still can. Already I take up
> Less emotional space than a snowdrop.
> My father in his last illness complained
> Of the effect of medication on
> His *real self*—today Bluebeard, tomorrow
> Babbitt. Young chameleon, I used to
> Ask how on earth one got sufficiently
> Imbued with otherness. And now I see.[3]

On its most direct level, the trilogy asks to be read as a demonstration of the way its two mediums, JM and DJ, receive and render in human terms invisible, otherworldly forces. Pushed in an interview to attribute actual existence to the bats and angels that "speak" to them through the ouija board, Merrill suggests instead that we look at the work as a study in indirection, those ghostly presences existing only "in the realm of, oh, cosmic forces, elemental processes, whom we then personify, or tame if you like, through the imagination. So, in a sense, all these figures are our creation, or mankind's. The powers they *represent* are real—as say gravity is 'real'— but they'd be invisible, inconceivable, if they'd never passed through our heads and clothed themselves out of the costume box they found there. How they appear depends on us, on the imaginer, and would have to vary wildly from culture to culture, or even temperament to temperament. A process Einstein could entertain as a formula might be described by an African witch doctor as a crocodile."[4] The poem's central image for the "forces" that speak through the board is light— light which, since its "Comings and goings in black space remain / Unobserved . . . / Until resisted" (S, 285), becomes visible only upon contact with the trappings of our world. "RECEIVE US," one of the powers commands in its indentifying uppercase, "WE ARE YR LIGHT" ("BORN AD 8") (S, 127). As that light is received and resisted, what was strange and without expression becomes visible, vibrant, even familiar:

> Earlier we'd been admiring an inch-high
> Prism set in noon light on the sill.
> Outflung, slowshifting gouts of color stain
> Ceiling, walls, us. DJ: It's really how
> His lessons flow through us. JM: And will
> Forever be deflected by the grain
> Of imperfection in that quartz capstone,
> The human mind—
>
> (S, 227)

We are encouraged at crucial points in the poem to understand the conversations reported and the heavenly systems described as beautifully colored, "slowshifting," *changing* deflections of a light which, inaccessible on its own, is given dimension through its two mediums.

So, for example, we gradually come to understand, in the initial installment of the trilogy, *The Book of Ephraim*, that the first voice from the board to make extensive contact, Ephraim (BORN AD 8), is in fact Merrill's and Jackson's own richly idiosyncratic, language-bound translation of a force passing through their skulls:

> As through smoked glass, we charily observed
> Either that his memory was spotty
> (Whose wouldn't be, after two thousand years?)
> Or that his lights and darks were a projection
> Of what already burned, at some obscure
> Level or another, in our skulls.
> We, all we knew, dreamed, felt and had forgotten,
> Flesh made word, became through him a set of
> Quasi-grammatical constructions which
> Could utter some things clearly, forcibly,
> Others not.
>
> (S, 31)

More directly, the bats who dominate the messages of the second book, *Mirabell's Book of Numbers*—derived, Merrill suggests, from the "limber, leotarded, blue-eyed bats" (S, 98) of the carpet in the room in which he works with the board—insist that their words as well are translated, explaining that "ALL / THESE OUR CONVERSATIONS COME FROM MEMORY & WORD BANKS / TAPPD IN U" (S, 140). More elaborately, in Book 3, *Scripts for the Pageant*, the departed spirit of Maria Mitso-táki (MM)—who, along with the spirit of W. H. Auden (WHA), is imagined as sitting in on the seminars in which the mediums communicate with the angels Michael, Gabriel, Emmanual, and Raphael—explains, also in uppercase, that one of her tasks throughout that book has been to render these "inexpressible" angelic forces in the deflecting terms of their human receptors: "WE CAMOUFLAGED U AS IN JUNGLE WARFARE / TO INFILTRATE THE INEXPRESSIBLE. / U SEE THOSE 4 ARE TERRIBLY STRONG DRINK. / KNOWING IT ALL, THEY TEND TO OVER-LOOK / THE IMAGE-THWARTED PATHS BY WHICH WE THINK." Asking for permission to "DECODE" the angels' thinking, MM and WHA were accordingly assigned to "BRING BACK A HUMAN LANGUAGE WE CAN USE"—to which JM responds:

> So that from the first
> They spoke to us through *you*—LANGUAGE THE WHOLLY
> HUMAN INSTRUMENT, REMEMBER   YET
> THEIR EVERY 'WORD' WAS (HOW TO SAY IT) HOLY
> Even in translation.
>
> (S, 413–14)

Decoding, translating, limiting, infiltrating, and rendering the "HOLY" in terms of the senses—these tasks taken on here by WHA and MM are, we are meant to see, the means by which the entire poem's taming of "cosmic forces" has taken place.

If we add to this account of the poem's conscious rendering of forces otherwise invisible a second idea—Merilll's suggestion that the source of those powers could as easily be the "elemental processes" of the psyche as the "cosmic forces" of the universe—it becomes clear that a useful way of reading the poem is as a sustained demonstration of how the "Darkness impenetrable . . . / . . . Impenetrable brilliance" of the self is refracted and made visible (S, 74).[5] Merrill encourages us to make such a connection between cosmic and personal forces in a number of places. In an essay on Dante, for example, one of the poem's most obvious sources, Merrill notes the way a divine "laser show" was "projected through Dante's human senses and image banks," identifying that initiating force as a "sustaining divinatory intelligence which spoke to him, if only (as Julian Jaynes would have it) from that center of the brain's right hemisphere which corresponds to Weinecke's area on the left."[6] A similar slide from divine light to deepest self marks Merrill's response to an interviewer's query about his choice of such a patently odd discipline as ouija communication: "Well, don't you think there comes a time when everyone, not just a poet, wants to get beyond the self? To reach, if you like, the 'god' within you? The board, in however clumsy or absurd a way, allows for precisely that. Or if it's still yourself that you're drawing upon, then that self is much stranger and freer and more farseeing than the one you thought you knew."[7] Perhaps most convincingly, musing in the poem itself about a new voice that had suddenly begun dictation ("By What? or Whom? . . . / Broad strokes, deliberate, / Of character unknown" [S, 73]), Merrill refers to Jung's merging of God and the unconscious—"It is only through the Psyche that we can establish that God acts upon us, but we are unable to distinguish whether these actions emanate from God or from the unconscious. We cannot tell whether God and the unconscious are two different entities"[8]—in order to alert us to this other possible interpretation of that source of power, concluding simply: "Jung says—or if he doesn't, all but does— / That God and the Unconscious are one. Hm" (S, 74). What this long poem gives us, then, is an extraordinarily elaborate demonstration of the way that dimensionless inner forces, passed through the deflecting "temperaments" of the two mediums, issue forth in gaudy, substantial, strange (and yet holy) representations. This odd rendering of spirit voices is another variation of the pattern described previously—Whitman's ensemble through which the "Me myself" is made visible having been, like Ashbery's everyday voices, deposited in the word-banks of JM and DJ.

Further, as the following reading of the trilogy is designed to point out, the poem is also organized as a careful, quite serious meditation on the very problem of indirection that it so colorfully demonstrates.[9] Merrill, of course, has always been a poet whose intricately textured work deliberately calls attention to itself as mediated experience. Robert von Hallberg, for example, describes him as a poet of "dazzling surfaces" and "quiet evasions"—suggesting that Merrill's foregrounding of the "contractual 'in other words'" of his language quite knowingly consigns certain aspects of experience to silence.[10] It is a habit of mind with which even Merrill's best reader, Helen Vendler, expresses occasional impatience; discussing Merrill's "conscious artificiality," she writes: "often, perhaps even too often, Merrill refuses the potential transparency of the written word, and reminds his readers that this is writing they are reading, not a window they are privileged to see through."[11] Does such relish for language's glittery

surfaces imply a too-easy acceptance of the medium's built-in limitation, a simple retreat from "signification" into "energy, invention and
ornamentation?"[12] Might one complain, as Ashbery did to Parmigianino, that "your hand is big enough / To wreck the sphere, and too
big, / One would think, to weave delicate meshes / That only argue
its further detention"?

Merrill has been confronted with such questions throughout his
career, perhaps most severely by himself. An essay in the *New York
Times Book Review*—"Condemned to Write About Real Things"—
recalls an early classmate whose scornful "Write about *real things* for
God's sake" attempted to point out the inadequacies of such topics as
masquerades and mad crones, distant subjects which "allowed us to
polish without much thought for what (if anything) we were communicating."[13] Dismissed at the time, that criticism of indirection sur-
faced again in a psychiatrist's office, four years after Merrill graduated
from Amherst: "The doctor wanted to hear about my life. It had been
flowing along unnoticed in my absorption with the images that came
and went on its surface. Now its very droplets were being studied on
a slide. 'Real things'—was I condemned to write about them, after
all?" These are criticisms countered only by a careful analysis of the
access to "real things" that polished surfaces provide: "Of course I
had been doing nothing else. Symbolist pastiche or makeshift jotting,
our words reveal more than we think." Merrill's example—an artless
diary entry about a visit to Florida: "Silver Springs—heavenly colors
and swell fish"—suggests that indirection renders visible and generative subjects too powerful and too complex for a direct gaze:
"Two banalities, each by itself bad enough, and hopelessly so in con-
junction. Yet in their simple awfulness they *broach* the issue most
crucial to this boy not quite fourteen. Two years earlier my parents
have been divorced. . . . What is this phrase but an attempt to bring
my parents together, to *remarry* on the page their characteristic inflec-
tions—the ladylike gush and the regular-guy terseness."[14] We see
just the same questions in *Sandover*: Of what value is indirection in
approaching and remarrying inner forces that by their very nature
threaten to separate and whirl apart? How can "slowshifting gouts of
color," organized into what Merrill calls "the plus and minus signs of
a vast evolving formula,"[15] make sense of a world that they are unable
to render directly? Is that world lost, or is it thereby found? What
these insistent questions do, however, is more than just signal Merrill's characteristic concerns. Their effect—like Ashbery's constant
self-assessment or Duncan's obsessive marking of potential conflicts—
is both to call attention to the tension between inner forces and me-

dium *and* to open up the terms by which that medium might be engaged and entered. For example, questions about the triviality of a parlor game, when held up against the painfully dissolving relationship that it mirrors, lead in time to a reworking of those apparently trivial elements and of the eroding relationship itself.

The very first words of the poem, from section A of *The Book of Ephraim's* alphabetical divisions, establish the device with which I am concerned:

> Admittedly I err by undertaking
> This in its present form. The baldest prose
> Reportage was called for, that would reach
> The widest public in the shortest time.
> Time, it had transpired, was of the essence.
> Time, the very attar of the Rose,
> Was running out.
>
> (S, 3)

"This," we soon learn, is Merrill's attempt to set down twenty years' worth of evenings "Spent / With David Jackson at the Ouija Board / In Touch with Ephraim Our Familiar Spirit." His error, which like Ashbery's Parmigianino he begins his work by foregrounding and insisting that we ponder, is a refusal of the apparently unmediated presentation of prose reportage in favor of the deliberately impure, attention gathering, glittering artifice we are about to encounter. That decision, he continues, was prompted by an earlier failure to present this material in the form of a novel—for whose prose he had had similarly naive ambitions: "I yearned for the kind of unseasoned telling found / In legends, fairy tales, a tone licked clean / Over the centuries by mild old tongues, / Grandam to cub, serene, anonymous" (S, 3). Such an anonymous prose, he writes in section S, would have provided the "neutral ground" necessary for disentangling the spirits' messages from the necessarily personal "stains" of their human mediums: "So as to measure by triangulation / Heights up there beyond the height of self, / Or so that (when the fall rains fell) would go / Flashing through me a *perfected flow* (S, 66, emphasis mine). Admitting error, on the other hand, is to abandon clarity for temperament, the illusion of the unobstructed "flow" of powerful forces for the play of deflection. Merrill begins his work, this suggests, as Duncan did—acknowledging that his speech is all indirection, drawn from "The company of the living" rather than from the oracular access of a "crevice in the ground between / mid-earth and underworld" (BB, 9). And he does so fully aware that the crisis referred to throughout the trilogy—literally, the threat of nuclear annihilation, but as it gets developed metaphorically, the constant threat of internal "fission" as delicately balanced forces are jostled and allowed to "run out"—must still be addressed, if not by prose reportage then by the glitter of artifice. Abandoning the illusions of prose means: "I alone was left / To tell my story. For it seemed that Time— / The grizzled washer of his hands appearing / To say so in a spectrum-bezeled space / Above hot water—Time would not" (S, 4). This image is itself an example of Merrill's obsessive indirection. Washing his hands and preparing to shave, he sees at the same time images of impending crisis (grizzled time is washing its hands of us, indicating that humanity has finally run its course) *and* of the activity to be pitted against it: the reflective, "spectrum-bezeled space" of a mirror whose glittering, framed errors must somehow stand "above [the] hot water" of disaster. Each book of the trilogy uses this same threat of dissolution to spur a sustained meditation on the value and power of indirection—a meditation, in turn, which prompts the cascading self-renderings of Merrill's exercise in seeing.

DJ and JM began making sporadic contact with a number of other-wordly voices, primarily Ephraim and those he ushered into their presence, in 1955. The first book of the trilogy narrates a year-long attempt (January–December 1974) to organize and present that material. Although it only gradually becomes clear, the impetus for this shaping and rehandling of years of transcripts is a threatened undoing of the lovers' long-standing relationship—the records of past encounters with the ouija board being one continual translation or rendering of the finally hidden bond between the two. Setting out straightforwardly to summarize his "research"—"huge tracts of information," he writes at one point, "Have gone into these capsules flavorless / And rhymed for easy swallowing" (S, 9)—Merrill inexorably finds himself describing two crisis periods in the union of his lover-mediums.[16] The first, occurring in the early stages of that relationship (Summer 1955–Summer 1957) is presented through the art of "timeskip and gadabout" in sections G–L, which we watch being written during the first half of 1974 while the two are still united in Stonington, Connecticut. If we are thus assured that the first threat of fission was successfully dealt with, the absence of such assurance in the presentation of the second, present-tense crisis—they are separated as the remainder of the poem is being written during the second half of 1974—suggests that the power of artifice to overcome "the dim wish of lives to drift apart" (S, 25) is still a live question. As did Parmigianino's riddling eyes or Duncan's Vietnam, the question continues to prompt Merrill's work with the medium rendering their shared world. The "hot water" that *Ephraim's* "spectrum-bezeled" dazzlements are mounted above, then, is the constant, and potentially final, eroding away of their relationship—as in this ceremonial heart, created for them in 1955, reduced in the present to:

> a ghost of roughness underfoot.
> There it was, the valentine that Maya,
> Kneeling on our threshold, drew to bless us:
> Of white meal sprinkled then with rum and lit,
> Heart once intricate as birdsong, it
> Hardened on the spot. Much come-and-go
> Has blackened, pared the scabby curlicue
> Down to smatterings which, even so,
> Promise to last this lifetime.
>
> (S, 25)

The narration of that first, resolved crisis is set up by a present-tense account (April 1974), in section F, of a visit with a scientist experimenting with chimpanzees' ability to master and transmit human language to their offspring. One favored chimp, Miranda, greets both the scientist and JM with "uncritical eyes" and "one great / Open-jawed kiss that threatens to go on / And on . . . / But for her manners" (S, 18–19). Manners—a set, systematic, even artificial relationship between parties—will be the subject of sections G through L which, as Merrill notes explicitly, describe various attempts by the mediums to work out some sort of systematic relationship "Between one floating realm unseen powers rule / . . . And one we feel is ours, and call the real" (S, 20). It is an account marked by positions tentatively taken and then radically revised: "All those years . . . / . . . Weren't we still groping, like Miranda, toward / Some higher level?" (S, 19). Those unseen powers, I have suggested, might usefully be located within that shared "Heart once intricate as birdsong."

Section H describes an abortive attempt in the fall of 1955 to make direct contact with this unseen "presence / Everywhere felt, who never showed his face" (S, 26). This, of course, is the dream worked through by all portraitists—to embrace that unseen world directly. If Ephraim's world, sensed to this point through tea cup and ouija board, can be compared to the "rosy-lit interior" of Merrill's Stonington tower as reflected at night "on a pane's trapeze / . . . swung beyond the sill . . . / . . . a pied-a-terre / Made for his at-homes" (S, 26), then the two mediums had grown hungry for more than this world of "insupportable hypotheses / Hovering there," insubstantially sketched "upon darkness, emptiness" (S, 26). Following Ephraim's suggestion, Merrill invoked the spirit's actual presence by hypnotizing Jackson, who then claimed to see Ephraim, in the following italicized incorporation of DJ's notes, step out of a window's reflective frame:

> The room
> Grown dim, an undrawn curtain in the panes'
> Glass night tawnily maned, lit from below
> So that hair-wisps of brightness quickened slowly
> *the limbs & torso muscled by long folds of*
> *an unemasculated Blake nude. Who then*
> *actually was in the room, at arm's length,*
> *glowing with strength, asking if he pleased me.*
>
> (S, 27)

Not himself hypnotized, Merrill sees only DJ, rather than Ephraim, who, himself stepping from the window, begins speaking in "a voice not his" and moves toward an embrace:

> Whose for that matter was the hand I held?
> It had grown cool, impersonal. It led
> Me to a deep black couch, and stroked my face
> The blood had drained from. Caught up in his strong
> Flow of compulsion, mine was to resist.
> The more thrilled through, the less I went along,
> A river stone, blind, clenched against whatever
> Was happening that once.
>
> (S, 27)

Backing off from the embrace, JM's instinctive resistance to direct contact with that powerful, compulsive "flow" of energy immediately sends DJ's vision "back into the glass-warp" and signals the pressing need for a more indirect relationship between the two realms. Merrill's love game recreates and comes to much the same conclusion as Whitman's experiment with embracing his boundlessness directly in sections 25 through 29 of "Song of Myself," or Roethke's abortive move toward the sea.

Section I builds on an argument put forward by an ex-analyst who, in too-easily dismissing their ouija communications as an elaborately masked way of speaking to each other, gives a skeptical turn to their assessment of the value of indirection. If a mask isolates and makes visible an aspect of an impossibly complex and volatile relationship, so too Ephraim's uppercase outpourings, like other indirect interpretive schemes, could be said to provide one possible means of reading that larger world beyond them:

> Hadn't—from books, from living—
> The profusion dawned on us, of "languages"
> Any one of which, to who could read it,
> Lit up the larger system it conceived?—bird-flight,
> Hallucinogen, chorale and horoscope:
> Each its own world, hypnotic, many-sided
> Facet of the universal gem.
>
> (S, 31)

The single, slanting world of Ephraim's dictation, then, might provide them with tangible access to—"we had them / For comfort, thrills and chills, 'material'"—and a means of "conceiving" of, that larger flashing gem. But, as we learn in the "flying trip / Round the world" recounted in section K, a grand tour stretching from 1956 to spring 1957, the dizzying profusion of other facets of that gem (the "market, mackerel, minaret / Simmering mulligatawny of the Real" [S, 38]) soon reduces Ephraim's thrills and chills to a simple, persisted-in, mannered formality they "chafe" against and compare to "Chairs like brocaded tombstones, or 'French Forms' / Squirmed from, at twelve, in my Verse Manual" (S, 38). Although Ephraim continues to view them through the medium of various reflective surfaces—a way of suggesting that, like Duncan's recessed voices, his interpretive scheme continues to be potentially available—his presence is not sought in turn by the travelers. Having now taken the opposite tack in dismissing as empty form the "language" they had previously tried to go beyond, the two discover that the only depths exposed and illuminated now are their own self-eroding "depths / . . . of unreflecting."

To name such unreflective, corrosive dailiness "life," section L suggests as it describes "that summer we came back" (1957), seems an admission that time is in fact inevitably running out: "Life like the periodical not yet / Defunct kept hitting the stands. We seldom failed / To leaf through each new issue—war, election, / Starlet" (S, 40). So, too, the once-intricate texture of their shared lives seems only, at best, not yet defunct: "Tediums / Ignited into quarrels, each a 'scene / From real life,' we concluded as we vowed / Not to repeat it" (S, 40). This dissolving heaviness is broken, however, by their attention suddenly snapping back to the world of Ephraim, not the actual force beneath his voice but that spectrum-bezeled reflective space whose indirect access to "some higher level" transforms their rutted, daily lives into a kind of garden:

No, no! Set in our ways
As in a garden's, glittered
A whole small globe—our life, our life, our life:
Rinsed with mercury
Throughout to this bespattered
Fruit of reflection, rife

With Art Nouveau distortion
(Each other, clouds and trees).
What made a mirror flout its flat convention?
Surfacing as a solid
Among our crudities
To toss them like a salad?

                                             (S, 41–42)

A mirrored ball not unlike Parmigianino's, flouting its inherent distortions, Ephraim's "material"—what has been brought to the surface "as a solid" through his costume—is at the same time a means of tossing the crudities of their daily lives, revealing more there than was expected. (An earlier poem about such voices put it this way: "once looked at lit / By the cold reflections of the dead / Risen extinct but irresistible, / *Our lives* have never seemed more full, more real, / Nor the full moon more quick to chill" [FN, 67].) The results of that reflection are life heightened ("What was the sensation / When stars alone like bees / Crawled numbly over it?"), or life made more terrifying—as in the death vision granted on one "occasion / [when] fatigue or disbelief / Mottled the silver lining" (S, 42). In either case, that created world's opening up of what seems almost another life ("Then, as it were, *our life* saw through that craze / Of its own creation / Into another life" [S, 42, emphasis mine]) staves off the inclination to drift dully apart. Neither "lost" nor "found," neither an array of discarded forms nor an overpowering entrance to another world, the globe is a made thing—in Ashbery's terms, "a metaphor made to include us."

Section L functions as a kind of hinge for the poem; in it Merrill not only remembers the triumph of reflection over fission or drift in 1957, but also, by linking that troubled time with the present July ("Remembered, is that summer we came back / Really so unlike the present one?") suggests the need for a similar imaginative counterpressure:[17]

The whole house needs repairs. Neither can bring
Himself to say so. Hardly lingering,
We've reached the point, where the tired Sound just washes
Up to, then avoids our feet. . . .

> Three more weeks, and the stiff upper lip
> Of luggage shuts on us.

(S, 41)

As the last two lines suggest, the major difference here is that this second crisis is not resolved: unable to speak directly, drifting toward exhaustion, the two separate for six months—JM to Greece, DJ to his parents in the Southwest—and, in a sense, put the problem aside for a time while Merrill tinkers with the issues raised by his ouija notes. Exactly the same move has occurred throughout the other poems in this study. Here Merrill declares the distance between his work with these voices and the actual world they speak for by literally setting an ocean between the two, then finds himself encouraged to enter the medium itself by teasing out the complexities of his relation with it.[18]

A series of related passages about power failure—the potential shattering of the delicate balance of "Powers of lightness, darkness" (S, 54)—serves to expand the threat of undoing being meditated on beyond the pairing of JM and DJ. In section O, alone in bed on a "breathless August night," JM remembers waking in a similarly empty bed in Athens on a winter morning years ago: "Upstairs, DJ's already at the simmer / Phoning the company. He gets one pair / Of words wrong—means to say 'kalorifér' / (Furnace) but out comes 'kalokéri' (summer): / Our *summer* doesn't work, he keeps complaining" (S, 53). The point of that memory's occurrence now, of course, is JM's waking to the threatened failure of *this* summer, which doesn't seem to work. Section P links that personal crisis to another potential failure, the kissed-awake sleeping beauty of nuclear war. And the stroke of that "doomsday clock"—unleashing the powers of undoing—is echoed, two sections later, by the remembered mind-cancelling stroke suffered by a friend, Maya Deren. As we are reminded throughout the second half of *Ephraim*, then, the delicate, inexplicable workings of minds, marriages, and worlds are constantly threatened with undoing. Time runs out.

JM begins his solitary examination of this problem, in Athens, by musing about his abandoned novel. In section M, he recounts a dream of Maya's which, according to Ephraim, was a vision of the hidden forces of heaven—or, in our terms, the potential, not-yet-printed, recesses of the self. Joined at a formal gathering by "one she seems to know," Maya, in her dream:

> alone wears mourning weeds
> That weigh unbearably until he leads

Her to a spring, or source , oh wonder! in
Whose shining depths her gown turns white, her jet
To diamonds, and black veil to bridal snow.
Her features are unchanged, yet her pale skin
Is black, with glowing nostrils—a not yet
Printed self.

(S, 44)

But, where Maya had been able to craft something out of her dream's insistence that in the "shining depths" of our deepest "source" resides a power able to reverse the unbearable weight of "mourning," translating her vision into a film in which a "young white actress gowned and veiled in black" becomes, "in phosphorescent negative / . . . a black bride" (S, 45–46), JM remembers himself hopelessly bound up in his novel's "shortsighted" insistence on truth. Committed to working out a relationship between "Earth, Heaven; / Reality, Projection," he found himself on "unsteady ground" with no useful counterbalance to the problem of separation save "A new day's quota of shortsighted prose" (S, 46).

Now, in Greece, as in that summer of 1957, the poet turns again from the impossible desire to "truly" scratch an account of the depths to an acceptance of artifice—the "illusion of coherence" generated, for example, by the reflective play of a candle's light on a mirror's random scratches: "A candle / Haloing itself, the bedroom mirror's / Wreath of scratches fiery-fine as hairs / . . . Making sense for once of long attrition" (S, 48). And just as, here in section N, this admittedly not truly scratched surface renders the light visible in a way that makes a kind of "sense" of "attrition," so, in one of the quotations assembled in section Q, a reference to Pope's magical grotto, he finds another image for the power of sparkling artifice to create a "new existence" fully responsive to the world's pressure:

> *Here Pope had constructed a private underworld . . .*
> *encrusted . . . with a rough mosaic of luminous mineral*
> *bodies . . . On the roof shone a looking-glass star;*
> *and, dependent from the star, a single lamp—'of an*
> *orbicular figure of thin alabaster'—cast around it 'a*
> *thousand pointed rays.' Every surface sparkled or*
> *shimmered or gleamed with a smooth subaqueous lustre;*
> *. . . Pope intended . . . that the visitor, when at length*
> *he emerged, should feel that he had been reborn into*
> *a new existence.*

(S, 61)

And much the same point is made in the last reference to the abandoned novel—in section T. There, Sergei, one of the *novel's* Merrill-like figures, is staring at himself in a mirror and is granted the following mirror-reversed revelation from a "voice" deep within himself:

> "Contrary to appearances, you and I,
> Who pick our barefoot ways toward one another
> Through playing cards and grums of class
> Over checkerboard linoleum
> Have not seen eye to eye. We represent
> Isms diametrically proposed.
> You clothe my mowing as I don your flask.
> Our summit meetings turn on the forever
> Vaster, thinner skin of things, glass blower's
> Tour de force—white-hot, red-hot at dusk,
> All that we dread by midnight will have burst
> Into a drifting, cooling soot of light . . ."
>
> (S, 69)

Once we switch the reversed consonants, we read that the opposed prisms of the human and the divine do not see "eye to eye": the invisible is accessible only through such indirect forms as cards or, as we have seen, reflecting crumbs of glass. Clothing its flowing through masks or the "skin of things," we render its potentially dreadful powers visible and stable in a "cooling soot of light." And it is this combination—the "vocal, comic member of the team" deflecting and shaping the unseen "slitherer / tombless, untamed"—Merrill suggests, which produces "Orderings of experience" perhaps sound enough to stave off disaster (S, 70–69).[19]

This pieced-together meditation ends as JM concludes his six-month residence in Greece and prepares to return home to Stonington, determined now to "face" and make something of the "Darkness impenetrable . . . / . . . impenetrable brilliance." A side trip to Venice—"A whole heavenly city / Sinking, titanic ego mussel-blue / Abulge in gleaming nets of nerve" (S, 75)—reminds him of his task of saving heaven (and his inner paradise) from drowning. The ludicrously inadequate attempts by camera-wielding tourists to respond to the crisis of time's running out ("this need of theirs / To be forever smiling, holding still / For the other, the companion focusing / Through tiny frames of anxiousness" [S, 75]) momentarily expose his own slowly arrived at recommitment to artifice as deeply limited:

> I thanked my stars
> When I lost the Leica at Longchamps. Never again
> To overlook a subject for its image,

To labor images till they yield a subject—
Dram of essence from the flowering field.
No further need henceforth of this
Receipt (gloom coupled with artifice)
For holding still, for being held still.

(S, 76)

This temporary abandonment of artifice is halted by a sudden thunderstorm whose violently protean shape-shifting Merrill reads as a kind of oracle—"Cold hissing white—the old man of the Sea / Who, clung to now, must truthfully reply" (S, 76)—his lightning-punctuated message suggesting the possibility of a different kind of artifice:

crack! boom! flash!—

Glaze soaking inward as it came to mind
How anybody's monster breathing flames
Vitrified in metamorphosis

To monstrance clouded then like a blown fuse
If not a reliquary for St. James'
Vision of life

(S, 77)

The storm's movement from the flash of lightning to the glaze of "water blown glass-hard" to the steady presence of clouds suggests a model for art: an art working that destructive potential (that "monster breathing flames") into form (in this case, a sacred glass "monstrance"), while acknowledging that the form's cloudy, indistinct nature makes its ritual display both a "blown fuse" and a captured "vision of life."[20] Such an acknowledgment, it seems, shifts Merrill from the incessantly anxious framing of "gloom coupled with artifice" back to a more lightly held, admittedly erroneous notion of framing whose artificial structures—like Whitman's "outlines," Duncan's "fictional ensemble," Ashbery's "metaphor / Made to include us," or his own mirrored ball—can be worked in mastering forces dark and impenetrable: "how Venice, her least stone / Pure menace at the start, at length became // A window fiery-mild, whose *walked-through frame /* Everything else, at sunset, hinged upon—" (S, 77, emphasis mine).

Merrill demonstrates what he means by such a reflective "frame" in section W, when he brings to life Ephraim's current "representative," JM's nephew Wendell, and places him in the midst of the post-storm "pink-and-golden calm." Wendell is clearly a device to work with in refining a theory of art. Their meeting is a contrast in styles—the "melon with ham, risotto with shellfish, / Cervello fritto spitting fire at us" Merrill springs for versus the "pack and staff" of the nephew who "though omnivorous / . . . rather looks down on the scene" (S, 79)—and of artistic programs. An artist himself, Wendell, under urging, produces a sketchbook of portraits in which "pain, panic and old age / Afflict his subjects horribly." Wendell's argument is that the afflicted, screaming self he is forced to render seems the only response to his catastrophic sense of time running out. JM's view, developed earlier, that a mannered, indirect account of the self's terrors and glories is a sounder approach to impending catastrophe, clearly has taken form as a reaction to this position. The "frame" allows him to dramatize his thinking on this subject. Reluctantly acknowledging the incompatibility of their views, JM soon finds himself alone with the sunken ("betided") heaven of Venice—its covered maze as much an image of time's threatened end as of heaven's—stubbornly holding onto his own poetics:

> our struck acquaintance lit no drowned
>
> Niche in the blue, blood-warm Palladian
> Sculpture maze we'd surfaced from, which goes
> Evolving Likeness back to the first man,
>
> Forth to betided lineaments one knows
> Or once did. I lose touch with the sublime.
> Yet in these sunset years hardly propose
>
> Mending my ways, breaking myself of rhyme
> To speak to multitudes and make it matter.
>
> (S, 82)

That same coolness of tone—artifice may be inadequate, but finally it's all I know—is carried through the book's conclusion and marks the problem as not totally resolved. Suspended between "blue time zones" flying home, Merrill, in summary form, reiterates his commitment to indirection:

> What I think I feel now, by its own nature
> Remains beyond my power to say outright,
> Short of grasping the naked current where it
> Flows through field and book, dog howling, the firelit
> Glances, the caresses, whatever draws us
> To, and insulates us from, the absolute—
>
> (S, 84)

The question with which Merrill is left, having returned home, is whether the play of indirection is adequate to face Stonington's marshalled reminders of the threat of nothingness. Facing the end of the year, another power failure ("Zero hour. Waiting yet again / For someone to fix the furnace. Zero week / Of the year's end"), and musing over the apparent entrance of a thief two nights earlier ("The threat remains, though, of there still being / A presence in our midst, unknown, unseen, / Unscrupulous to take what he can get"), Merrill resists the temptation to use Ephraim's transcripts for fuel, reminded by an interrupting telephone call of the need to make something of those cryptic messages: "Wait the phone is ringing: / Bad connection; babble of distant talk; / No getting through. We must improve the line / In every sense, for life" (S, 91). And here the first book ends—committed to working with art ("the line") in the name of life, but with the question of its efficacy unresolved. Another call comes, starkly exposing this final position: "It's Bob the furnace man. He's on his way. / Will find, if not an easy-to-repair / Short circuit, then the failure long foreseen / As total, of our period machine" (S, 91).

Neither the walked-through "frame" of mysterious, otherwordly communication nor the problem with which it is designed to work are abandoned in the dizzying multiplication of otherwordly voices in the next two books of the trilogy.[21] One of the poem's conventions is that all ouija sessions are to be conducted before a mirror, the reflective surface of which makes it possible for the spirits to see themselves and subsequently describe themselves to their mediums. The spirits becomes visible only as they are reflected upon—they are reflective creations.[22] What Merrill does repeatedly in these next two books is acknowledge that these figures exist "in the mirror only / of a live mind" (S, 105), then assent to that fiction. MM, for example, describes her heavenly "appearance" in this, at first confounding, way:

> I RATHER SEE MYSELF
>
> PALE LILY ON THE CALLA SIDE: THICK LEGS
> BUT A DEEP CANDID WONDER OF A FACE
>
> You see yourself . . . Maman, not that it matters,
> You see with our minds' eye, with nothing else.
> You've said as much (0.6). Let me acknowledge
> Belatedly that awful truth, then go
> Right on pretending that it isn't so.
>
> (S, 152)

So, too, we are reminded that the various settings described are, in reality, a "FICTIVE SPACE" (S, 451), a "*framed world*" (S, 450) of mental reflection. When the talk turns to the problems in inviting a new spirit to the radiant world of Book 3's seminar, for example, DJ makes the following comic slip, showing us the seams of this creation:

THE PROBLEM NOW IS CHIEFLY WHERE HE'LL SIT
(DURING THE LESSONS) OUT OF RADIATION . . .
THE REST OF US OF COURSE IMMUNE TO IT
DJ: Are *we*? DEAR BOY TRY TO REMEMBER
THIS IS ALL IN A MANNER OF SPEAKING

(S, 421)

It becomes clear, then, that the remaining two books of the trilogy—whose outpourings were initiated by the installation of an "immense / Victorian mirror"—function as an elaborately framed, reflective world. The masques and seminars of these books, like JM's solitary meditation in Greece or his creation of "Wendell," take place solely in the "spectrum-bezeled space" of mental reflection.

If the problem left unresolved in *Ephraim* was whether the play of indirection—what I have called a mannered, medium-bound approach to the self's terrors and glories—was adequate to stand against the threat of nothingness, the reflective work of the next two books attempts that defense by responding to the two different ways that *Ephraim* framed the question: What does art give us instead of the threatening directness of the hypnosis scene? What does it give us instead of the form-weary skepticism of the world tour? In a sense, these were also the questions in mind when Merrill described his boyhood diary's ability to "broach" an impossibly charged subject and then "remarry" its warring, self-critical elements. The argument framed in Book 2, *Mirabell's Books of Number*, is the first of these—the need for and the effects of "broaching" the self's secrets through the dispersing, insulating devices of language. Its primary narrative occurs in the summer of 1976 when, rather idly resuming their parlor game, JM and DJ are visited by a number of bats who demand that the mediums absorb a series of revelations in order to write "POEMS OF SCIENCE." JM's acceptance of this new task makes it clear that this subject is finally a "pretext"—a frame—for once again making visible the changing play of light's contact with *our* atmosphere:

> Science meant
> Obfuscation, boredom—; which once granted,
> Odd lights came and went inside my head.
> Not for nothing had the Impressionists
> Put subject-matter in its place, a mere
> Pretext for iridescent atmosphere.

(S, 109)

The book is organized as an "imagined" seminar in which DJ and JM, joined by the human spirits of WHA and MM, are, through discussion and lecture, prepared to halt time's "running out": "About us, these bright afternoons, we come / To draw shades of an auditorium / In darkness. An imagined dark, a stage / Convention: domed red room, cup and blank page / Standing for darkness" (S, 147). Their primary instructor is a bat who, under their speculative attention, metamorphoses into a peacock they name Mirabell. The bat identifies himself at first as a kind of fallen angel—"BEZELBOB," he says, "SYLLABLES THAT TO A CHILD SPELL WICKEDNESS" (S, 115)—but he is later, and more properly, identified as one of "THE BOBS THE FURNACE MEN" (S, 131): that is, Bob the furnace man at the end of *Ephraim*, coming to assist in the repair of their many-faceted power failure. He is coming, we now see, to assist in that repair by adding the glinting "BEZELS" of his defracted revelation.[23]

The tale that Mirabell gradually unfolds for them is a version of *Ephraim's* struggle to understand the interaction of fission and artifice, dramatized now, however, on the microscopic and mythic levels. It is as much a frame to be "walked-through" as was the invention of a Wendell: Roethke would have called this a "rehearsal," Whitman an "Outline." Fission, according to Mirabell, occurs when the unseen powers of the atom ("INTENSE FISSIONABLE ENERGIES BLACK & WHITE / WHICH EITHER JOIN & CREATE OR SEPARATE & DESTROY" [S, 119]) are tampered with improperly. This possibility exists on both micro and macro levels:

> His whole point's the atom's .
> Precarious inviolability.
> Eden tells a parable of fission,
> Lost world and broken home, the bitten apple
> Stripped of its seven veils, nakedness left
> With no choice but to sin and multiply.
> From then on, genealogical chain reactions
> Ape the real thing.
>
>   (S, 192)

Mirabell tells them the following parable of the "lost world." God first created on the earth an immortal race of centaurs who, in turn, invented an atomic race of "FEATHERD / WINGD CREATURES[S]" (S, 167) to serve as messengers and, in time, to "RID THEM OF THEIR RELICS" (S, 168)—older centaurs who couldn't die off on their own. These feathered creatures eventually gained, in time, enough wisdom about the atom to enslave their former masters and use its powers to build a glorious "CRUST WORLD" above the earth, ministered to by the earth-bound centaurs. Their eventually incautious handling of the atom's previously inviolate power, however, was disastrous. In time despising that crust world and, "WITH A LAST THRUST OF ATOMIC FISSION," destroying it utterly, those creatures now acknowledge: "THERE IS AN EVIL WE RELEASD   WE DID NOT CREATE IT / CALL IT THE VOID   CALL IT IN MAN   A WILL TO NOTHINGNESS" (S, 120).

Those winged creatures, of course, are the bats now dictating the poem, given "A 2ND CHANCE" to redeem themselves by deterring God's newest creation from the "devil" of naive meddling:

> WE TRIFLED & FELL   NEGATIVE ENERGY THE BLACK HOLE
> WAS BORNE   WE BURN   YET THERE IS MERCY   & HAVING SUFFERD
> IT IS OUR DUTY TO WARN MAN AGAINST THE CHAOS ONCE
> WORSHIPT BY US . . .
> & NOW WE GUARD THE EMBERS WHICH ARE MIND   THEY ALONE WARM
> GOD BIOLOGY & SHOW MAN THE WAY TO PARADISE
> . . .
>
> THE DEVIL HAS BEEN DRIVEN FROM US INTO MAN   WE NOW
> MUST DRIVE IT OUT OF HIM   OUR TOOLS ARE MIND WORDS REASON
>   LIGHT
>
>   (S, 113–14)

This new project—humanity—was itself almost a victim of a parallel form of self-destruction. At a crucial point in history, during the rule of Akhnaton in Egypt ("the first individual in history"), the bats' task was shifted from the simple one of developing the rudiments of intelligence ("WE WERE MESSENGERS / TO WHOM GOD GAVE THE PASSKEYS TO THE MIND OF MAN   WE ENTERED / A JUNGLE OF GREENERY FRESH, QUIVERING WITH TRAPT LIGHT, / & SLOWLY LEST WE FRIGHTEN HIM CLEARD PATHS" (S, 241) to that of guiding culture. Akhnaton and Nefertiti learned, like the bats, how to use atomic power and built a kind of glorious crust world, then, like JM and DJ trying to embrace the force called "Ephraim" directly, overstepped their bounds—unleashing a "NUCLEAR EXPLOSION" and coming close to another release of "PERFECT FISSION":

>   IT WAS THE DAWN
> OF ARCADIA & GOD SMILED LIKE THE SUN UPON THEM
> Then in one wasteful flash it ended—why?
>
> THEIR OWN BATTERY CELLS CD NOT BEAR THE STRAIN
>   (S, 227)

To say that they couldn't "bear the strain" of direct contact with the atom is to say that at the moment of this crisis God "UNDERSTOOD / THE LIMITATIONS OF THE NEW EARTH MASTER" (S, 179).

What Akhnaton and Nefertiti did, according to the poem, was to make a structure whose capstone, a polished quartz pyramid, was designed, through its reproduction of the "EXACT PRISM OF LIGHT ENERGY" (S, 126), to let that energy pass directly into the world. That is, like Roethke initially approaching the sea or Whitman in the crisis sections of "Song of Myself," they naively attempted to embrace that flow of energy directly, despising the mediation of a crust world. Realizing human limitation ("INSULATING & TRANSMITTING / DEVICES WERE NEEDED ON THE NIGHT OF HIS DISASTER" [S, 179]), God interfered in the process by substituting a flawed piece of quartz (S, 227) to deflect that power, leaving only a pair of slightly mismeasured clear diamonds to touch the power directly (and "THOSE MINUTE DIAMONDS NEARLY DESTROYD WORLD" [S, 195]). And realizing that that stopgap, almost accidental, insulating measure wasn't enough, God, or God B as he is called here, instituted a role for the bats: to guide the building of a new pyramid—that of the "many uttering tongues" (SM, 6) of culture which, as has been suggested by many of the writers examined here, might properly receive that powerful light and set it shimmering in an intricate web of defracted light:

>   & THEN? U SAY IT
>   Dawn
> Flowing through the capstone at an angle
> Such as to lift the weight of the whole world
> Will build—ah, I can't think . . . Arcadia?
>
> PARADISE
>   (S, 165)

The bats, then—through their work of recycling the "densities" of significant creators back into earthly circulation—work to direct the building of a new, flawed pyramid. We call it language: "MANS TERMITE PALACE BEEHIVE ANTHILL PYRAMID JM / IS LANGUAGE   USE IT: (S, 118). Through their lab work, through a parcelling out of densities they call "cloning," these bats guide the work of culture building. Culture, then, is a "WORK GUIDED BY HIGHER COLLABORATION":

ALL CULTURE FOCUSD ON ONE
GLOWING UNIFYING VISION B4 THE VIOLENT
LIDDING OF REASON U KNOW OF, WHEREFORE GOD B SENT MAN

THE IDEA: TO CREATE, A REASOND INDIRECTION.
NOW THRU THE ARTS OF SCIENCE   POETRY   MUSIC   IN SLOW
ACCUMULATIVE FASHION MAN'S GARDEN TOOK SHAPE. CULTURE
& LANGUAGE NEED ALWAYS THE MESSENGER AT THE ELBOW.

(S, 242)

To complete this history, we need only add that the bats' task of per-
fecting such a flawed, indirect approach to hidden powers is, in the
"atomic age," a particularly crucial one. In contrast to the danger-
ously direct access pioneered by our atomic scientists—we are reminded of this by Laura Fermi's self-assured statement at the beginning of *Mirabell*: "*They were the first men to see matter yield its inner
energy, steadily, at their will. My husband was their leader*" (S, 94)—the
bats seek the "slow, accumulative," indirect showing forth of paradise. They repeat, again and again, that man must "STOP / PLAYING
WITH HIS DANGEROUS NEW POPGUN. THE ATOM MUST / BE RETURND TO
THE LAB & THE USES OF PARADISE" (S, 247).

Near the close of *Mirabell*, we are reminded that this entire history—the perils of direct contact, the need for cloning—serves as an
amazingly elaborate frame for working out the need for indirection in
touching the self. The heart of the bats' revelations is that our significant writers have "BEEN IN EFFECT CHOSEN & CONDITIOND" (S, 260)—
conditioned in that they express themselves through "composite /
Voice[s], . . . formula[s]" (S, 266) granted to them through the mix-
ing of ancestral densities before birth, a situation, of course, exactly
parallel to that of the artist who, as Duncan and Ashbery suggest,
makes contact with his or her "powers" by means of inherited poetic voices.[24] So, for example, when JM complains of the dictation of
his poem, "it's all by someone else! / . . . I'd set / My whole heart,
after *Ephraim*, on returning / To private life, to my own words" (S,
261), WHA makes it clear that this lack of free will is caused by a
limitation in humanity—the inability to approach those powers in
any other way:

YR SCRUPLES DEAR BOY ARE INCONSEQUENT
IF I MAY SAY SO   CAN U STILL BE BENT,
AFTER OUR COURSE IN *HOW TO SEE* PAST LONE
AUTONOMY TO POWERS BEHIND THE THRONE
ON DOING YR OWN THING . . .   . . .
                              THINK WHAT A MINOR
PART THE SELF PLAYS IN A WORK OF ART
COMPARED TO THOSE GREAT GIVENS   THE ROSEBRICK MANOR
ALL TOPIARY FORMS & METRICAL

MOAT ARIPPLE! FROM ANTHOLOGIZED
PERENNIALS TO HERB GARDEN OF CLICHES
. . .

IT WAS THE GREATEST PRIVILEGE TO HAVE HAD
A BARE LOWCEILINGED MAID'S ROOM AT THE TOP

(S, 262)

With this, Mirabell's flawed pyramid of culture is changed into the inherited manor house of poetry, set about with the elaborately trimmed shrubbery of form, its inner rooms ringed by the crowned figures of still-useful ancestors—with the individual poet's work, then, forming its top room, the capstone, to the already-existent structure. And what has seemed a limitation of language—that the self can only be grasped through such inherited indirections—is now seen as a response to human limitation, shielding us from powers too explosive for direct contact. Admittedly I err, says this long parable, and then passionately defends that acknowledgment.

Scripts for the Pageant, Book 3, works the tension involved in indirection from a second direction. If the parable in *Mirabell* argued that an awareness of tension saves one from naively attempting to grasp what is hidden directly, that in *Scripts* warns against the reverse— entirely avoiding the impulse to touch in the name of an equally naive skepticism. The danger in both cases—as in the attempt to "see" Ephraim or in his dismissal as an empty form, or for that matter, in the two lines of response to Whitman sketched in my introduction—is that the tension simply dissolves and disappears. In this version, the "INTENSE FISSIONABLE ENERGIES BLACK & WHITE / WHICH EITHER JOIN & CREATE OR SEPARATE & DESTROY" discovered at the heart of matter are now seen as orginating in the grander, but equally precarious pairing of God B's positive "whirling point of Light" (S, 517) and a negative force called the "Monitor"—a contrasting "Point, dimensionless and black" (S, 454).[25] According to the "walked-through frame" of *this* volume, "THE ORIGINAL / PACT WAS BETWEEN GOD BIO & THE BLACK / . . . BLACK OF THOUGHT UNTHINKABLE" (S, 440)—a coming together of unseen and opposing energies in which the "CONTRARY RUB" (S, 458) of that negative force, "A RUB AGAINST IMPLACABLE / CONTRADICTION" (S, 397) forces the positive force into a visible, material-making action in order to hold its own. From this act of resistance came the earth, or the greenhouse; each version of *Genesis* in this volume reworks that formula:

IN THE BEGINNING GOD
WAS GIVEN, TO SHAPE HIS WORLD, A TWO-EDGED GIFT.
HIS BROTHERS OF THE PANTHEON ALLOWED
MATERIALS, BUT WITH THIS PROVISO: 'GO
BUILD, YOUNGEST BROTHER, ONLY TAKE THIS ONE,
OUR MONITOR, TO DWELL WITHIN YOUR BALL.'
. . .
FROM THIS OPPOSITION, WHICH HOLDS SWAY
NO LESS WITHIN MAN'S SOUL, LORDS, CAME THE FIRST
MINUTE PASTE THAT WAS GOD'S MATERIAL.
IN SHORT: THE ELEMENTS FROM A 'WHITE' SOURCE
RESISTED THOSE OF A 'BLACK' OR 'SHADOW' FORCE.
. . .
IN HIS JOY, HIS CRAFTSMAN'S EAGERNESS TO BEGIN, OUR FATHER
    TOOK FRICTION INTO HIS HANDS
AND FROM A STARRY MIX GROUND UP A PASTE OF LIVING MATTER,
    MUCH AS THE BAKER KNEADS HIS DOUGH.
YEAST OF LIFE! DOOR FLUNG OPEN INTO THE FURNACE, OUT CAME
    A LOAF WE'VE ET ON SINCE.

                                    (S, 392, 396, 458)

Matter, then, issues from and stabilizes that original tension, a union based on a "LIMITED CHARTER / . . . [in which] THERE IS, SIMPLY, NO 'QUARREL' BETWEEN LIGHT & SHADOW, SO LONG AS SUBSTANCE (PSYCHE OF MATTER) STANDS / BETWEEN THEM" (S, 460). If the universe is made up of opposing "powers of darkness, powers of light," that "innermost dichotomy / [is] RESOLVED BY SUBSTANCE, EVEN BY THE STUFF / OF OUR 'CREATION'" (S, 461). Substance not only saves us from overpowering contact with those dimensionless forces, but, as we saw earlier with the DJ-JM relationship, in its roundabout detour it also keeps them married.

As this last phrase, spoken by WHA, suggests, culture-making humanity, in this schema, has a crucial role to play in God B's continuing act of resistance. According to the four angels who take over the mediums' instruction, God has always employed helpers in His creation of substance:

HE LONG KNEW THE FORCES ARRAYED AGAINST HIM: THE NEGATIVES,
    THE VOIDS. HE HAD BEEN BESTED BEFORE.
THESE HAD DESTROYED OTHERS OF HIS WORKS BY *EXPLOSION* AND BY
    BLACK *SUCTIONING*, AND HE NAMED THEM EVIL.
HE WAS EVER ON GUARD, HE SET ASIDE FOUR QUANTA OF ENERGY AND
    FIRST CREATED HIS HELPERS.

                                    (S, 293, emphasis mine)

Those four angels assisted in the original creation of the world, but they now function as overseers of the continued substance-making of humanity's mental creations that now holds back "THE NEGATIVES, THE VOIDS." The mechanisms for that supervision are quite various, but all involve nudging humanity into sense-making, tension-responsive activity. One of the bats, for example, makes a brief appearance to describe his understanding of that mechanism. The angel Michael, he says, sends him into dreams to "ENTHRALL & INSPIRE ALL THOSE / WHO DO IMMORTAL WORK." However that supervision is described, it always involves humanity's making of meaning or substance. Michael himself insists:

> WE BROTHERS HAVE THIS POWER, THIS DUTY, EVEN AS SPOILERS &
>   MADMEN TO DESCEND,
> TO FOUND RELIGIONS, TO MISRULE, TO TICKLE
> INTO GENIUS MAN'S GENIUS
> MAKING THE LONG & SHORT OF IT Human dimensions?
> SCRIBE, THE SUBSTANCE AND THE SENSE OF IT.
>
> (S, 550–51)

Following the last ouija divisions—YES & NO—*Scripts* is organized as a three-part meditation on humanity's sense-making activity. The instruction in "YES," dominated by the angel of light Michael ("A MONUMENT TO CIVILIZED / IMAGINATION" [S, 286]), focuses on our use of intelligence; that of "NO," dominated by the angel of death Gabriel ("THE SHADOW OF MY FATHER"), examines the black threat of skepticism that calls forth and defines that activity; "&" serves as a bridge, detailing the same two-part design within the human psyche. WHA's address to Gabriel at the beginning of "NO" establishes this distinction—"LORD MICHAEL SWITCHED ON A LIGHT / AND ILLUMINED OUR HUMAN MIND. / . . . LORD GABRIEL, HELP US NOW TO UNDERSTAND / THIS BLACK BEYOND BLACK" (S, 438)—which God B's summary at the end of the section confirms: "MY SON MICHAEL LIT UP YOUR MINDS   MY SON / GABRIEL TURNED THEM TO THE DARK FORCE WE / CONTAIN   POET FROM THIS MAKE A V WORK" (S, 493). Taken together, the three sections form another elaborately clothed defense of the error of "REASOND INDIRECTION."

"YES" is imagined as a kind of seminar, its circle—"A CLOSED CIRCLE   A BOCCACCIO / WE 8 AMID TIME'S HOWL SIT TELLING TALL / TALES TO AMUSE & AMAZE & WITH LUCK INSTRUCT US ALL" (S, 324)—made up of the two mediums, two shades (WHA & MM), and the four brothers. It begins, as seminars do, with a text and responsive commentary. Michael sets the first text:

> AS SEARCH FOR ENLIGHTENMENT IS OUR OBJECT, LET ME POSE A
>   FIRST, AFFIRMATIVE TEXT:
> THE MOST INNOCENT OF IDEAS IS THE IDEA THAT INNOCENCE IS
>   DESTROYED BY IDEAS.
>
> (S, 321)

This is an appropriately riddling text whose key terms—*innocence, idea*—are twisted and redefined by each participant, but in time a kind of consensus is achieved: far from destroying humanity's original, unrealized (and therefore "innocent") potential, "ideas" (made sense) make something useful of it. In the impassioned commentary that follows, we are given a history of humanity's attractions to, and fears concerning, such made ideas. Raphael, angel of the earth, for example, gets at the text affirmatively with an account of cave paintings: "O THE BEAUTY OF THOSE INNOCENT IMAGES LIT BY THE *IDEA* OF MAN / KNOWING HIMSELF, THERE IN A CAVE, IN A CHASTE WOMB OF HISTORY" (S, 324, emphasis mine). The act of knowing oneself, of bringing what was unrealized to light, Raphael insists, is an act of enhancement not destruction. Gabriel makes the same point with his negative example—suicide, the act of relinquishing hold of that known, living self and mistakenly attempting to return to unmarked, no longer morally obligated innocence:

> NO MATTER HOW INTELLIGENT, HOWEVER UNPREPARED, AT THAT
>   MOMENT WE CLASP HANDS, THE SUICIDE & I,
> & DO YOU KNOW I LOOK STRAIGHT INTO *INNOCENCE*, MICHAEL,
>   STRIPT OF *IDEA* AS MORALITY IS SHED.
> AT THAT MOMENT, IN THE RED DEBRIS OF RUIND CELLS, I KNOW
>   INNOCENCE.
>
> (S, 333, emphasis mine)

Ideas, then—light, morality, self-knowledge, things to be made and added to, the whole ensemble of creative activity—are, according to this seminar, to be celebrated, not feared.

Once the importance of "ideas" has been established, the angels begin to explain the complicated mechanism that makes "immortal work" of man's use of "HIS MOST DELICATE MACHINE . . . / . . . THE MACHINE OF THE MIND DRIVEN BY WORDS TO MINE MEANING: / MAKE SENSE OF IT" (S, 346). We discover now that the "5," those dense, reissued souls who, when reborn, remember their previous existences, act as scouts for the angels, each associated with a single sense. Akhnaton (or the figure who had at one time taken that form) appears and explains that in his various lives (Curie, Galileo, etc.) his work has been to turn visual observations into patterns: "TO SEE AND MAKE SENSE OF IT" (S, 337). Likewise, we discover that "Mon-

James Merrill's The Changing Light at Sandover   197

tezuma" investigates through the (broadly defined) instrument of touch: "FIRST AS HEALER, THAN AS CLAPPING MINSTREL, THEN AS THE / KING CALLED MONTEZUMA, WHO SUFFERED THE IRON GRIP / OF THE NEW WORLD, & HANDED OVER HIS GOLD TO NO AVAIL, / AS TOUCH I FINGER THE STUFF OF THINGS, LORD, AND MAKE SENSE OF IT" (S, 339). After the procession of costumed "reports," Michael explains: "WE HAVE BROUGHT YOU OUR SCOUTS, THE IMMORTAL FIVE. THEY REPORT TO MY BROTHERS & ME THEIR FINDINGS" (S, 350). The brothers, in turn, each take one of these figures (Gabriel takes two, to make the arithmetic come out) and work with his findings, functioning as "THE SENSES OF OUR FATHER" (S, 350). Michael, for example, is reported to by Akhnaton, sight, and does some of his own "looking" as well; the result: "I LOOK, I READ, MAKE SENSE OF IT, AND REPORT TO MY FATHER" (S, 351). And God, after taking in this "made sense," makes His own art form, successfully resisting the black force pressing against Him, and making substance of their opposed natures: "TURNING OUTWARD HIS MULTIPLE ATTENTION FORTIFIED BY THE GREAT ORCHESTRA OF THE SENSES, / OUR FATHER SINGS, / SINGS, ALONE, INTO THE UNIVERSE" (S, 351). Taken alone, this first section of the meditation is as impassioned an account of the possibility of singing the self as found in this study.

Appropriately, this section ends with a grand celebration of the senses, its occasion the twenty-fourth anniversary of the two mediums—of their not giving into fission.[26] They are instructed to make the following preparation: "SALT. A SPICE OF YR OWN CHOICE. / A SCENT. ICE IN A BOWL. A CANDLE LIT / & A LIVE FLOWER" (S, 353) and later, completing the ceremonial welcome to the senses, a record: "STRAUSS . . . / . . . ROSENKAVALIER / SIDE ONE GO PUT IT ON DEAR BOY" (S, 355). Once the preparations are made, we see, in a kind of demonstration of how God B's invisible "*light takes form*" (S, 356) through its contact with various reflecting mediums, the following clothing of the unseen:

> Music, A single pure white beam one knows
> Floods the mirror room, which undergoes
> Instant changes. Dewy garlands deck
> The staircase. Statue, pictures, candlestick,
> Each is prismatically multiplied.
> The Ouija Board drifts upward on a tide
> Of crystal light—ethereal parquet
> Where guests will presently join WHA
> and MM.
>
> (S, 354)

That is, the multiply refracted light, split into an intricate "parquet" of interwoven impressions, turns schoolroom into stage, and stage into the floating paradise—the crust world—almost achieved then scorned in *Mirabell*. This is only one side of the story, of course, but as the guests to this celebration—the angels, the 5—insist, that, in fact, is the task that humanity is being called to do: "It's as we were told at the outset—every grain / Of dust, each waterdrop, to be suffused / With mind, with *our* minds. This will be Paradise" (S, 308).

The "&" section is a self-conscious bridge between Michael's and Gabriel's lessons. It begins with the two mediums traveling to the island of Samos, their arrival celebrated in a wonderfully elaborate lyric wherein the repeatedly entwined end words (*light, land, fire, water,* and *sense*) present a correlative for, and a commentary on, the multiple directions possible as humanity makes sense of the world's elements. Stones along the island's shore, for example, are described in this manner:

> Fire-wisps were weaving a string bag of light
> For sea stones. Their astounding color sense!
> Porphyry, alabaster, chrysolite
> Translucences that go dead in daylight
> Asked only the quick dip in holy water
> For the saint of cell on cell to come alight—
> Illuminated crystals thinking light,
> Refracting it, the gray prismatic fire
> Or yellow-gray of sea's dilute sapphire . . .
>
> (S, 369)

Each of these stones, dead in the flat light of day, weaves a "string bag of light"—thinking it, refracting it, knotting it, making colored sense of it—as the waves wash over and back, turning them into reflective surfaces. The stones, that is, do for sunlight what humanity (and these meditations) has been called to do for God's dimensionless power. We learn later in "&," when Nature (God B's twin who, along with him, created the earth) enters the seminar and begins to explain the source of humanity's sense-making powers, that the "quick dip in holy water" needed to make man a reflector—or as Ashbery would have it, a mirror, a speculator—involved more than a dash of sea water. Nature quotes God's thinking:

> LET US DIVIDE THE FORCE OF HIS NATURE, JUST AS WE WILL MAKE
>   TWO SIDES TO ALL NATURE,
> FOR IN DUALITY IS *DIMENSION*, TENSION, ALL THE TRUE GRANDEUR
>   WANTING IN A PERFECT THING.

SISTER, TAKE COMMAND OF HIS . . . RESISTANCE? HIS 'UNGODLY'
   SIDE. MAKE HIM KNOW DARK AS WELL AS LIGHT, GIVE HIM
   PUZZLEMENT, MAKE HIM QUESTION,
FOR WOULD WE NOT LIKE COMPANY? I AGREED.

                                         (S, 408)

In order to make a viable partner in his sense-making task, God grants to humanity the same conditions that spur Him to creative activity: an opposing side, in this case internalized, whose dark questions and insistent doubts call forth resistance. Man, like God B, is burdened with a "TWO-EDGED GIFT": an opposition between song and skepticism resolved only by substance or dimension. It is the dark edge of this gift to which we turn in "NO."

The seminar in "NO" is directed by Gabriel; his lesson—making a loop all the way back to the opening lines of the poem—is that the force of the Monitor, the "black beyond black," is linked with the problem of time running out. He announces: "MY THEME IS TIME, MY TEXT: / OF ALL DESTRUCTIVE IDEAS THE MOST DESTRUCTIVE IS THE IDEA OF DESTRUCTION" (S, 438). As with Michael's text, this seems riddling at first: what does the "idea of destruction" have to do with time?, and how does time understood in this way function as the negative energy that calls forth a resisting, substance-making activity? As before, Gabriel's point gradually becomes clear. In response to a query from WHA ("LORD GABRIEL, HELP US NOW TO UNDERSTAND / THIS BLACK BEYOND BLACK. IS IT AN END TO DREAM? / AN HOURGLASS EMPTY OF SAND? [S, 438]), Gabriel replies: "IS IT THE HOURGLASS DRAINED OF TIME? / NO, FOR IT IS THE HOURGLASS IN WHICH SAND RUNS UP!" (S, 448). Surprisingly, the "black" that humanity, the atom, history, the earth all contain ("history's great worm / Turns and turns as it does because of twin / Forces balanced and alert within / Any least atom" [S, 478]) is not the forward march of time, taking up and discarding the selves, structures, and ideas that we dream; rather, it is another sort of dream, a dream in which the sands of things accomplished run back up the hourglass.

And what does *that* mean? Examples are provided by two new members of the seminar, Robert Morse (RM) and George Cotzias (GK), friends recently dead. RM presents, in effigy, the figures of Caligula and Hitler, two "SOULS DIPPED IN A BLACKENING DYE" who were cloned with the high densities of previous human achievement, but who gradually "CHANGED, CHANGED," giving up those slowly accomplished human densities in what can be seen as a sudden reversal of time:

WHAT YOU, DEAR SCRIBE & HAND,
NOW LIVE IN IS TIME'S FORWARD RUN. THE BLACK
BEYOND BLACK IS OF TIME SET RUNNING BACK.
THESE SOULS WERE CAUGHT IN THE FRICTION, STRIPPED LIKE GEARS,
GIVEN VAST POWERS THAT COLLAPSING WERE
SUCKED DRY OF EVERY HUMAN DENSITY.

(S, 451)

Like all human achievers in their making substance of the friction established between God B's intelligence and the Monitor's will to nothingless, these unfortunate souls separated themselves by eventually giving too much attention to the "SIREN" song of the black and converted their world-making task of thinning the earth's unruly garden to a world-destroying drive to "TERMINATE!" That is, giving ear only to one dimensionless force, the "idea of destruction," they were "sucked dry" of all human densities and reduced to human black holes—running time backward, and in place of substance making an entrance for vacuum.[27] GK uses current concerns with sources of power to create a second example of time's reversibility. If coal and oil are seen as the compressed histories of living substance, then their use can be said to be a tapping of time's forward movement. In contrast is atomic power which contains the potential undoing of what has been accomplished in time:

NOT FORWARD TIME COMPRESSED (COMBUSTIBLE
OILCAN OF 'THINNER') BUT ATOMIC BLACK
COMPRESSED FROM TIME'S REVERSIBILITY,
THAT IDEA OF DESTRUCTION WHICH RESIDES
BOTH IN MAN & IN THE ACTINIDES.

(S, 453)

In both of these examples—humanity, the atom—when Gabriel speaks of time as the negative force to be resisted by substance, he means, in fact, time's potential reversal, a one-sided giving into the Monitor's opposing dream of destruction or the suck of nothing's vacuum.

How, then, do the "TWO MINDS OF MATTER" become combined? What is the substance that their friction creates? The best example, as I have been suggesting, is this long poem itself, which repeatedly tells us it is suspended between YES and NO—a walked-through frame which, like Ashbery's "postures of the dream" or Whitman's "outlines" or Duncan's fictional "ensemble," we use without wholeheartedly believing in. All of the poems in this study, in fact, are examples that call attention to, and exploit, their limitations in embracing an external medium. We are directly encouraged to make this connection near the end of "NO" when JM realizes that if all of the trilogy "COMES DOWN TO THE NATURE OF THE ATOM" (S, 461), then all of the angels, bats, and centaurs he has worked with are simply creations spun off from that original play of opposed powers. His momentary inclination, however, to give in to "THE MONITOR'S BREATH, THE SHADOW WHICH TRAILED OWR FATHER FROM THE HALLS OF HIS BROTHERS, / THE JUDAS, THE CAIN, THE GREAT OPPOSING FORCE TO MATTER ITSELF, / THE CHALLENGE TO THE MAGICIAN'S ART, THE RAGE TO PROVE IT WAS, IS, ALL DONE BY MIRRORS" (S, 476), is nudged back to a more generative double-minded attitude by WHA, who counsels him to appreciate the "errors" of substance:

> But if it's all a fable
> Involving, oh, the stable and unstable
> Particles, musn't we at last wipe clean
> The blackboard of these creatures and their talk,
> To *render* in a hieroglyph of chalk
> The formulas they stood for? U MY BOY
> ARE THE SCRIBE   YET WHY? WHY MAKE A JOYLESS THING
> OF IT THRU SUCH REDUCTIVE REASONING?
> ONCE HAVING TURNED A FLITTING SHAPE OF BLACK
> TO MIRABELL, WD YOU MAKE TIME FLOW BACK?
>   (S, 461–62)

The point is, then, to join all the writers examined thus far by admitting that it was done by mirrors—that it is an "error"—and to find in that admission not the siren call to demolish the work of self-reflection, but a tension that forces us to explicate, examine, and defend the value of error. Discovered in Whitman but put into play in a multitude of contexts, such a tension animates this trilogy and the other long poems examined here. In Merrill's poem, it produces a sustained meditation on the two-edged necessity of working through indirection: a work of substance, both monstrance and blown fuse, which broaches and, for a time at least, marries the psyche's opposing forces.

Fittingly, the book ends with a pair of ceremonies that make this doubleness clear. *Scripts* concludes with a ritualistic shattering of a mirror—a breaking of the reflective surface that acknowledges both the nature and limitation of this poem's incarnation of the light. MM instructs: "JM WILL TAKE THE MARBLE / STYLUS & GIVING US THE BENEFIT / OF A WELLAIMED WORD, SEND OUR IMAGINED SELVES / FALLING IN SHARDS" (S, 516). A similar ceremony occurs at the close of the brief "Coda" to the volume, a section primarily concerned with the preparation of RM's soul to descend to earth and continue the poem's task of "MAK[ING] SENSE OF IT, MAKING MY REPORT TO GOD" (S, 530), but which concludes with JM's ritualistic reading of the entire trilogy to an audience of shades *and* and their heartbroken Greek friend Vasíli Vassilikos, who has just entered their house, bringing news of his wife's sudden death. Momentarily embarrassed by the mirror game in the presence of *real* grief, they try to back away from the reading:

> —Vasíli, drink your brandy, get some sleep,
> Look, we've got these great pills . . . No; he asks instead,
> Anything, *anything* to keep his head
> Above the sucking waves, merely to listen
> A little while. So in the hopelessness
> of more *directly* helping we resume.
>
> (S, 559, second emphasis mine)

And as the first words are read—"Admittedly I *err* . . ."—we come full circle, realizing now the necessity for such a ritualistic admission in all works of art *and* the manner in which such indirection neverthe-less takes on and makes something of hidden and potentially over-whelming problems. JM and DJ admit error and go on nonetheless, convinced that, in a small, indirect way, the forces Vasíli struggles with will be stablized and made momentarily accessible, his head thereby held above the "sucking" force of nothingness. And the circle we have just travelled back to the book's opening lines is, in fact, ringed by another circuit we have also negotiated—for Merrill's ar-gument suggests not that unstated personal limitations (as in Berry-man and Kinnell) keep Whitman's embrace of the other from allowing us to sing the self fully, but that the mechanism of the embrace is *itself* unavoidably limited in its indirection, and, remarkably, that because of such a "weakness," those very same personal terrors and tensions might yet be shaped and made substantial. Admitting such tensions offers Vasíli and other readers not "the absolute," but a manner of drawing near to it.

NOTES

1. Ross Labrie, "James Merrill at Home: An Interview," *Arizona Quarterly* 38 (1982): 28. See also his remarks in David Kalstone, "An Interview with James Merrill," *Saturday Review*, December 2, 1972, p. 45: "You hardly ever need to state your feelings. The point is to feel and keep your eyes open. Then what you feel is expressed, is mimed back at you by the scene. A room, a landscape. I'd go a step further. We don't know what we feel until we see it distanced by this kind of translation."

2. James Merrill, "Lost in Translation," in *From the First Nine, Poems 1946–1976* (New York: Atheneum, 1982), p. 352. Cited in the text as FN. For strong readings of this poem, see David Kalstone's *Five Temperaments* (New York: Oxford University Press, 1977), pp. 125–27 and Helen Vendler's "Chronicles of Love and Loss," *The New Yorker*, May 21, 1984, pp. 127–28.

3. James Merrill, *The Changing Light at Sandover* (New York: Atheneum, 1983), p. 89. Hereafter cited as S; emphasis mine.

4. J. D. McClatchy, "The Art of Poetry XXXI: James Merrill," *The Paris Review* 24 (Summer 1982): 196–97.

5. Helen Vendler, reviewing the first installment of what was to become this trilogy, identifies this as the use of "a voice recognizably [his] own but bearing a different name," *Part of Nature, Part of Us* (Cambridge: Harvard University Press, 1980), p. 212. Samuel E. Schulman takes note of Vendler's remark and links the device to Whitman, finding in Merrill "a willingness to see himself dissolved into elements, cast into other voices, represented by other styles and people," "Lyric Knowledge," in *James Merrill: Essays in Criticism*, ed. David Lehman and Charles Berger (Ithaca: Cornell University Press, 1983), p. 114; cited in the text as JM. For more on refraction in this poem, see Richard Sáez, "'At the Salon Level,'" in *James Merrill*, ed. Lehman and Berger, pp. 222–230.

6. James Merrill, "Divine Poem," *The Nation*, November 29, 1980, p. 30.

7. McClatchy, "The Art of Poetry," p. 194.

8. My attention was drawn to this statement by Stephen Yenser's "The Fullness of Time: James Merrill's *Book of Ephraim*," *Canto* 3 (Spring 1980): 155–57. Another confirmtion found within the poem is Mirabell's description of "THE STRUCTURELESS STRUCTURE OF THE SOUL CELL, / OR MORE PROPERLY THE SUBLIME STRUCTURE OF THE CELLS OF GOD BIOLOGY" (S, 290).

9. Both Sáez, "'At the Salon Level,'" p. 235 ("By the third volume of the trilogy the reader should be well aware that he is dealing essentially with a poetics") and Yenser, "The Names of God: *Scripts for the Pageant*," in *James Merrill*, ed. Lehman and Berger, p. 275 ("we might even think of his metaphysics as his rhetoric and his prosody writ large") make this point.

10. Robert von Hallberg, *American Poetry and Culture, 1945–1980* (Cambridge: Harvard University Press, 1985), pp. 95, 103.

11. Vendler, "Chronicles of Love and Loss," p. 124.

12. Von Hallberg, *American Poetry*, p. 105.

13. James Merrill, "Condemned to Write About Real Things," *New York Times Book Review*, February 21, 1982, p. 11.

14. The preceding four quotations are all from Merrill, "Condemned to Write About Real Things," p. 33.

15. McClatchy, "The Art of Poetry," p. 213.

16. I have been aided in identifying this two-part structure by three readings of the poem: Judith Moffett, "*The Changing Light at Sandover: The Book of Ephraim*," in *James Merrill: An Introduction to the Poetry* (New York: Columbia University Press, 1984), pp. 174–88; Henry Sloss, "James Merrill's 'Book of

Ephraim,'" *Shenandoah* 27 (Summer 1976): 63–91 and (Fall 1976): 83–110; and Stephen Yenser, "The Fullness of Time."

17. Sloss also reads "L" as a hinge between the two periods, but because he takes the *past-tense* description of the mirrored ball to somehow be a reference to a "sense of finality, and even dread" in their shared life in the *present*, he then must read the second half of the poem much more negatively—as a dismissal of Ephraim. See "James Merrill's 'Book of Ephraim,'" pp. 87–90.

18. Sloss rightly speaks of these sections as a series of meditations, ibid., p. 78., but does not accept their temporary nature, which I see as crucial. This side-stepping of an emotional crisis is paralleled by their "put[ting] on ice," that same June, a sudden, chastening call to face the threat of global disaster (Merrill, *Changing Light*, p. 72). That problem, too, is faced indirectly.

19. Yenser, "The Fullness of Time," pp. 141–44, reads this untamed figure as Time, but the trilogy as a whole seems not to support such a precise designation for the "unseen."

20. For more on this passage see ibid., pp. 149–51.

21. Two useful sources for working out the "content" of what is revealed in these next two books are Moffett's "masterplot" summaries in *James Merrill: An Introduction to the Poetry*, pp. 189–228, and Yenser, "The Names of God," pp. 246–81.

22. David Lehman, in "Elemental Bravery," ibid., p. 35, and Peter Sacks, in "The Divine Translation," ibid., p. 163, both make note of the mirror-mind connection I discuss here.

23. A connection pointed out by David Jackson in "Lending a Hand," ibid., pp. 298–99.

24. It is possible, I think, to insist too much on the literal notion of a controlled universe and thus miss its use as a metaphor. Richard Sáez does this, in an otherwise powerful meditation on the trilogy.

25. Yenser, "The Names of God," p. 265, notes that Merrill's essay on Dante also calls attention to these dimensionless points. This same essay (p. 260), contains a survey of Merrill's references to the "Monitor."

26. See Vendler, *Part of Nature, Part of Us*, pp. 227–28, for a discussion of Merrill's conviction that "the sensual and spiritual are indivisible."

27. Yenser, "The Names of God," p. 270, usefully describes time's backward run as "evolution inverted."

Index

Numbers in italics indicate individual poems

A Note on the Author

THOMAS GARDNER is an associate professor of English at Virginia Polytechnic Institute and State University. He received his M.A. from Syracuse University and his Ph.D. from the University of Wisconsin. His essays, reviews, and poems have appeared in such journals as *American Poetry, Contemporary Literature, The Georgia Review, Poesis, Poetry Northwest,* and *Sagetrieb.*